APHRODITE AT MID-CENTURY

CARYL RIVERS

Aphrodite at Mid-Century

Growing up Catholic and Female
in Post-War America

DOUBLEDAY & COMPANY, INC., GARDEN CITY, NEW YORK, 1973

ISBN: 0-385-05632-X
Library of Congress Catalog Card Number 73–79706
Copyright © 1973 by Caryl Rivers
All Rights Reserved
Printed in the United States of America
First Edition

CONTENTS

APHRODITE AT MID-CENTURY

1 *Prelude*

It seems to me that my earliest memory is of Pearl Harbor. That cannot be so; there must be things I can dredge up from the past that go back beyond December 7, 1941. But if that date does not exactly live in infamy, it is surely graven forever in the storehouse of my brain.

Pearl Harbor was thirteen days before my fourth birthday. I remember the small details of the day with an icy clarity. I can see the Paisley swirls of the Kirman rug in our living room—I was sitting on it—and the smooth mahogany grain of the radio with its slim Hepplewhite legs that were visible between the legs of the adults who gathered around it.

There was an electricity in the air that I could feel. It seemed to crackle and jump between all the familiar things in the room and it suspended time and space around me. I knew, without having to be told, that something incredibly important had happened. I don't remember the words coming from the radio. I would have had only a dim comprehension of the words "bomb" and "war" and "Japan." It was the unseen current that froze the moment for me, and the rug, the radio, the legs. I think I felt it more intensely than anyone else in the room. Like the blind man whose body mysteriously compensates for the loss by sharpening his ability to hear, a child vibrates with a subvocal emotional current in a way that adults can understand only by remembering their own childhood.

The war had come at last, and it was to spread its thunderous shadow across the childhood of my generation. As we gestated, as we kicked in our cribs, as we cooed and learned to step, the war was gathering like some great tidal wave above us.

Our lives, in its shadow, ticked on, as ordinary lives do. Our family—my father, my mother, and I—were in most ways an average American family in 1941. We lived in a pleasant colonial house on a quiet street in a town called Silver Spring, Maryland, a suburb of Washington, D.C. When my parents moved to the street in 1939, they thought of it as the country, for nearby were woods and streams, and the center of town had one movie house and a shopping center. Today Silver Spring has a skyline of office buildings, 250,000 people, and a drug problem. But in 1939 it was the country.

My mother and father had been born in Washington and grew up within a few blocks of each other. Her father was German-American, a printer by trade. He left the Catholic Church, vowing never to return after the family had quarreled with a priest at the time of his mother's funeral. (My mother never knew the details of the quarrel.) He raised his children as Protestants. My paternal grandmother was the daughter of an Irish Catholic blacksmith, who eloped with a young man of Protestant English extraction (my grandfather). He worked for the Federal Bureau of Engraving and Printing and, as the drum major of a local band, cut a dashing figure in his uniform. Her family refused to speak to him for eighteen years after the wedding, even though my grandfather converted to Catholicism.

My mother (German-American Protestant) and my father (Irish-English Catholic) met in law school and were married in a small Catholic ceremony. My mother left work when I was born, but returned to practice at a large law firm in Washington shortly afterward.

In the zeal that comes with the early stages of mother-

hood, my mother began a journal of my life. Reading
through it now, I can watch the development of an oddly
matched set of twins: the war cloud and me.

> *January 1940: Expiration of six months notice required to
> abrogate our commercial treaty with Japan.*
> *January 1940: Caryl's blandishments. When I get angry
> with her, she says: Are you sick?" Pause. "Are you well?"
> Pause. "Are you provoked with Caryl? Hug!"*
> *March 12 1940: Peace concluded between Finland and
> Russia.*
> *March 21 1940: Bought skates. You shuffle along but can't
> skate.*
> *May 1940: Germany invades Holland and Belgium.*
> *May 1940: Curls cut off. They were practically non-
> existent.*

The War, to my generation, means World War II. It is
said that way, in capital letters, and our youth was wrapped
inextricably around it. Its cataclysms happened too far away
to be comprehended, but its tentacles crept into the minutiae of our daily lives. To me, at four, the war offered small
adventures. The blackouts that began shortly after Pearl
Harbor were full of delicious excitement, grand games invented by adults solely for the pleasure of children. Black
shades had to be pulled down, fathers prowled the streets
in white helmets. My mother's journal tells of one night
when she tucked me in bed when the alarm sounded:
"You put your arm around me and said, 'I'll take care of
you, mommy.' And as we lay there just talking you said to
me in a soft little voice, 'I'm very good to you, aren't I,
mommy? I take care of you during blackouts and cover
you with blankets when you lie down' (referring to a
previous evening). As I whispered, 'You're so good to your
mommy,' you continued, 'You didn't think I'd turn out this

way, did you mommy? When I was three years old I was naughty, but now that I'm four I'm very good.'"

The first summer the war was on my parents took me to Ocean City, Maryland, and I was enthralled by the new kinds of lamps that had been installed along the boardwalk. The side of the lamps that faced the sea were solid metal so that no light would be visible to prowling U-boats. On the side that faced the boardwalk the light shone through two luminous panels that to my four-year-old eyes became a pair of feet. I named them "the dead lighted feet," and I was enthralled with them, and talked of them for years afterward.

One night, we had a special visitor at our home for dinner. His name was Murray Bernhardt, a friend of my parents', who came over with my uncle Dick, my mother's younger brother. He was home on leave from Camp Shelby, Mississippi. I have always remembered the name: Murray Bernhardt. It has about it the unmistakable scent of mystery and romance. The good China and the silver were on the table, glinting in candlelight, and Murray Bernhardt had on his uniform and he wore a short, clipped mustache, terribly exotic in those days. He was immensely impressive. Wherever he is today, he is thirty years away from the lean, mustached man of my memory, and he must bear little resemblance to him now. But in my mind he did not age and he will not. He is preserved there, like a mastodon under the ice cap, exactly as he was on that evening in 1942.

In her journal, my mother described the conclusion of that evening, a romantic gesture that will seem incomprehensible to the generation whose War is Vietnam:

"We all scratched our names on a piece of sealing wax and put them in the desk for Murray to collect when he comes back from the war. Sort of unfinished business for Murray."

The real change in my life came when my father went

into the Navy. He was in his thirties, past draft age, but he
volunteered for the officer corps in the Navy. He wanted
sea duty, but was assigned to a naval air station, Barin Field,
near Mobile, Alabama. My mother and I set out to join him
in a secondhand Plymouth bought for the journey. At its
end lay a land that seemed to me as magical as the needle-
slim emerald towers that shone from the pages of my copy
of *The Wizard of Oz.*

The world that I came to know was a hybrid that existed
for a short period of time and then vanished utterly. It was
a combination of The South and The War, and the two are
twined in my memory the way the Spanish moss on the
southern oaks tangled in the leaves. It is composed for me
of the smell of magnolias and the look of a bleak wooden
administration building surrounded by a plot of parched
earth that was meant to be a lawn, and a profusion of giant
young men in khaki. A peculiar lassitude crept out of the
warm, damp Alabama earth, traces of which stay with me
still. As young as I was, I understood that time traveled
more languorously there than in Silver Spring, Maryland.
It lapped at one gently, like the waters of the Perdido Bay,
at the edge of which we made our new home. The chame-
leons ran across the grass and the dewberries grew in the
fields. Nature took its sweet time and there was inevitability
at the heart of the morning flowers that opened on fence
rails with the sun.

And yet, over the waters of our quiet bay hovered the
PBY's, the big-bellied amphibious airplanes whose pilots
sometimes swooped dangerously close to our pier for a look
at my mother sunbathing. She used a bottle of an orange,
oily-sweet substance called Gaby Sun Tan Lotion and when
I was walking on a city street recently I got a whiff of something—perhaps the perfume of a passing woman—that
smelled just like Gaby. For an instant the street vanished
and I was surrounded by the pier and the sound of the water

lapping its barnacled supports and the buzzing of a distant
PBY and my mother loosening the straps of her orange swim
suit to get a tan on her shoulders. I was gripped by a sudden,
powerful sense of loss because that world was so irretrieva-
bly gone—that I was no longer five years old and my mother
thirty-two and the PBYs buzzing in the air. I suppose they
are all junk, now, the PBYs, rotting in some scrap yard or
moldering in mothballs. But in those days the languor of
the southern earth and the noisy power of even a small sliver
of a giant war machine blended into a peculiar oneness.

Absurd juxtapositions seemed normal. I was catapulted
from the world of middle-class kindergartens, where everybody played tamborines and wore little black aprons for
painting, to a one-room schoolhouse in Alabama that
housed all eight grades and offered outhouses in the yard.
I was an interloper there, clearly, and the children were
skittish with me at first. But the industrial might of the North
came to my rescue with one of its sublime achievements.

Toilet paper.

Inside the wooden outhouses at school were stacks of
pages torn from the Sears, Roebuck catalogue. Then, as now,
the pages were glossy and stiff, offensive to my pampered
border-state bottom. I began taking a roll of toilet paper
to school with me along with my lunch. My popularity took
a quantum jump. I stood by the outhouse door at recess,
doling out luxurious squares of toilet paper with all the
enlightened self-interest of a Chicago ward boss.

I did not stay long in the one-room school. My parents,
concerned about my education, enrolled me in a parochial
school. By the standards of the region, it was progressive—
two rooms, only four grades in each.

There was a small church across the street from the
school, and it was there I gleaned my first knowledge of the
Catholic Church: the mingled smell of incense and flowers
and new grass and a sliver of warm sunlight staining the

wooden back of the pew in front of the one where I sat. I had no sense of a mighty institution rooted in the ages; just of a place that was warm and smelled good and was tinged with mystery. I went to Mass sometimes with my father and he would leave me in the pew to go to confession, and now and then I could hear indistinct whisperings from the box that had swallowed him up. It was a tantalizing area of the adult world I was not permitted to enter.

We drove to the church across a shining, rippled body of southern water, and its dazzle in the sunlight, seemed an accessory to the service, a setting designed to show it off, as if the Mass itself was a jewel. But I always fidgeted during the Mass. Even mystery cannot transfix a five-year-old for long.

I remember that I was happy in the small parochial school, except for the area of the day that stretched between twelve and one. As a part of a campaign to convince me of the merits of vegetables, my parents decreed that I would eat the hot lunches served by the nuns each day. It was the era in which cleaning one's plate was a moral duty for a child. My uneaten vegetables lay on my plate, each one an accuser. They would, by some process unknown to me, be transmuted into fodder for the minions of Hitler and Tojo. I argued that the logical thing to do would be to put the peas and the beans and the carrots into an envelope and mail them directly to the Allied front lines. My parents would not listen to logic.

In the lunchroom, I gulped peas whole with a mouthful of milk; I hid carrot pieces under potato skins. The peas were mushy and disgusting when I bit into one by accident. Beets felt like tiny pieces of frozen snake against the tongue; green beans crunched like little bugs, but I could get them down. It was the nuns' sweet potatoes that did me in.

I could not bring myself to put the yellow, pulpy mass in my mouth. I was told I had to sit at the table until I ate them. I sat through lunch, through afternoon classes. I heard the happy squeals of the other children at recess, and I began to cry. The tears slid down my face, dropped off into the sweet potatoes, making the yellow mush look like Alabama mud. Finally the nun relented and let me go. Who but a sadist would make a child eat her own tears?

The next time sweet potatoes were served I threw up on my plate.

I was ordered to march out to the drain in the yard with my plate of throw-up. I said a prayer as I slid the yellow mess off the plate and tried to stuff it through the grates of the drain. My prayer went thus (we had just heard stories about The Flood from the nuns):

"Please, God, send another Flood. Don't hurt the people or the animals, God. Just get the vegetables. Drown every rotten vegetable, God, especially the sweet potatoes. Get the stinking sweet potatoes. Amen."

Then there was the time I was almost murdered by getting stuffed down the hole in the outhouse.

For some reason, two second-grade girls had selected me as their particular victim. Perhaps it was random cruelty, or just the fact that my accent was peculiar. One day when I went into the outhouse at recess they whispered through the door that they were coming in to push me down the hole. Terrified, I began to cry, and I braced myself against the door as the whispered threats continued. I tried to close my nostrils against the smell, seeing in my mind's eye the waves of slop. Who knew the depth of it? Perhaps it went all the way to China. I would never be found.

The bell rang, but I dared not move. I stayed in the outhouse for what seemed eternity before I ventured to open the door a crack. I peered out and saw no one in the schoolyard. I ran as fast as I could back to the classroom.

I learned a lesson that day about adult justice. My tormentors had to kneel in the corner for the rest of the afternoon. So did I, for being late after recess. The wooden floors were rough and hard and I kept trying to shift from knee to knee, but I found no position in which they did not ache. I was totally confused about why I was kneeling in the corner. All I had done was to protect myself against murder most foul. Was self-preservation not allowed by adults? I did not understand.

At home, I was secure from such conflicts. Sometimes my parents entertained other officers and their wives from the field. Sometimes, as a special treat, I was allowed to stay up and greet the guests. I remember them—my parents included—as the most glamorous people in the world, the men resplendent in their blue uniforms with the gold braid and the women in their long gowns. I watched them with envy one night, observing that when any of the women entered the room, the men stood up. I was enchanted. I walked into the room, then out again. Nothing happened. In, out. In again. No reaction. Since the women were wearing long dresses and I was wearing pajamas, I deduced that the pajamas were the problem. Pajamas quite obviously did not rate a standing ovation.

I went back into my room and struggled into my little blue nightgown. My mother came looking for me and I explained my plan. She smiled and left the room. A minute later, when I padded into the living room in my nightgown, all those marvelous men in the navy blue and the gold braid, rose to their feet in tribute. I was thrilled to the nerve ends in my bare little toes.

I will remember that night all my life; and yet, when I try to see in my mind's eye the faces of the people who were at the party that night, all I can see are faces from a hundred movies I have seen in the years since, the men incredibly handsome, the women with the perfection of a ripe peach. My parents and their friends must have thought themselves ordinary people having an ordinary dinner party. But to me they are such figures of fantasy that they have merged in my consciousness with my generation's ultimate symbol of fantasy—the movies.

My Southern Idyll ended abruptly when my father was assigned to sea duty on the carrier Lake Champlain, a berth he was granted only after pulling all available strings at the Navy Department. My mother was expecting a baby who was christened "She-he" for my convenience. We dropped the She when my brother was born a few months later. We returned home, and my life slid into its old patterns. I resumed my friendships with my peers, members of a group with sociological significance. We were the last generation of kids Before Television.

2
The Beat Generation*

My best pal in Silver Spring lived directly behind us. She was two years younger than I, shorter and rounder. Her name was pronounced the same as mine, although spelled differently, so nicknames were in order to avoid confusion. Hers started out as Little Carol, and got shortened to Beano. Mine was Big Caryl, or more often, just Big. The name pursued me into adolescence, when the last thing I wanted to be called was "Big Caryl."

Next door to us lived David, who was a year younger than I and a year older than Beano. The three of us were inseparable. Since we did not have the Marvelous Machine to snap on with the flick of a tiny wrist when we got bored with each other, we indulged in a substitute activity: creative bickering.

We argued about everything. Incessantly. Automobiles were a favorite subject. We had a Plymouth, David's parents had a Chevrolet and Beano's parents a Ford. Our arguments were pressed with wit and style:

"Fords are stupid."

"Fords are neat. Plymouths are stupid."

"Plymouths and Fords are dumb. Chevrolets are neat!"

"They are not."

"Are too."

"Are not."

"Are too."

"Are not."

* Before Everybody Acquired Television

19

When our mothers could stand no more and ordered us out of the house, we stood at the point where the three yards joined and argued the territorial imperative:

"You can't come on my property."

"Well, you can't come on my property. My yard is bigger than yours."

"My yard is bigger than both of yours."

"Is not."

"Is too."

"Is not."

We argued politics; specifically Truman and Dewey. David was a Republican and Beano and I were Democrats. David was badly handicapped by having a candidate whose name rhymed with Phewey. We did not let him forget it.

"Dewey is a phewey, Dewey is a phewey, yah-yah-yah-yah-YAH-yah."

We sang:

> "Truman's in the White House
> Waiting to get elected.
> Dewey's in the trash can
> Waiting to get collected."

For every minute we spent playing, we spent five minutes arguing. First we argued about what yard we would play in. Then we argued about what we would play; usually War or Cowboys. Beano and I, as the only girls on a street full of boys, had learned early not to have any truck with dolls or house or sissified girls' games. I had been entranced with cowboys since my grandparents took me to see *They Died with their Boots On* on my fourth birthday (Errol Flynn perishing nobly as Custer). I much preferred rustling cattle to rustling of skirts. My prized possession was a white leather two-gun holster, studded with fake stones. It was the envy of the neighborhood. When I was sick, *it* went out anyway.

"Mrs. Rivers, can Big come out and play?"

"No, she has a cold."

"Can I use her gunbelt?"

I was convinced that being a girl was an O.K. thing. Could I not do anything the boys could do, and do it better? Except, of course, pee on target. Boys were admittedly better at that. Dickie Martin from up the street could hit the trunk of a skinny dogwood from six feet. But I could cartwheel off the five-foot-high driveway and land on my feet, and even Dickie Martin couldn't do that. I didn't suffer from penis envy.

My parents bought me a first baseman's mitt and a football. My father drew the line when I asked for shoulder-pads. He said girls shouldn't play tackle football. I shrugged and played without shoulderpads.

In my neighborhood we had a substitute for TV that occupied much of our time.

Clubs.

We formed clubs and broke them up and formed new ones with a speed that would have dazzled the Italian parliament. We even institutionalized our sexual curiosity. We formed the Peter Showing Club (Peter being the generic name for genitals of either sex).

Meetings were held at the bottom of a ravine several blocks away from our street. A cement drain pipe sloped from the road to the bottom of the drain, to carry rainwater from the road. We gathered at its base, perched on the cement, and proceeded with the agenda.

It consisted of pulling aside a pair of Brownie shorts (girls) or unzipping a fly (boys) after which the membership would peer at the unveiled Peter. A brave soul might make a tentative poke with a finger.

Club meetings were very short, since we couldn't think of anything further to do, and the sight of a six-year-old penis or vagina begins to pall after one has stared at it for more than forty-five seconds.

The best thing about the Peter Showing Club was the aura of forbidden fruit that lingered over the ravine as we slid down the pipe. The delicious scent of sin mingled with the smell of molting leaves. We were all sworn to secrecy. We were sure our parents would be horrified if they ever learned about Peter Showing.

The Science Club was more respectable. It met regularly in the basement of my house, under the watchful eye of Tonto. Tonto was six feet tall, his flesh was cardboard and he was smiling and holding a box of cereal. Beano, David, Wayne Robey, and I (the membership of the Science Club) liberated him from the corner market one summer's day and he stood for years in the corner, revered like some ancient Russian icon.

My specialty in the Science Club was dinosaurs. I gave lengthy and serious reports about them, to which the membership listened dutifully. I illustrated my lectures with genuine dinosaur bones I had collected (amazing how many Brontosauri had lived in Silver Spring). Each bone I found I carried lovingly home, oblivious to the fact that it was grungy, covered with dog slobber or maggots. I laid them all at the feet of Tonto.

In a short time Tonto was surrounded by treasure. There was the Chinese vase I had retrieved from Ronnie Yingling's parents' trash can. It was festooned with samuri and almond-eyed maidens and I thought it was beautiful, despite the broken handle. I labeled it "Ming vase."

When we were not preparing scientific reports or showing Peters in my neighborhood, we were on the prowl for Adventure. Now, there is a myth that has grown up about city children and the children of the suburbs. The former, it is said, grow up to be self-reliant because they have survived the dangers of the city. Suburban children are alleged to be cream puffs, having been surrounded by chain-link fence, greenery, and the watchful eyes of parents. But with danger not so readily at hand, we had to be as daring and resourceful as the Masked Rider of the Plains to find it. We sniffed it out in the storm sewers.

The network of storm sewers that ran beneath the streets of the area were built to carry off rainwater from the streets to the less-than-crystal waters of nearby Sligo Creek, which was polluted even then. The storm sewers were very small sewers, so we had to hunch down and duck-waddle through them. They were dark and dank and smelled fetid and musty, and God knows what manner of germs lurked there, not to mention the danger of a sudden storm. But we would hike as far as a half mile through them, munching on sandwiches as we waddled along, playing Intrepid Explorers.

One Saturday, Beano and I and my friend Sally from school and her sister Marybee planned a sewer hike, unbeknownst to our parents, who would have had coronaries on the spot. After a pleasant waddle through a length of pipe we emerged to dine on the lawn of a small bungalow, where a woman peered through the window in amazement as we came up through the manhole. After lunch, Sally tripped trying to climb down into the pipe and scratched up her back and arms. Marybee decided that would be a Safari-Getting-Wounded-Man Back to Civilization. We marched Sally, still sobbing from her wounds, through the streets, muttering such dialogue as "If we don't make the fort by sundown, we're goners!"

Marybee had a distinct flair for the dramatic. My friend Sally was a skinny blonde, whose knees, like mine, were always covered with bruises. Marybee, a year older than we, was dainty, with long chestnut hair. She was a devotee of the scary radio show, "Inner Sanctum." When the three of us played "Inner Sanctum," Marybee got the best parts. Her favorite role was that of a woman who thought (a) that she was going crazy and (b) that her husband had hired two men to kill her and they were at that very moment digging her grave in the back yard.

Sally and I were cast as the gravediggers.

Marybee raved, tore at her hair. "Oh my God, they're going to kill me. Oh help, I'm losing my Mind! Help, Help, somebody help me!"

If Sally or I tried to ad lib a line, Marybee would snap: "Shut up and dig."

One afternoon Sally and Marybee and I went on a hike through one of the stands of woods near her house that was stubbornly resisting the tide of suburbanization. We came upon a shack where an old man lived with a large, equally old dog. A pile of bones lay near the shack.

Marybee sized up the situation. The man lured innocent victims into the woods and set his dog on them to eat them up.

The old dog meandered out of the shack. We ran as fast as we could. Panting, we hid behind a clump of bushes.

"Did you see him foaming at the mouth!" Marybee asked, breathless.

Sally and I nodded. "Blood-flecked foam," I added.

We crept hunched over, Indian style, through the woods to escape the old man and the murderous dog. As we walked by the side of the road that bordered the woods, a teen-age kid driving a car too fast made a face at us.

We bolted into the woods. Obviously he was a crazed maniac escaping from the Washington Sanitarium. (The sanitarium was a local hospital. It was not a mental institution, but Marybee swore that when she rode by it on her bike crazy people screamed through the windows that they were going to knife her.)

Our danger increased. Obviously the maniac was in league with the old man and the rabid dog against us. We made our way stealthily to Sally's house.

We told the whole story to a boy that lived next door, John Grubb. He listened with wide eyes. John Grubb told his mother. She called the police.

We took it on the lam.

On the days that the scent of adventure was not so strong —particularly on the hot muggy stretches in July that drove the dogs, panting, under the houses—we settled on someone's porch with a stack of comic books. While the educators fretted about comic books destroying the moral fiber of American youth, we gobbled up the exploits of the one-dimensional characters we had come to know and love. Comic books taught me to read. Wonder Woman was more inspiring than Dick and Jane and Spot.

Not only was Wonder Woman gorgeous in her spangled short shorts, but she could stop bullets with her metal bracelets and toss 300-pound men around with ease. I adopted Wonder Woman as a role model.

Captain Marvel was my second favorite. A boy Broadcaster (Billy Batson of Station WHIZ) said the word— Shazam!—and an old guy who lived at the Rock of Eternity threw a thunderbolt and turned Billy Batson into Captain Marvel. I liked him better than Superman. It seemed to me you had to be pretty dumb not to know that Clark Kent was Superman with glasses on. Shazam had more poetry than dumb Clark running into a phone booth all the time.

The comic-book heroes spent a lot of time aiding the War Effort. The comic books clearly delineated the enemy for us. The Jerries were long-faced men with cruel mouths who wore monocles (officers) or thick-necked brutes (regulars.) Japs had bile-yellow skin and buck teeth, from Tojo on down.

Even the Heap helped the Allies.

The Heap was a World War I German flyer who crashed into a swamp, but—as the captions put it—a spark of life remained. Over the years the Heap merged with the swamp slime and he (or it) got up one day and shuffled out of the swamp, looking like a moving compost heap with beady eyes. We played the Heap a lot, snorting and grunting with gusto. I would root around under a log in the woodpile for a supply of mulch to put on my head for a realistic Heap. My mother never could figure out why my hair got so dirty.

I remember only one comic book that really upset me. It was called *The Green Hand,* and it was about an evil man who had a scaly green hand and went around strangling people with it. When he died someone chopped off his hand, and people kept it as a souvenir. (Not exactly the same thing as an ash tray with a picture of the Empire State Building on it, but there is no accounting for tastes.)

The original owner of the Green Hand came back and strangled each new owner in a graphic manner. I remember reading the Green Hand in the living room, shaking with terror. I didn't dare go through the dark hall to the kitchen where my mother was, or up the dark stairs to my father. True, I didn't possess the Green Hand, but maybe its owner might be lurking in the hall and decide he needed some strangling practice.

It was not until I was about eleven that the first television set appeared on the block. Wayne Robey's father was an electrician and he built a seven-inch set. I would stand in the back of the Robey's basement, trying to get a glimpse of the shimmering, snowy figure of Hopalong Cassidy. There was always a crowd, so I never saw much. I wished my father had taken up electronics instead of law.

But most of the time, my friends and I did not have an electronic court jester to cavort for us when boredom sat heavy on our shoulders. We had something else. We had a magnificent ritual, shared, unvaried, knitted tight into the fabric of our childhood. It was an experience that still leaves its shadow across the way we perceive reality.

We had Saturday Afternoon at the Movies.

Now, it may be said that today's kids still go to the movies, but it is not the same; not the same at all. By Saturday today's kids are sated. The TV has been at them all week and the movie is just more of the same. I took my son to a children's matinee recently and the theater was never quiet at any time during the film. The kids talked and played exactly the way they do at home when the TV set is on. But for us, Saturday afternoon from one to three was *it;* all we had. (More often than not it was one to five, or six. We would sit through the serial and the reviews and the cartoons and the feature twice, and when darkness fell, irate fathers prowled the aisles, calling children's names. My father was often among them; we would promise faithfully to call him when the movie was over and when the dinner began to boil on the stove he would come and root us out of the movie. We would say, with wide-eyed innocence, that the movie wasn't over yet. We considered the fact that it was the second time around a mere technicality.)

I have heard people say that television is making us a nation of sharers; and it is true that our children all know about the Cookie Monster and can count in Sesame Street cadence. But they are separate sharers. They sit in their own houses, linked to other children only vicariously by the image flickering simultaneously on ten million television sets.

But for us, Saturday Afternoon at the Movies was a highly social event. Going to a movie alone was unthinkable, perverse. To this day I cannot walk into a movie house alone without feeling utterly depressed. Anyone who can't find *someone* to go to a movie with has truly experienced rejection.

When our group had assembled—three to seven being the median range—there was the question of logistics. In bad weather, that meant figuring out whose father could be conned into driving us to the movies (usually mine).

In good weather it meant choosing a route. Though the theater was only ten blocks away, different routes offered different attractions. One enticed us with houses under construction to climb into; another offered a dandy sewer; a third had a vacant lot to mess around in; and a fourth had a genuine boarded-up haunted house. The choice was not simple.

The movie theater we frequented on Saturday afternoons was called the Seco. There was another in town called The Silver which had flashier decor and showed the good movies our parents went to see. The Seco was moviehouse baroque gone to seed, and it suited us. There were rumors that rats lived in the Seco, but I never saw one.

The theater manager was a fat man with a mustache, and about his bulk floated an air of seediness that matched precisely the quality the Seco had achieved. He was our natural enemy, and tormenting him was a sacred duty. The American ingenuity that propelled us to the moon may well have been nurtured in the Secos of the nation, where the children of the Republic matched wits with the theater managers.

Our schemes to avoid paying the twenty-cent tariff were elaborate and unrelenting. If the manager threw us out, we would reappear in exactly the same seats five minutes later. A tap on the Seco's rear door would always call some kid inside the theater to open the door a crack while we slipped in. The theater manager would see the light cracking in through the door and hurry to try to grab us. But once the lights were out, we could melt in with the crowd, perched in our seats with our feet on the backs of the seats ahead, surreptitiously munching hamburgers.

The Seco had a rule that no one could eat anything in the theater that did not come from the vending machines in the lobby. We padded our coats with hamburgers from the Little Tavern next door, and when the ushers instituted about-the-waist frisks, we shoved the hamburgers in our underpants.

Bean shooters were in vogue for a time, followed by paper clips, which, propelled by rubber bands, made a delightful ping against the screen. A local bread manufacturer once made the disasterous mistake of handing out to each child a miniature loaf of bread. Chaos followed. The screen *wanged* each time a loaf hit it, and the shadow of falling bread slices flickered like a flight of swallows across it. The air was thick with the spongy pieces of white bread. The Seco, for the first time in recorded history, capitulated and cleared the theater.

But while all this was a part of the Saturday ritual, at the heart of it was the movie itself. Fooling around was expected during the previews, Hearst's movietone news, even during the "mushy" parts of the movie or when Gene Autry sang. But for the movie itself—always a B movie, for the Seco showed no others—we had respect.

Our parents did not have to worry that we would learn anything much about the Facts of Life from the Seco. (My mother-in-law took my five-year-old to a Saturday matinee one day to see *Smokey the Bear*—great for the kiddies. The previews were for *The Marquis de Sade*.) Westerns were the staple of the Saturday fare, and if the hero fondled anybody, it was his horse. Action was the ingredient of both the movie and the serial that always preceded it. The serials went on endlessly, each week leaving the hero in some impossible predicament. They did not generate much suspense; we knew the hero was going to be O.K. and the devices for his salvation were extremely transparent. At the end of one sequence the hero would put his hand on a box containing dynamite and it would blow up immediately. But at the beginning of next week's episode, the hero would be out the door before it blew.

Few adults patronized the Seco, for obvious reasons. One

day Beano and I sat in back of one man who had ventured in to see a war movie. I had lost my nickel for a candy bar and I was telling Beano it was her moral duty to lend me one. She refused.

"I'll never be your friend if you don't."

"I don't care."

"My father won't give you a ride home. He won't let you in the car. You'll have to walk home in the rain."

"I'll call *my* father."

"You can't be in the Science Club if you don't."

"Says who?"

"Me. I'm the president."

"I'll vote for David to be the president."

"You can't do that. I'm already the president."

"Yes I can."

"No you can't."

"Yes I can."

"No you can't."

The man turned around in his seat, thrust a coin into my hand and growled, "There's your goddammed nickel, kid. Now take it and shut up!"

The names of the cowboy heroes who were my favorites on Saturdays at the Seco have vanished completely from public mention. When film buffs talk with nostalgia about the great cowboy heroes, they talk of men who rode before my time—Hoot Gibson and Tim McCoy. But I cannot forget Charles Starrett as the Durango Kid, who wore a black mask and went around Doing Good. Lash La Rue was a forerunner of the non-violent philosophy. He had no qualms about smashing any bad guy in the teeth, but he never shot anyone. He had a whip as fast as a cobra and he disarmed the forces of evil with his lightening wrist. Pieces of clothesline vanished mysteriously from backyards whenever the Seco featured Lash La Rue.

Tim Holt had a Mexican sidekick and "Wild Bill" Elliot

(who played Red Ryder) had Li'l Beaver, an Indian boy, as a sidekick. Johnny Mack Brown was on the side of the angels. When our fathers told us he had been an All-American, we were not impressed. We had seen him drill three villains with a single shot. Anyone could throw a football. Roy Rogers and Gene Autry were tolerated, but were considered too effete to be greatly admired. Their clothes were too clean and they wasted all that time singing.

The Good Guys were sometimes the Bad Guys. Jesse James was the ultimate Western hero. We never tired of movies about him: *I Shot Jessee James; The James Boys; The Return of Jessee James; Frank James Rides Again.* (Since Jesse didn't have any children, the producers of the B movies couldn't use a favorite ploy—the "Son Of" films. If a hero was a popular draw, why not his progeny? We sat through *Son of Lassie; Son of Robin Hood; Son of Frankenstein.* If they had made *Third Nephew Twice Removed of Robin Hood* we would have sat through that, too.)

Among our favorite bad guys were the Daltons and the Youngers, Sam Bass and Belle Starr. The generation that was nourished on these tales is now on the far side of thirty; we are generally presumed to be among those who cherish law-and-order. But I wonder. For in those B movies that are still a part of us, however minuscule, there was a remarkable cynicism about The Law.

As often as not, the man who wore the badge was a paid lackey of the Establishment. He took his orders from Brian Donlevy—wearing a flowered vest and a mustache—playing either the railroad owner out to cheat the farmers or the banker foreclosing mortgages on widows. Our heroes often had a price on their heads; but it was a price set by a corrupt and cynical elite who richly deserved the comeuppance they were sure to get.

Our heroes, it seems to me, were a great deal more like Bobby Seale or Daniel Berrigan or Daniel Ellsberg than

John Mitchell. (In fact, I can never look at John Mitchell without seeing a fancy vest and a mustache.)

The B movies contained a lot of what we would now—being much more sophisticated—call the sociological explanation of the roots of crime.

The James boys or the Daltons did not rob banks out of sheer avarice. In the prologue to the film we saw them as children, watching in horror as their farm was burned and their father murdered by the agents of People in Power. Vengeance was their motive, pure if misguided. While the movies could not go so far as to let unrepentant bank robbers triumph, when they fell dead in a hail of lawmen's bullets, we knew they were as much victims as predators.

The war movies were second in popularity to the Westerns, followed by swashbuckling pirates. The pirates, like the Bad Guys, were often heroic rebels; but the war movies, churned up in the wake of World War II, were locked into a more predictable mold. The Westerns might present the outlaw as hero, but the Bad Guys in the war movies had few redeeming virtues. We never wept when a Zero went down in flames. We applauded, in much the same spirit that we would have clapped for a home-team double. War was utterly synthetic in the movies. It was a grand game, riskier, perhaps, than baseball, but filled with more opportunities for glory. The advertisement that appeared in *Life* magazine for MGM's *Battleground* gives a good idea of Hollywood's version of war:

"Scenes like these from *Battleground* fasten themselves vividly in your mind . . . Denise, a lovely French girl, who is *very* friendly—Holly (Van Johnson) dodging snipers' bullets but worried about his six stolen eggs . . . snow . . . fog . . . dawn attack . . . disaster . . . then, shadows on the snow . . . sunshine . . . planes . . . droves of them . . . a skyfull of billowing parachutes—ammo . . . rations desperately needed . . . 'Hey wiseguy, who said it didn't do any good to toss in a prayer once in a while' . . . Here is excitement! Belly Laughs in the midst of Terror!"

John Wayne and Alan Ladd single-handedly killed more Japs and Jerries, sank more ships, blasted more fighters, slogged through more jungle, than any five regiments. Sometimes they perished (nobly, with violins) and sometimes they survived, but the picture always closed with the fleet streaming toward the sunset ("Anchors Aweigh") or the B-29's filling the sky ("Off we go, into the wild blue yonder") or the landing craft hitting the beaches. ("From the halls of Montezuma to the shores of Tripoli.") If the recruiters had been waiting outside the theater they would have been swamped by eight-year-olds, Beano and me among them.

If the war movies are to be faulted, it is most probably for this—letting us grow up believing that war was the way Warner Brothers showed it to us. If the movies were propaganda for the American way of life, well, so were our textbooks. If they were racist, they were no more so than the rest of our society. There was no public outcry against the image of a bile-yellow, buck-toothed Hirohito. The roots of My Lai and all the other horrors we never heard about in places like Korea or Laos or Vietnam lie far deeper in the fabric of the Republic than a John Wayne movie. But we *can* tell John Wayne he Lied in *Fighting Leathernecks,* and all the others. The power of the lie endures because the Grand Game in technicolor stays in the mind when the small black and white news photos and the grainy sixty-second television news films recede.

The grip the Saturday movies fastened on our imagination was due perhaps to sheer lack of competition. Our children are fed image sandwiches by the television. Layer is heaped on layer so fast that the flavor of each is erased by the new slab that is slapped on. We had seven days to digest the Saturday movie. We began by playing it on the

33

way home. (How many movies are there today that kids could play on the way home without getting arrested by the morals squad?)

The walk home was usually taken up by the argument over who got to play what part. I remember once that I made a hasty choice early in a movie called *The Death March on Bataan*. My character got bayoneted through the heart in the second reel. Beano and David insisted I had to stick with my original choice. I refused. The arguments were always resolved exactly the same way each time. Jesse or Robin Hood became triplets—or quadruplets, or sextuplets, depending on our number. The only exceptions were the Daltons and the Youngers, because there were enough of them to go around.

Girls were entitled to be Jesse as well as boys; female role models were scarce. Most of the women in the movies were always standing around screaming, cringing, kissing, or something stupid like that. The only movie females I deigned to emulate in my entire childhood were Esther Williams and Belle Starr. (Belle not only could ride and shoot and rob banks, but she looked like Yvonne De Carlo to boot.)

On the days that followed Saturday we galloped across back yards, stripping leaves from my mother's best rhododendron bush to use for money, then stuffing them in the mail box on David's front porch. Then we robbed the bank. We sat in the sandbox carelessly slinging sand into tin cans, muttering about "Havin' some Grub," and we bailed out of the woodpile at the back of my yard.

The sandbox is gone now—it was ripped up years ago. No one bails out of the woodpile, and the rhododendron thrives, although how it survived, I will never know, having supplied the funds for so many daring bank robberies. And the Seco? Its insides have been ripped out, and with them the Seco's magnificent seediness and the rumored resident rats.

They were replaced by reclining seats and modern art. The theater has a new name and it serves expresso coffee and it shows "films," not movies. The movies we watched on those Saturday afternoons are moldy pieces of celluloid in musty warehouses. Most of them are not considered of sufficient interest to be dredged up for the "Late Late Show" on television, even by the most penurious UHF operation.

I suppose it is absurd to mourn them. The Muse will not have been dealt a blow when these moldering pieces of film crumble into nothingness. But somehow, it seems that it is the trivial things that mark the childhood of a generation, rather than the great events. The storms of the adult world are perceived dimly by children, much as a cod in the half-light of ocean deep might sense an April gale. The things that touched our everyday lives remain in memory. If the psychiatrists are to be believed when they say that the vertebrae of our psyches form and stiffen when we are very young, there may be a high celluloid content in those vertebrae. The flesh of the creature we knew as "Saturday Afternoon at the Movies" may lie amoldering in the warehouses; but its spirit marches on, somewhere in the collective subconscious of a generation of Americans.

3
God's Kingdom

I spent one year in the public schools in Silver Spring, the second grade. It was the year of my first—and last—step Outside the Law.

David and I missed the bus one morning, and we decided we would not, like dutiful children, go home to our mothers. We would defy the law; we would be daring, like the James brothers.

Stepping Outside the Law was great for forty-five minutes, mildly diverting for another hour, and after that, miserably boring. At 10:15 we went into the corner market, where the grocer made us sandwiches, which we ate crouched in the parking lot. We tried to think of a way we could go home without arousing suspicion.

We decided to tell our mothers we had been let out of school early because the furnace had broken down. It sounded logical and it had historical precedent. The furnace was notably erratic.

There was only one small detail we had not considered. The month was May and the temperature was 85 degrees.

I blurted out the truth after an interrogation by my mother which consisted of one raised eyebrow. I had to go back to school. My little painted chair was put in the front of the classroom while my teacher explained my sin to my peers. I was an outcast, a criminal. I never tried to step Outside the Law again.

The next year, my parents decided to enroll me in the parish school. I remember standing in the schoolyard behind a boy holding a sign that said: THIRD GRADE and feeling like an immigrant fresh off the boat at Ellis Island. A nun walked to the steps of the school and began to wave a large hand bell, and the line began to move. We all marched together into the school, a large beige brick building that looked like a combination of a packing crate and a Babylonian ziggurat with the top layers sliced off. I stared at the madonnas in the niches in the hallway as we marched by. I did not know it then, but it was a new world I was entering as I marched into the beige brick building; not merely the third grade but the dominion of the Holy Roman Catholic Church.

I had arrived in God's Kingdom.

Growing up Catholic in mid-century America was both absurd and marvelous. Absurd, because as I look back from a distance of some twenty years, I see a world of changeless truth, simple moral choices, and nodding assent that seems as distant from contemporary reality as the age when crossbreasted crusaders whacked heathen skulls in the name of Jesus Christ. I cannot imagine that it has vanished so utterly; it seemed so durable. The jut-jaw of John Foster Dulles loomed from the cover of *Time*, immutable as Gibraltar. Fulton Sheen surely should have outlasted Ed Sullivan, with his laser-beam eyes and that small, pleased smile that crept across his finely cut face when he made a point particularly well. And now brave Dulles is merely a crusty curmudgeon of a memory, the pronouncements so admired now extinct as the Brontosaurus. Fulton Sheen, so daring then, seems small potatoes. Today's priests get hunted by the FBI, agitate to get married and disagree with the Pope.

Nothing like that happened at mid-century. It was a time when priests went to Wednesday night bingo, nuns wore their skirts to the floor, rock and jazz were for bars, not churches, and the Godless Atheistic Communists were excoriated from the pulpit Sunday after Sunday after Sunday.

It was marvelous, because the Catholic Church has always had an instinctive sense of style. It melds the pizzaz of burlesque piano with the unsullied ice of Gregorian chant. Consider, for example, incense. Catholic incense is not the same clammy-sweet stuff that teen-age heads use to mask the smell of burning grass. It is at once sweet and smoky and it tingles the small hairs in your nostrils. How did the Church happen on the peculiar power of that smell? Who in some murky Gothic yesterday understood that a smell is the closest thing human beings have to a time machine?

I can never smell Catholic incense without being snapped back to a small and crowded church on an afternoon that is so warm it weights my eyelids. I can feel the ache in my back from kneeling straight, and the delicious relief of dropping my buttocks back against the seat; still kneeling technically, just cheating a bit. My skin is damp beneath the green serge parochial school uniform I am wearing, and I am singing, "Holy God, We Praise Thy Name/All in Heaven Above Adore Thee/All on earth Thy Sceptre claim."

The incense runs up my nose and coils down into my lungs, the physical manifestation of the grace of God. It is good to know that I am in the state of grace and that if I get hit by a truck as I step off the curb in front of the church I will go right to heaven to sit among the Thrones and Dominations.

Being very young and Catholic was filled with delights. The theology presented to the Catholic child could have sprung from the gentle brain of Walt Disney, with the dreadful coyness of Bambi sifted out. The kingdom of God was more magical than *Fantasia*. Presiding over it all was God the Father, a kindly old man with a white beard, who gave us each day our daily bread, which I assumed was wrapped in cellophane and had the word WONDER printed on it. Jesus was the man in the picture in the third-grade classroom in the parochial school, with the melted chocolate eyes and the neatly trimmed beard, surrounded by smiling children. Mary, his mother, was a porcelain statue with the skin of a Revlon ad, streaming God-grace from down-turned hands. Looking at her, we knew she had never screamed at *her* son: "Damn it, clean up this room this instant or no movies for a month!"

God's intentions were totally benign.

"Why did God make us?"

"To know Him, love Him and serve Him and to be happy with Him forever in heaven," cooed the children, reading from the little green catechism.

The Holy Family was an integral part of our lives in parochial school, although Joseph tended to be a bit player compared to Jesus and Mary. We nodded our heads gravely every time anyone spoke the name of the Son of God, and at the top of all our papers we wrote J.M.J. If we forgot, the papers were handed back and we were gently chided. In my neighborhood there were only two children who went to parochial school, my classmate Tony and myself. It so happened that in one of the neighborhood clubs we formed, I was elected president and Tony was vice-president. We named our group the Victory Club, since World War II was still fresh in our imaginations. As executives, Tony and I got to design the club pennant. David's mother (Protestant) volunteered to make the pennant on her sewing machine. He was the treasurer of our collective fortune, which amounted to fifty-four cents which the membership had earned by scrounging old Coke bottles and taking them back to the store for the two-cent deposit.

David's mother brought the finished pennant to show my mother. It was red, and it said VICTORY CLUB in large white letters, and above that, in smaller white stitching, were the letters JMJ.

"Do you know what that stands for?" My mother asked.

"No," said our neighbor. "David said it was a secret code and only Tony and Caryl know what it is."

"Jesus, Mary and Joseph," said my mother, and they both cracked up.

As Catholic children we had a companion at our side, more constant than Lassie, more vigilant than the school-boy patrol. We had a Guardian Angel.

I walked home from school some days listening intently for the flapping of wings. It (the gender was not clear) looked like the picture on my favorite Holy card of two children crossing a rickety bridge over a swift current. The G.A. levitated just behind them, its silvered wings hovering about them like a mother's hands. Some children were very dutiful about their angel, sitting on only half the chair at suppertime and carefully pushing a clump of food to one side for it, which drove mothers to distraction. Cunning children second-guessed the angel palate.

"I'm giving the angel all the broccoli. Angels like broccoli."

It is a difficult point to debate with a seven-year-old.

Legend, fact, and myth blended effortlessly in God's kingdom, and the saints did battle with Satan in epics that dwarfed the Brothers Grimm. St. George slew a dragon, St. Christopher waded across a stream with the Christ Child on his back, a shower of rose petals fell at the death of the Little Flower, St. Theresa, the sun whirled in the heavens for Our Lady of Fatima, the birds spoke to Francis of Assisi.

There were pictures of the saints, as well as those of the Holy Family, all around me in parochial school. Every classroom had a crucifix, a twin of the ones the nuns wore at their breast, a statue of the Virgin and assorted pictures of the saints. Usually there was a calendar supplied by Hanlon's funeral home, which featured the Martyr of the Month. In January we watched the days march by under St. Sebastian, tied to a post with arrows protruding from his appendix. In February it was St. Lawrence being roasted alive, in March St. Peter crucified upside down, in April St. Joan burning at the stake, and so on through the year.

I don't remember being distressed by all this gore. Perhaps it was because through it all the victim's expression remained one of mild vexation, eyes rolled upward and a slight frown, as if he was annoyed by the possibility of rain.

The tales of the martyrs were, in fact, no more grisly than the beloved fairy tales of our early youth, in which people were constantly being dismembered, eaten by ogres, or otherwise coming to unpleasant ends. It was also true that martyrdom did not exactly threaten us in a suburb of Truman's Washington, despite the rhetorical questions about How We Would Behave If Told to Renounce Our Faith. I knew all along what I would do if the commies told me to renounce or else. I would cross my fingers and say Karl Marx was great. After that, I would take to the hills with a Thompson submachine gun and become the tough-but-beautiful leader of a group of Free Fighting Catholic Democrats. I was a great believer in the motto: "She Who Lies and Gets Away, Lives to Fight Another Day."

We had numerous discussions about martyrdom in the schoolyard that would have chilled the blood of any adult walking by. We debated, in a detached way, about which was the best way to get martyred. Getting shot and freezing to death were the popular choices. Legend had it that the latter was very pleasant; you just got a warm feeling all over and went to sleep. Nobody opted for burning or getting eaten by Lions, though if pressed, we would have given the Lions a slight edge.

The Catholic Church knew how to manipulate even our budding human defects for the greater glory of God, interpreted, in one particular case, as a larger subscription for the diocesan newspaper, *The Catholic Review.*

Prizes were offered to the children who sold the most subscriptions. I can still see the two prizes that brought the saliva of material lust pooling to my mouth. There was an altar perhaps two feet square, made of imitation marble with candles that lit up when you plugged it in. There was also an infant Jesus of Prague, a statue of the infant in an outfit that could have come from the MGM wardrobe for a movie about Queen Elizabeth. Tiny Christ was choked by a lace ruff. The God-man who said "Blessed are the poor" was smothered in a red satin dress with ribbons, geegaws and fake precious stones. I thought he was gorgeous. Children usually have lousy taste.

I tramped through my neighborhood trying to sell *The Catholic Review* to Lutherans and Methodists. The altar and the infant were lugged off by children blessed with Catholic uncles, cousins, and neighbors.

The great difference at mid-century between public and parochial school—besides the omnipresence of God in our schools—was the nuns. The fifties were the high-water mark of religious recruiting in American Catholicism. There seemed to be no end to the great stream of girls that flowed to the church each year to yield brides of Christ. The nuns were the shepherdesses of our education. They dressed like Mary, and if the children confused the two, no harm done. The nuns were creatures somehow apart from time, or so it seemed to me. Time's motion is not the same for children as it is for adults. It hovers, drifts, speeds alternately. Sometimes it stops completely, as on a May afternoon in arithmetic class with the siren smell of warm air and earth wafting through the classroom window. The wait for the bell is an eternity.

The nuns shared our time zone, because they were so much a part of our lives and because they were not anchored in the past. Their own personal past was obliterated for us by the habit. They did not talk of their mothers and fathers or sisters and brothers, so we assumed they had none. They were invented just for us.

In those years there was a spate of priest-and-nun movies (*Going My Way, The Bells of St. Mary's*) with Bing Crosby's larynx moving tunefully beneath the Roman collar and Loretta Young, all white teeth and eyelashes in her habit. It was all a con job, of course. Not many priests could sing like Crosby and the nuns did not have Loretta's cheekbones or her cardboard sweetness. I remember one nun who punished us for talking in class by making us stand in a corner holding all our books. The geography alone weighed half a ton. Another hiked up her skirts with a safety pin to kick a football twenty yards. The principal of the parochial school was a nun who listened to us as if we had opinions of consequence; I never remember her being unfair. And there was my sixth-grade teacher who marked me down for arguing that Cheyenne, Wyoming, was pronounced Shy Ann and not Shane. Any kid who went to Westerns knew it was Shy Ann.

The nuns who taught me in my earliest years have receded back into a general memory of nunnishness. I can remember the rustle of a skirt, a voice, white hands beneath chalk-white cuffs, nothing more. But my fifth-grade teacher, Sister Francette, I can see in my mind's eye as clearly as if I left her yesterday. There she is, tiny and wrinkled, a face all nose and the iron rims of spectacles. She was an instinctive teacher. I don't know how she did it, but she even coaxed from me an enthusiasm for the geography book that said things like: Sao Paulo is in the coffee-producing region of Brazil.

Sister Francette was also a health fanatic. Every now and then she would tell us to close our books and fold our hands, and she would begin one of her health stories.

There was a young girl, she said, who worked as a cashier in a luncheonette. The girl handled money and was careless about washing her hands. She got leprosy. First her fingers rotted, then her toes, then her nose. They turned yellow, smelled, and finally dropped off.

A young boy who constantly used profanity got his come-uppance. He got cancer of the tongue. He repented, and his last words before they cut out his tongue were "Jesus, Mary and Joseph."

One story that did not seem to have a moral was about the Pig Baby. It seems that when Sister Francette was a young girl, a mysterious baby was born in her neighborhood. She sneaked a look at it in its carriage one day. She saw, she told us, a baby dressed in ruffled white with dainty pink human hands and the head of a pig. (I have often wondered about the genesis of the Pig Baby. Did Sister Francette as a child happen on a deformed infant that to her young eyes was not quite human, or did she invent the pig baby in her own lively—if macabre—imagination?

I had nightmares. My fingers rotted, my tongue was cut out. Finally I told my mother about them. She said, very sensibly, that I couldn't get all the diseases, so if I had to worry I should pick out one and worry about it exclusively. There were parental rumblings about Sister Francette's health stories, but I do not recall that they had any effect upon the storyteller.

It was in the fifth grade too, that I first remember a real comprehension of death. I suppose I had assumed, as children do, that the fact of my existence was proof of immortality. On one of those warm afternoons I always associate with going to church, the entire class was ordered into a single line and marched three blocks to the Warner E. Pumphrey funeral home. I would go there again from time to time. My grandfather and both grandmothers were buried from Pumphrey's, and the atmosphere inside the colonial brick building, with its lawns manicured as neatly as the fingernails of the deceased, was always consistent.

Inside might be the blaze of summer noon or the dark winter rain, but in Pumphrey's it was always a dusk of dim lights and hushed voices. It was as if the management felt it had to please its clients, the quick and the dead, by creating a limbo, a place of half-life where they could mingle on equal terms. The air was drenched with the scent of flowers. To this day I am convinced that death smells like carnations.

The fifth-grade class filed wordlessly into one of the carpeted rooms at Pumphrey's and we were prodded gently into a circle around a small casket. A first-grader had died of leukemia and we had come to pray for the repose of his soul. He wore a striped blazer and his still, small hands were draped with a rosary and beneath his eyes were shadows that the cosmetician had not been able to conceal. The Hail Marys droned on until we forgot where we were and started to fidget. The rosary ended and we filed out, and when the sunlight hit us we began to chatter and jump so nosily that Sister Francette had to snap her clacker at us. Pumphrey's limbo was a hostile environment. The life in us propelled us through the door and spilled out through high, clear voices.

Walking home from school that day, I did not see the tan cement of the road or the forsythia bushes blooming on every lawn. I saw the dead boy, and I gazed at him both terrified and fascinated as intimations of my own mortality vibrated through me. I think I prayed, but not the words of the countless prayers we learned by rote. God was the father of us all, and my own father was good and gentle, so could God be less? I addressed him without hesitation.

"Don't let it happen to me, God. Dear Mary and Jesus, I promise I'll be good and say the rosary and go to mass. Don't let it happen to me."

There was an intimacy in our relationship with the nuns that persisted through my years in the parish school. The priests, who we saw often, did not share our daily routine, and so they were more remote, if familiar. The boys, I think, felt closer to the priests than the girls did, simply as fellow members of the great male fraternity. The priests sometimes horsed around with the boys, roughhoused, tossed baseballs, but they were more circumspect with the girls. Priests were authority figures; the nuns deferred to them, and we were properly respectful. We might snap back an impertinent answer to a nun, but we were conscious of the exalted station of the priests.

They lived in a small beige brick house, with only the black-topped school yard separating the rectory from the school building. We children never saw more of it than the parlor if we had occasion to stop by on an errand. A housekeeper, well past middle age, always opened the door when we rang. I don't remember ever hearing her speak. I don't remember her at all, except as a mumbling presence.

The rectory seemed to us a place of mystery, unknowable. I know now that there was no mystery there at all, just medium-sized rooms, comfortably but plainly furnished. The house that was the rectory has since been sold, but when I drive by it now I can think of it as nothing else but "The Rectory." It seems small and forlorn now, not at all exotic, and I cannot help thinking as I pass it that the men who lived there through the years must have spent many lonely hours in those plain-but-comfortable rooms.

The rooms the nuns inhabited in the large convent building around the corner were doubtless smaller and plainer. But despite the restrictions of convent living there seemed to be a centrifugal force of community that pulsed through the white frame building; a sense of a sheltering, shared world within the walls that the nuns always spoke of in the plural possessive: Our Parlor, Our Chapel, Our Garden.

The priests did not speak so of their rooms in the rectory. They came as strangers to a strange place, not knowing how long they would stay. If they got on with the other men in the house, well and good. If not, it was a situation that had to be borne for an unknown period of time. The priest might indeed make friends in the parish, but often he would find an invisible barrier standing between his friends and himself. It was a curtain of subtleties, of inflections in the voice, of things unspoken in the presence of a priest. The priest may not have wanted it there, but the parishioners thought he would expect it.

In their eyes, he was not like them. He stood higher. They called him "Father" and the word must have been as often a strait jacket as a tribute. Idiosyncrasies were acceptable in priests, but certain kinds of human weakness were not. I remember one priest, matinee-idol handsome, who was a great favorite with the boys in the school. He always wore an aviator's jacket, World War II style, and with the touches of gray at his temples, he was a dashing figure. It seems to me that he simply vanished one day. Rumors filtered down to us that he had a problem with drink, but no one spoke of it except in whispers. A priest with such a problem would be a scandal to the Faithful.

Another young priest who came to the parish was noted for his anti-Communist fervor. He was a handsome six-footer, an ex-Marine, and the intensity of his fervor seemed to vibrate the pulpit on Sunday morning, especially when he preached on the Red Horde. He left, suddenly, and again there were rumors: nervous breakdown.

I have no idea if the rumors about these two priests had any truth to them. But I know that we expected that a priest who bent under the pressures of his life would be taken suddenly from our gaze, as if the sight of his pain would tarnish our shiny, mind-held image of A Priest.

What a burden it must have been to them—nun and priest alike—to have to be better than we were. I can imagine how often the priests sat in their-plain-but-comfortable rooms in the rectory and wondered how the glowing dreams of serving God dwindled to paying repair bills for church roofs, swallowing creamed chicken and peas at the Men's Club Dinner and ordering warm-up jackets for the school teams in the store of a parishioner who hinted that he was storing up Brownie points in heaven by his largesse.

The priest I remember most vividly from the parish was the pastor, Father Ziep. He was such a commanding figure that one tends to remember him only in vivid blacks and whites, the way children store memories of special people from the past. Years later, I drew on those memories to write a piece that appeared in the New York *Times* Magazine about the parish school. This was my portrait of him:

On a certain day the classroom would be cleaned with particular care and the nuns oversaw the fresh lettering in colored chalk of the Biblical saying on the blackboard. Father Ziep was coming to give out report cards.

Father Ziep was the pastor and I believe he was Andrew Carnegie re-incarnated. He built a fine new church when the parish outgrew the old one, and paid off a staggering debt in three years. There was no subtlety in him. Parishioners who were irked with him muttered, "That Damn Stubborn Dutchman!" His face was intransigence in the flesh. Rembrandt would have cherished it. A great winged nose swept down it and he would stand in the pulpit at Christmastime and lean over, nose dipping to the faithful like a Boeing 707 in a climbing turn.

"I hear a lot of talk around here about a white Christmas. What I want around here is a GREEN Christmas. (Pause for effect) A GREEN Christmas."

He had no patience with latecomers at Mass, and would often interrupt the Latin prayers to point at them and holler at them to come up front and take a seat. Once he saw a boy sitting in the choir loft lean out and swing the chandelier that hung from the church ceiling. The pastor was at the place in the Mass where he turns to the congregation to begin a Latin prayer.

He swung around, palms upward, and said, "Oratre Fratres. There are two people in this congregation who have a jackass for a son."

Father Ziep's face was the mirror image of his will. He fought and did not yield. Lose, maybe, but yield never. His enemies were formidable: The Hecht Company (a department store) and the Federal government.

Father Ziep's magnificent nose quivered like a tuning fork when it caught a whiff of socialism. He was a champion of Free Enterprise. He turned down government aid for the school lunch program. Parents gnashed their teeth. Father Ziep stood firm as Gibraltar. The school launched its own independent and non-socialistic lunch program.

The bill of fare was memorable. One day it would be bread and gravy, a watery brown sauce dribbled over white bread that had been sliced so thin it was barely visible. On another day it was franks and beans—very heavy on the beans. Another menu was scalloped potatoes and something, but all I ever got were potatoes.

The Hecht Company was the town's first department store, and it went up a block away from the school. Between the store and the school was the field, a few precious acres of dust, dying grass and weeds that was a great playground for kids with imagination. It was where we played at recess. It was county property, and both Father Ziep and the Hecht Company coveted it. The company wanted a warehouse and Father Ziep wanted a county park. After a protracted struggle, the county made it into a parking lot.

Father Ziep railed from the pulpit about the clinking of cash registers at the materialistic Hecht Company and complained that there was no Nativity scene in the windows at Christmastime. When he had lost the field, his vendetta endured. On Friday nights, when the parking lot was overflowing with shoppers, he stood with a lantern at the entrance to the school's black-topped yard. "No Hechters here," he would call out. "No Hechters here."

He remains in my mind an epic figure, solitary and un-
bowed by the forces of mammon.

Father Ziep's visits to the classroom were viewed as visitations from God the Father, armed with the book of everyone's sins. As he swept in we jumped to our feet and
sing-songed, "Good MORning FAther. He sat at the big desk
in the front of the room fingering a stack of white cards.
Stomachs lurched. Mouths dried. He read the names in al-
phabetical order, offering comments.

"Now you have a D in spelling. Why do you have a D?"

"I don't know, Father."

"Don't know? What do you mean, you don't know? You
haven't worked hard enough, isn't that right?"

"Yes, Father."

"Well, you had better get to work. Next time I want to
see a B. Am I going to see a B?"

"Yes, Father."

There were no underachievers in Catholic School. Either
you were a dumb kid or you were lazy. Catholic school did
not traffic with such notions as traumatizing the child. A
little trauma was considered good for the soul as well as for
the report card.

* * *

In time, Father Ziep read my magazine article, and he
took great umbrage. He dispatched a letter to me from the
rectory—he is now in his eighties and retired—and I was
delighted to see that time had not staled his fighting spirit.
He recalled that I had not won any of the school essay contests, and observed that my "present dribble" vindicated
the judgment of the school. He proceeded to set me straight
on a few things. First of all, he was no Andrew Carnegie.
Far from being a champion of Free Enterprise, he had
often entertained the notion that some form of communism,
divorced from Russian atheism, might be a good thing for
the world. He remembered that the Damn Stubborn Dutchman wouldn't start building a new church until he had $200,-

ooo cash, because he didn't believe in paying a lot of money
to banks. When one parishioner grumbled, he got his money
back from Father Ziep.

The pastor did not recall the incident with the kid and
the chandelier. Any kid who tried such a stunt would not
have been dignified with the name jackass, he said. A jackass has sense.

I wrote back to Father Ziep, explaining that my portrait
had been an admiring one. Mid-century was the time of
the gray flannel suit and the pervasive flavor was bland. In
such a time a man of Father Ziep's unique personal traits
was to be cherished, and if some of my facts were askew,
it was due to the child-lens of my memory.

In another letter he told me something of his life as a
priest, and it was not just a life but the story of the immigrant church. We knew little of it when Father Ziep was
our pastor. The Catholic heroes we learned of in school
were saints facing lions or bishops wrestling with commis-
sars, events so far detached from our daily lives as to be
almost mythical. We did not understand that in a time not
long past, people who professed the faith we were learning
lived lives of such desperate hardship that they clung to
the rock of the Church as shipwrecked sailors might clutch
onto a floating spar. We could not comprehend a life wrung
dry of its energy by the struggle for the next meal or a roof
to keep out the rain. We thought our scrambled eggs and our
Kix and Wheaties at the breakfast table were as inevitable
as the sunrise. We may not have been exactly children of
affluence, but we regarded a certain modicum of comfort
as an unquestioned part of our lives—and we assumed, of
everyone's. If, as we were growing up, we discovered that
there was a simplicity, a lack of sophistication in the institution that nurtured us, we simply put it down to the many
peculiarities of the adult world. We did not know that the
people the Church had served for so long had needs much

more primal than ours. A man with no job and no schooling and a sick child does not care about theology. A simple prayer, a simple faith, will serve.

Father Ziep grew up among such people, in the coal fields of western Pennsylvania, and it was the oppression and the suffering that he saw there that led to his contempt for the Carnegies of the world. He says (in words that sound more like a Progressive Labor Party brochure than the opinion of a parish priest, that all their foundations, museums and institutions cannot atone for their heartlessness toward the poor. They were built on the sweat, health, life, and death of the exploited worker.

He saw there, too, a strong and steady faith. He took part in a Corpus Christi festival one year, and watched whole families who had walked fifty miles to the festival, sleeping at night by the side of the road.

He entered the seminary as a young man, trying to hide from his superiors the symptoms from a case of rheumatic fever he had contracted when he was nine. His first parish was a black parish in Washington where he had to walk miles every day to make sick calls to the only city hospital that would admit Negroes. His second parish was in western Maryland; when he arrived there on the train there were no taxis or buses, so he had to walk to the rectory, carrying all his luggage. When he arrived, the housekeeper would not let him in, telling him that he had to go immediately to the hospital for a sick call. The pastor had steak every day but Friday, but his assistant never saw a piece of steak the entire time he was there. One Christmas day he felt so ill he had to clutch at the altar to keep from falling when he was saying Mass.

At another parish near the Pennsylvania border in Maryland he took only eight hundred dollars of his twelve-hundred-dollar salary, in order to build up a reserve for the bankrupt church. He raised chickens and sold eggs to make money, grew vegetables, and did all the painting and repairs on the church himself. At another church, in the slums of Baltimore, he discovered that the nuns who taught at the parish school were sleeping on mattresses filled with corn husks. The strain of conducting services, making sick calls, hearing confessions, struggling to shore up a crumbling church, haggling in vain with the archdiocese over money to make repairs, was destroying his health. The next parish to which he was sent had a church and school buildings with roofs that leaked so badly that there was sometimes three feet of water in the cellars. His predecessor used to sit on the stage in the school building and pick off rats with a .22 rifle. Father Ziep put out poison and got eight bushels of rats in two days.

There was a time, he says, when he was so fed up with being shuttled from one broken-down parish to another that if he had had a way to make a living, he would have left the priesthood. But then came Silver Spring, Maryland, and the years of struggle were over.

He says he does not regret the deprivations of his life; he is thankful for them, for they helped to mold him. They brought him closer to people and their problems. He kept in mind always, he says, that even when he had to spend much of his time raising money to keep parishes alive, he never forgot that it was the spirit that was at the center of his world. Now, he can look back on fifty years as a priest with peace of soul.

We would not have understood such things, we children who sat and shivered as we waited for Father Ziep to hand out report cards. Our most pressing concern was the mark we were about to get in deportment. The Church he had known—the one that housed people who slept on roadsides to attend festivals and nuns who slept on corn husks—was not our Church. His world would not be our world. We would find, many of us, that simple faith was not enough for survival in a time when a planet could be split at the punch of a series of buttons.

I often wonder what happened to my companions of those days in the ordeal of report cards. I went to high school with most of the girls, but the boys scattered to a dozen schools. I can look at my eighth-grade graduation picture and say each one of the fifty-five names. I remember them that clearly. I wonder what happened to Johnny, a small Greek statue masquerading as a CYO football player. He had hair so golden the sun seemed to fire it and a grin at once cocky and innocent, melting girls and nuns into love that ran out through their eyes when they looked at him. The cheerleaders sang, "'Oh Johnny, Oh Johnny, how you can run!'" when he trotted out onto the field. I wonder if he was able to cope with a life that had to lead downhill from that apex of love and admiration.

What happened to Joe, who repeated the seventh and eighth grades, and who crammed his six-foot rawboned body into one of the small desks and sat all day cracking his knuckles? I remember Bobby, with that peculiar face that was half angel, half storm trooper. He climbed out of school windows and was considered a hopeless discipline problem. Is he an ex-con or an accountant?

There are others about whom I do not have to wonder. Cynthia, with her bobbed hair and freckles, could have been drawn in an earlier age by John Held, Jr. She missed a turn driving her boyfriend's car one night and hit a pile of bricks at sixty. Tommy had an open Irish face, the kind that in later life squares off and reddens easily. Not long after Cynthia died he was watching two of his friends horsing around in a mock duel with two wooden sticks. A flying sliver lodged in his brain.

Soon after Tommy there was Theresa, sweet and pretty, whose veins had not grown strong enough to hold the blood pumping through her body. Nobody knew it until she crumpled, dying on a counter at S. S. Kresge. And we, Catholic and enlightened, whispered of things happening in threes and heard the sweep of the wings of the dark angel at the backs of our necks.

The rustlings came and went quickly. It was not death that terrified me. It was ringworm.

RINGWORM. The word struck terror in my heart. Ringworm. A fate more horrible than death. When you got it, your hair was shaved off and you had to wear a little cap made out of a woman's nylon stocking.

Every day at recess in the parochial school we had to line up by grades when we heard the bell. A boy in the line next to mine had one of the little caps. I stared, repelled but fascinated. We always marched back into the school to the strains of the "Washington Post March" played over the PA system. I would march along, watching the boy's head in the stocking bobbing along to the crescendo of the brass. To this day, I cannot hear the Washington Post March without thinking of ringworm. It is not exactly what John Philip Sousa had in mind, but there it is.

It was an article of faith that ringworm was spread by the backs of theater seats, so whenever I went to the movies I spread my jacket carefully over the back of the seat. If, in my absorption in the film, I forgot and rested my head against the naked seat, panic would clutch at me. I would imagine the little ringworms snake-dancing their way across my scalp.

I was immensely pleased that one of my classmates was spared the ravages of ringworm. He was a boy with a magnificent thatch of red hair, who stood a full foot shorter than I. He sat across from me, and when things got dull in class he would bend his head close to the desk and comb his hair vigorously until a neat little pile of white flakes rested on the desk. He made extremely clever designs in the dandruff.

I was captivated. What mattered twelve inches of height when he was so imaginative an artist?

It was only occasionally, however, that the opposite sex could draw my attention from a more pressing concern: basketball. It was basketball that filled my mind and my afternoons, basketball that I talked about at the dinner table. Basketball was what counted.

4

The Sporting Life

"Sacred Heart of Jesus, I adore Thee. Please let us beat Blessed
   Sacrament."
"Sacred Heart of Jesus, I adore Thee. Please let us beat Blessed
   Sacrament."
"Sacred Heart of Jesus, I adore Thee. Please let us beat Blessed
   Sacrament."
"Sacred Heart of Jesus, I adore Thee. Please let us beat Blessed
   Sacrament."
"Sacred Heart of Jesus, I adore Thee. Please let us beat Blessed
   Sacrament."

I said it when I genuflected in church, I said it on my
knees in my room, I said it pedaling my bike on my way to
school, I said it at any odd time I could fit it in. We needed
all the help we could get to beat Blessed Sacrament.

I had been to my first girls' basketball game in sixth grade.
I remember the day well, because everybody in the class
was going to the game and I was in despair. My mother
got out one of the dresses I always wore, with the ruffled
hem and the sash that tied in the back. I wailed in dismay
when I looked at it. Everybody was going to wear skirts
and blouses to the game. I *had* to wear a skirt and blouse. It
was the first time I had evinced any interest in such things;
suddenly it was imperative. How could I go to a basketball
game with a dress that had a sash that tied in the back.
Ukkkkkkkkk.

My mother rummaged around in her closet and came up
with an old black pleated skirt. It hung nearly to my ankles,

but it was a skirt, a bona-fide skirt. I wore my tan puffy-sleeved uniform blouse with it, and my saddle oxfords. I felt that I was at the height of fashion.

I sat in the crowded stands at the Silver Spring Armory, a red brick structure with the obligatory turrets that festoon American armory Gothic and house basketball courts instead of weaponry. I watched the team members thudding heroically along the court, white thighs flashing under the yellow gym suits, and watched the cheerleaders gyrate for them with as much vigor that they expended when it was the boys that were playing. I was smitten. I sat and chanted GO GO GO and wished it was me on the court, white-thighed, thudding, cheered.

Girls' basketball was big time in parochial school. While the girls in public school were shunted off to intramural volleyball, the parochial schools worked up an egalitarian lather for both its boys and its girls teams. Little girls didn't have to be cheerleaders. We could be stars! Women's Lib would have approved. At the age of thirteen I would have preferred, given a choice, Bob Cousy's jump shot to Ava Gardner's sensuous mouth.

I went out for the team in the seventh grade, and I made it, an honor granted to few seventh-graders. I was tall and I could run fast, so I became a guard. Girls' basketball was played in those days with six players on a team, three guards and three forwards. We only played half court—three forwards from one team and the guards from the other in one court, and the other guards and forwards in the opposite court. The center line could not be crossed, so it was the job of the guards to get the ball away from the enemy forwards and pass it to the home-team forwards in the other half of the court. Guards couldn't shoot, they were purely defensive players. Playing guard wasn't exactly stardom, but it was a start.

As members of the school team, we had a special responsibility. We carried the honor of the school on the backs of our yellow gym suits. The nuns were careful to lecture us about our fine families and the advantages we had, things that were not available to some of our opponents. The nuns did not say so, but we understood that we were in a class above some of the girls on other teams, who lived in neighborhoods where Negroes were moving in and the trash was not collected regularly. Our opponents might show up in scruffy, mismatched jerseys and their sneakers might be the shade of a tenement façade. Our yellow, one-piece uniforms had to be freshly starched and laundered and our sneakers had to be polished before every game. If they were not, we didn't set foot on the court. I was very careful every Friday night (our games were on Saturday) to apply white polish and set the sneakers in a dust-free spot. Our gleaming sneakers were the badge of middle-class virtue.

I began a diary when I was in the eighth grade, and in it my first season (49–50) is summed up in a footnote:

"I was the only seventh grader to make first string. Best Guard on team. Modest aren't I. Lost playoff to Blessed Sacrament. Referee was Nuts. Everybody mad."

When I got to the eighth grade, I was tired of being a guard. Why should all my hard work end up as somebody else's basket? I hungered for glory, and I was not alone. We all nodded our heads at the teamwork lectures our coach gave us, but within each breast under the little yellow snaps that fastened our gym suits hummed the basket-hunger. We all wanted to shoot. *The Catholic Review* mentioned only the High Scorer each week. I began to suspect that some of my teammates were not passing the ball to me at times when it was appropriate. I noted darkly in my diary:

"Sick and tired of being stooge. Gonna assert myself. I'M PLAYING FORWARD."

The psychologists who blithely claim that little girls are not competitive, that they are in fact "sugar and spice and everything nice," should spend an afternoon at a CYO basketball game. We wanted to be stars, all of us, and we wanted to win. We competed against each other and against the enemy. Our natural hunger for self-esteem and our instincts to compete were given a healthy outlet on the hardwood floor. Off that floor, our arena narrowed to a single word: boys. We could not do battle with our wits; to be too smart, to accomplish too much in school was to bring on the dreaded label, "Brain." A brain had weak eyes, glasses, and was probably ugly.

We had already begun to perceive, at our tender age, that off the basketball court the only competition approved for girls was for the favor of the opposite sex. We had begun to see that victory in that competition offered status. If the boys had begun to dehumanize us by ranking us according to mammary development or the sweet curve of a girlish buttock, the symmetry of a face, we in turn had begun to dehumanize them. We judged their value by how many points they scored on whatever team they were on, by the popularity they had won from their male classmates, and by the regularity of their still-smooth young faces. They learned early that success was the way to court female favor; we learned early that it was wise to attach ourselves to the scent of success that clung to a male. To be the girl friend of the best-looking boy on the football team was Achievement. The best-looking boy on the football team became a commodity, a thing with a definable market value; self-aggrandizement had become, by the eighth grade, an overriding part of male-female relations. We would not have understood it; we believed our motives to be pure, but they were not.

On the basketball court, we controlled our own destiny.

Success or failure depended solely on our actions. It did not depend on our parents or our bra size or on other external factors we could not govern. I remember standing at the foul line, breathing the close air of a crowded gym, waiting as the roar fell to a hush, feeling the ball in my hands. I remember knowing as the ball left my hands that it was true, hearing the crowd roar approval. It defined me, gave me value. I did not have to be a nymphet, budding in a sweater, teasing and afraid of giving too much or too little. The nuns may not have understood this, but they were aware that the energy expended in tossing a basketball was better invested than in other activities that could be indulged in by nubile girls.

The nuns talked to us often of sportsmanship, of The Game being all, not the winning of it; but they were as happy as we were when we won. We wanted to win, passionately. It was the sort of passion that might have crippled something in the boys, who felt the same way; for they were on the verge of being locked into a system that would brutally process them to an endless treadmill of required victories. But it was good for us; it diluted the passiveness that society urged on females; there was nothing passive about the way we played basketball.

Our games were marvelous primal contests. Despite the nuns' admonitions, we were not ladies. Once, a burly guard from another team snarled that if I elbowed her she would smash me in the mouth.

Did I keep a dignified silence, as a lady should? Did I bring honor to my parish, my fine family, the sisters who taught me, by ignoring such crudeness? I did not.

"Try it, you creep, and you won't have any teeth left," I snarled back.

My father, who had played semi-pro basketball and often helped coach the team, had taught me a marvelous repertoire of dirty tricks, subtle things one could do with hips and elbows. After hipping an opponent and making it appear that she had fouled me, I would step to the foul line and piously make The Sign of the Cross.

There were times when our games looked more like revival meetings than athletic contests. Just before the games began, both teams would kneel in a huddle on the court, Hail Mary-ing. It seemed somewhat presumptuous to assume that God was leaning down from his throne to get a better look at round one of the CYO tournament, but if he saw every sparrow, might he not also see a set shot from mid-court? We took no chances.

The Hail Mary was just an extra for me. The night before, I had addressed a number of pleas for victory to the entire celestial spectrum. Blessed Sacrament might outplay us, but they would never outpray us.

"Blessed Sacrament" is the name of the sacred body and blood of Christ in the Eucharist; but to me the words bring to mind only one image—a group of tall, willowy girls in gym suits the shade of a glass of burgundy. Blessed Sacrament parish was near ours in suburban Maryland. They were like us, only richer. A Blessed Sacrament forward's father was likely to be a doctor; our fathers were somewhere in the middle range of the G.S. (federal government) scale.

With us and Blessed Sacrament, there was none of the It's-not-whether-you-win-or-lose-it's-how-you-play-the-game nonsense. We were out to kill them and they were out to kill us. Our coaches eyed each other across the width of the court like a pair of mountain lions after the same hare. They were in the grip of a controversy that year about a particular style of guarding used by Blessed Sacrament, which made our team's parents froth at the mouth and introduced us to the omnipresence of politics.

The Blessed Sacrament coach was named Mrs. D., and

she shared the philosophical convictions of Vince Lombardi (The Name of the game is WIN). She had taught her guards to stand as close as possible to an opposing forward, and put their arms as far around the forward as possible without making body contact. This left the forward only a small opening through which to move—backward. Since it was a foul under our rules for a forward to bump into the arms of the guard, this style of play nearly immobilized the forward. But this "close guarding" was clearly outlawed under CYO rules.

In the middle of the season, CYO officials suddenly announced that the rules had been changed, that the close guarding that Blessed Sacrament had perfected was now kosher. Our coach was outraged; a delegation from the parish protested to the league, to no avail. There were mutterings about Mrs. D.'s use of "influence," but the rule change held. We gritted our teeth and prepared for Blessed Sacrament. My diary tells the tale.

Dec. 1: Stayed after school 20 minutes for talking. Found out schedule. St. Bernadette's comes first. We'll slaughter 'em.

Dec. 9: First game. We won 49–14. Passing much improved.

Dec. 15: Day before St. Ann's game. Tough opponent. Laying for our traditional rivals, Blessed Sacrament.

Dec. 16: We won, 39–18. Smeared 'em. Bring on Blessed Sacrament. Me and Sally went to movies in afternoon. Saw "Kim." Planned to sneak in but line stretched past exit.

Dec. 20: No game today. Nothing much to do but stick around and do nothing much of anything.

Dec. 30: No game. Practice. Went to see "Pagan Love Song" with Diane. Carleton Carpenter and Debbie Reynolds. Neat.

Jan. 5: Beat St. Thomas 36–5. Look Out Blessed Sacrament!

Jan. 7: Practice. Sweeney and Alexander filled Grosses shoes with water. She was mad. Saw "Pagan Love Song" second time. Neat picture.

Jan. 11: Day filled with expectation of Blessed Sacrament Saturday. Can't wait. We'll slaughter 'em.

Jan. 12: Team went to Mass and communion. We'll slaughter 'em.

Jan. 13: CRAP! CRAP CRAP CRAP CRAP CRAP CRAP. We lost.

Blessed Sacrament beat us, as they always did, by a tiny margin in the last seconds of the game as partisans of both teams screeched on the sidelines. We didn't win the championship that year, but I did get picked to the city All-Star team, and I got a silver and blue warm-up jacket that had ALL-STAR emblazoned on it. I would have slept in it, if I hadn't been afraid of getting it mussed. I wore it everywhere that summer; it still hangs in the cellar of my parents' house in Silver Spring. The silver is turning yellow with age now, and the jacket smells of mildew and must. But I could never bear to throw it away. Sic Transit Gloria Mundi.

The winters were filled with the blazing passions of CYO basketball at my school at mid-century. But when the snow melted to muddy slush and the forsythia bushes began to sprout small green buds, the hoops and the balls and the yellow uniforms were packed away. Spring is a short season in the outlands of Washington, D.C. There are a few weeks of rain and the cherry blossoms come out for the tourists to flood in and gawk at, and then the hot weather rolls in and stays through mid-September. For us, the Sporting Life did not abate in the summer. It just found different, more individual forms.

The county public school department, realizing an obligation to its constituents even during the vacation months, set up a summer recreation program at the high school around

66

the corner from my house. Beano and I often went there on hot summer afternoons, though the facilities could hardly be described as elaborate. The program was held in the gym, an old brick building that reeked of the pungent odor of male sweat. There was a good softball league set up for the boys. They had equipment and umpires and buses to ferry them to the games. It was thought that such things were necessary to keep boys "out of trouble." Since girls didn't get into trouble—at least not the kind that caused any property damage—we were generally left to fend for ourselves. There were several basketballs and a few volleyballs bouncing around the gym, and we could use the softball equipment when the boys weren't using it—which was rarely. There was a swimming session every Wednesday morning at a pool in nearby Washington, but it seemed that every child within a radius of a hundred miles was in that pool on Wednesdays. Finding an inch of pool that was not filled with dripping child-flesh was nearly impossible. There was pulling and shoving and noise enough for a minor riot. A boy drowned one afternoon when I was there. He hit his head on the pool and no one saw him on the bottom until it was much too late. Beano and I sat on the grass after the pool had been cleared and watched the members of the rescue squad roll out a stretcher with a canvas-covered form. We stopped going to the pool for at least two weeks.

"Arts and crafts" was on the agenda for the recreation program, and now and then we were able to do some elementary woodworking. But arts and crafts meant, usually, gimp.

Gimp, for the uninitiated, is a strand of plastic material about the width of a shoestring. It came in four colors, red, blue, white, and green. Gimp was very useful. It could be plaited, using three strands, or boxed, a more complicated process using four strands. We could plait or box lanyards made of gimp, on which we could hang whistles, watches, or such cereal-box memorabilia as Tom Mix weather rings. My room was cluttered with lanyards. If all the gimp I plaited in those summers at the high school had been put end to end, they would have formed a plasticized highway from Silver Spring to Weehawken, New Jersey. Beano and I sat, day after day, in the stinking gym with the heat climbing to ninety-eight, putting the red piece of gimp over the blue piece of gimp and the blue piece of gimp over the red piece of gimp. It was like spending the summer in the Triangle Shirtwaist Factory.

Some days, when the heat got to us, we would set out on bike hikes to find people with swimming pools. There was no decent place to swim nearby, aside from the crowded public pool. The creek was buggy and polluted, and our parents had drummed it into our heads that its waters probably were infested with polio germs. Beano and I would ride around residential neighborhoods until we found the rare, affluent family that owned a swimming pool. We would park our bikes and press our noses against the inevitable chain-link fence that surrounded the pool, looking forlorn and bedraggled, all sweaty from pedaling our bikes, waiting for someone to take pity on us and invite us in. No one ever did.

The only day we got to the beach in the summertime was on Saturday. Going to the beach was a day-long expedition. It was only thirty miles away, but there were no freeways, just two-lane, winding roads jammed with families like ours fleeing from the heat. No one we knew had beach cottages or boats or went to Florida; those were the province of Rich People. We were not Rich People, so we went to the Chesapeake Bay.

The Chesapeake, for those who have not had the pleasure of knowing it, is a brackish body of water that slices into the state of Maryland and separates the Eastern Shore from the rest of the state. Its waters, seen close up, are greenish-brown in color, and by July they have warmed to the temperature of a tepid bath. The water at Mayo Beach, where my family always went, was so shallow that it took a fair hike to get the tepid water flowing at the level of one's kneecaps. In some seasons we had to brush away clusters of floating Japanese beetles with each stroke. By July, the jellyfish invasion had begun. There were millions of them, little floating umbrellas with stingy tentacles that left a red welt across your skin as they brushed across it. The beach management had to string up nets across whole sections of the water to keep the jellyfish out.

At the entrance to Mayo Beach there was a big sign that proclaimed these crystal waters for use by whites and gentiles only. Sometimes, on the way to the beach, cars would pass us—old cars crowded with black people, the car radios blaring Rhythm and Blues from a black station, the people drinking beer with gay abandon, oblivious of the car's fragility and the probability that a tire would blow before water's edge was reached. They were on their way to Carr's Beach or Sparrows Beach, slices of the bay allocated to Negroes. I used to watch the cars drive by and hear the music and imagine that Carrs and Sparrows beaches must be places of rare exotica. They were not, of course, places to which I would think of venturing.

I don't know how the management of Mayo Beach enforced its "gentiles only" provision. Each car had to stop at the entrance to the parking lot to pay an admission fee. I never saw anyone turned away, though it was rumored that an Italian family that lived down the street had been questioned. But it did not seem odd to me that Negroes had their own beach. I assumed, perhaps, that God had created a world full of places inhabited by black people and places inhabited by white people, and that the two groups kept apart by some kind of natural law.

Beano and I—and sometimes David or my friends from school—ran and plunged in the tepid waters as soon as we arrived at the beach and we had to be dragged out to eat the sandwiches that our parents had packed earlier that morning. After lunch we were forced by parental decree to wait one hour before plunging into the water again, so we whiled away the time unsuccessfully feeding nickels into the slot machines in the beach pavilion. Then it was back into the waters again until the sun began to slip behind the hills on the horizon; we would emerge wrinkled and waterlogged, dripping salty water from every bodily aperture. On the way home we would munch old ham and cheese sandwiches and sing "A hundred bottles of beer on the wall, a hundred bottles of beer, take one down, pass it around, ninety-nine bottles of beer on the wall," until my father could stand it no more and ordered silence. I can remember no weariness so delicious as the sort I knew in the back of the car on a summer Saturday, jouncing along through the darkening air, still digesting a great quantity of Chesapeake Bay along with my sandwich, skin tingling with the memory of the sun.

It was only on Saturdays that we could take the waters. Now and then we would go under the sprinkler, which was cooling, if not entirely satisfactory. When we were young enough so that it didn't matter whether we wore tops on our bathing suits or not, Beano and I would play Tarzan, jumping into the spray with a bloodcurdling yell. Beano had a two-piece suit, so she could take off her top and beat on her chest and holler WAH-WAH-WAH-WAH-WAH, just like Tarzan. I could holler too, but since I had on a one-piece bathing suit Beano said I couldn't be Tarzan. I said I could too, and I pulled down the top of my suit. She said it didn't count. I said it did too. She said it didn't. I threatened to expel her from whatever club I was president of at the moment.

But it was not the sprinklers and Tarzan that was the real game of summer, not gimp-plaiting, or even the immersion in the Chesapeake Bay. The game was baseball. Baseball was inextricably bound up with my summers as soon as I could lift a Louisville slugger. There was a sensuality, a ritual slowness to baseball that made it appropriate to the muggy Maryland summers. We had neighborhood games at the foot of the street, and when there were only the two of us, Beano and me, we would play endless games of catch. We would spend hours tossing official American League baseballs to each other, taking turns being pitcher and catcher. My fastball once went through the closed window of her father's '49 Ford. (The same year I hit a croquet ball through their basement window. My father spent a lot of time that summer putting in panes of glass.) Our windups were elaborate reconstructions of the ones we had seen on our heroes, the Washington Senators or their Big League compatriots. We studied the windups of various pitchers and copied them; Warren Spahn was a favorite, with his leg kicked high in the air before the pitch. I imagine we must have been ludicrous, with our disparate shapes; Mutt and Jeff on the mound. But we were in deadly earnest about perfecting our pitching form. Sometimes we would take turns doing famous windups and guessing whose they were.

I always imagined myself the first girl pitcher to make the major leagues. I would have a fastball faster than Walter Johnson's, faster than Feller's, a knuckleball that danced and floated, a curve that left strong men slack-jawed at the plate. I would stand on the mound (the imaginary one in my front yard) and hear the admiring murmurs of the crowd.

71

"She's the best thing to hit this town since Walter Johnson. No, she's even *better* than Johnson!"

I remember sitting in my room the first day I got my menstrual period—the summer I was twelve—in a blue funk, feeling that it was utterly beneath the dignity of a Big Leaguer to have to wear a Kotex. But the next day I was on the mound again (after all, I didn't have to wear the damn thing on my arm) whizzing them by the astonished—if imaginary—batters.

We did have a softball team in parochial school; but it was not the serious thing that basketball was. It was put together as an afterthought. Our team was pitiful. On the first sunny day the year the softball team came into existence, Sally and I, in an excess of zeal, went out and played softball for six hours. As a result I pulled the muscles in my back and had to take a hot bath every night for a month. I played first base, but since I couldn't bend over, I had a slight problem with ground balls.

At another practice session Sally collided with Dorothy Sweeney in the outfield and broke her shoulder. She played with a cast. Her boy friend, Jimmy Carey, had also broken his arm at about the same time, and since we were short a right fielder, we pressed him into service. The umpires agreed that a male right fielder with a broken arm was not an unfair advantage, so he was allowed to play. We were murdered in every game we played, but I won a trophy as Most Improved Player on the team. I suspect I won it by dint of the fact that by the end of the season my back had healed enough for me to catch grounders; at least I could get down to their level, which did not guarantee I would catch them. Ground balls were not my forte.

In the depths of the summer, the stretches of August which would send the dogs panting under the houses to lie against the cool earth, when it got too hot even for Beano and me to play catch, we would all sit around on the front steps and quiz each other on baseball trivia. Who completed the only unassisted triple play in baseball history? Who was called the Gray Eagle? What was Walter Johnson's lifetime batting average? Name the starting lineup of the 1950 Washington Senators.

The Washington Senators of mid-century were my team; I was devoted to them. There are men of my generation who fell in love with the Brooklyn Dodgers. They speak, the words almost a caress as their tongues slide over the syllables: Pee Wee Reese, Duke Snider, Gil Hodges. There are others who worshiped at the altar of the invincible Yankees, who memorized every motion of Joe DiMaggio's torso as the heavy shoulders with the number five between them rent the air with a piece of Louisville hardware. But it was my misfortune to fall prisoner in my early years to an infatuation with one of the sorriest teams ever to tread the infield turf. Let others cherish memories of DiMag, loping through center field, or Bobby Feller rearing back like a startled stallion to roar a baseball across a piece of rubber at 90 mph. I have my memories too: Sam Dente missing an easy roller at short; Sandy Consuegra throwing wild and cussing in unintelligible Spanish; Sherry Robertson striking out.

Let the others remember Mize, Rizzuto, Williams. I remember Carden Gillenwater.

Carden Gillenwater played second base, for a time, for a team of whom it was written:

WASHINGTON
First in war
First in peace
Last in the American League.

And if not last, then next to last. Each August it was a thrilling battle as the Senators and the St. Louis Browns

73

battled it out for the cellar. When one of the Senators' managers was fired after a last-place finish (it was Ossie Bluege, I think. Or perhaps Joe Kuhel), he snarled: "You can't make chicken out of chicken salad!"

I thrived on chicken salad. I was as devoted as if the pennant rode on every pitch. There was no more delightful way to spend a slice of an August night than stretched out under a cool, clean sheet, a pitcher of lemonade by my side, and the radio on, listening to the hypnotic tapping of the teletype that was dancing out the fate of the "Nats" that night in St. Louis or Detroit or Manhattan. In those days the road games were not broadcast live. The announcer sat at his microphone in Washington reading from the teletype, and there was a suspense-filled interval between the time the message was tapped out and the time the announcer read it. I could lie in bed and hear the tapping and know that something—perhaps something of great pith and moment—had already happened in St. Louis or Detroit or Manhattan. In the interval time stood still. Whatever it was that had happened, it had not happened yet for me. The game might have ended with a last fly ball or that same ball might have gone sailing into the stands with two men on, and victory was the message undulating through the air.

The Senators' announcers had a gimmick for announcing base hits. It was a gong, struck once for each base achieved by the runner. There was an auditory pattern to a base hit that held more delights than merely seeing it on the TV; a base hit on TV is like a slug of liquor swallowed quickly. On the radio there was time to sniff it, savor its bouquet.

First there would be a tap-tap-tapping and then Arch MacDonald would say: "Here comes the pitch." (Pause.)

"He swings." (Pause.)

And all my muscles would tense with that pause. I could hardly bear the suspense.

And then I would hear the gong.

One. (Pause.)

Two. (Pause.)

Three. (Pause.)

Four!

And then Arch MacDonald would say, in the calm, pleased voice of a seer, a man who knew it all along— "And there she goes, Mrs. Murphy!" and I would wiggle my toes in ecstasy and know that a home run must be the sweetest thing a summer night could offer.

My husband and I were talking recently about baseball, and how nobody seemed to miss it much when the players went on strike; how pro football, with its speed and the violent crunching of bodies and the Instant Replay of the crunch seems so much better suited to the pace of today. Would anyone today sit by a radio for two and a half hours listening to the clack of a teletype? Mid-century's delights were slower, less elaborate. Would I sit and listen to a teletype today? Would I swim with Japanese beetles? I no longer know the names of the young men who slide into third base and catch fly balls; they are younger than I am and that seems all wrong, somehow. There is professional baseball in Oakland and Atlanta and Houston and none in Brooklyn, and the Washington Senators have become the Texas Rangers. The ball parks are not filled and no one has the patience to watch the pitcher and the batter duel for thirteen long minutes while nothing very sensational or very violent happens, unless there is the weight of money hanging on every pitch. My era in baseball is gone, and with it my passion. My husband keeps up with it, however. He is an author and a TV news commentator and he goes into drugstores and buys packs of baseball bubble gum and lies and says he is buying them for our son. I tell him it is not a disgrace to be addicted to baseball, but he still lies about the gum. He chews it and says, "Christ, this stuff is as lousy as it used to be," and he spits it out and saves the cards. One night we were lying in bed and he asked me who was the best pitcher on the 1950 St. Louis Browns.

"Ned Garver," I said.

"Name the four starters for the Cleveland Indians," he said.

"Feller, Lemon, Garcia, and Wynn."

"What was Al Zarilla's nickname?"

"Zeke. Zeke Zarilla."

He looked at me in admiration. "I'm glad I married you," he said.

My friends and I did not go to the Nats games like any normal, sane sports fans. It was the players, as much as the game, we had come to see. When we reached a certain age we had a biological imperative to fall in love with somebody. A ballplayer was just right; heroic, ideal, and far enough away for comfort. Beano favored Junior Wooten, and later Gil Coan. Sally, if I remember, was partial to Sam Dente. Diane, whom I met in dancing school, and who played basketball for another parish, admired Eddie Robinson. I would not admit, however, that my passion for anyone in a Senator uniform was anything more than a pristine love of the game. My sighs were secret ones, if transparent. I would not swoon in public; it was not seemly for the first girl pitcher in the major leagues to do so.

Since it was the players we went to see, we were prepared to observe them for as long as humanly possible. On summer weekends that featured double headers, we pitted ourselves against the broiling sun and the painful hardness of the bleacher seats. If the game was scheduled to start at one, batting practice began about 11:30. We were there. It was during batting practice that a Senator in the flesh might turn and wave or even toss us a baseball. We cherished such moments, and recounted them, in every detail, afterward.

A wave from Sid Hudson, a smile from Irv Noren, a curious glance from Eddie Yost as our cheers rang out in the empty bleachers; we cherished them as if they had been the bull's ear granted us by the matador. Our arms and our faces turned the shade of broiled meat and our fannies ached. Loyally we sat, next to thin Negro men wearing open-necked sportshirts and hats, with brown bags by their feet with bottles of whiskey in them, or large-bellied white men in T shirts with bottles of beer in little brown bags. And when the epic contests were over and the Senators had gone down to ignominious defeat (as was usually the case) we repaired to the parking lot where we waited patiently, leaning on the fenders of cars, until the ballplayers came out, their hair wet and glistening from the showers. We would crowd around them and thrust our prized autograph books at them. Whenever the clubhouse door opened, all the kids waiting in the lot would close around it to see who was emerging. If it was a coach or a trainer, or worse yet, a civilian, there would be a collective groan of disappointment and we would fall back.

The general dispositions of the ballplayers were well known in the parking lot. We knew who would usually grunt and brush by us, pushing away the proffered autograph books with a forearm and disappear into a waiting car. Some of the bolder boys would make remarks: "You old grouch" or something equally devastating. The rest of us would just stare after the disappearing warrior, hurt and disappointed. We offered him the sort of blind adoration that one gets from only the rare dog. It is a scarce commodity in this world. I wonder if the ballplayers knew what it was they were rejecting.

But most of the ballplayers were gracious, they would

smile and sign our books and we would drink in the sight of the Washington Senators in the flesh, a sight more thrilling than if St. Francis of Assisi had materialized right in front of us. I am certain that if any saint took it upon himself to appear to mortals in the Griffith Stadium parking lot, he would be amazed to find himself playing a poor second fiddle to a third-string utility outfielder.

In the summer of 1951 I went to forty Washington Senator home games, a feat that some cynics might describe as an excess of masochism. I see in my diary that the day General MacArthur came to town and made his famous "Old Soldiers Never Die" speech to the Congress, Sandy Consuegra beat the Yankees on opening day. I gave MacArthur the barest of mentions, but spent considerable time analyzing the Yankee pitching. One June 4 I noted that the Nats lost by one run, and Irv Noren was in a hitting streak. Oh yes, I got 100 in my religion exam. The entry for June 8 reads as follows:

"Rats. Nats lost double header to Chisox. Noren got a double. I graduated today. Diplomas are neat."

On June 26, my diary notes, Diane and I took a two-day trip to New York with her mother as chaperone. It was a graduation present from my parents. After five hours on the bus from Washington to New York, we dragged the poor woman onto another bus—the one to the Polo Grounds. We saw the Dodgers beat the Giants.

By the time the Nats had returned from their first western swing (leading the league, the Senators, like Halley's comet, always flared brilliantly before plunging again to the void), I was in love.

His name was Irving Noren, the son of a Swedish baker from Pasadena, California, and he played center field. The Nats paid $70,000 to acquire him, an astounding sum for tight-fisted Clark Griffith, the Senators' owner.

I liked to sit in the front row of the center-field bleachers, to gaze adoringly at The Presence. Diane liked the stands along the first base side, nearer to Eddie Robinson. We were a pale imitation of the groupies who traipse around after the long-haired, doe-eyed rock singers of today and who, if reports are to be believed, keep score of how many singers they have slept with. We sublimated the sexual aspects of our passion for the ballplayers to the point where it was approximately the size of the official American League baseball. We did not lust after their bodies. Any experience we had with lust was tentative, confusing, and probably the result of a clandestine reading of *Kiss Me Deadly*.

There was certainly not much possibility of the ballplayers lusting after us. Thirteen-year-old girls in 1951 wore high white cotton socks that were folded down three times to make a bulge at the ankle, saddle shoes, wide-pleated skirts, and in my case—braces. We were content to worship from afar, much to the relief of the first basemen and center fielders.

I studied pictures of Irv Noren very carefully, trying to distinguish in the fuzzy newsprint whether the small patch of metal several inches under his Adam's apple was a miraculous medal or just a uniform zipper. A miraculous medal was the true sign of a Catholic athlete. Were Swedes Catholic? Ultimately I resigned myself to the fact that it was just a zipper, and I had fallen in love with a Protestant.

I religiously kept a scrapbook in which I preserved for posterity all the newspaper clippings that made even the barest mention of Irv Noren. It contained such information as the fact that he had his appendix out in May, that he was nervous before opening game, that he used to play for the Pasadena Plumbers, and that he was chosen Boys Ballplayer of the Year by Police Boys Club Number Four. The book is filled with the dreadful posed pictures newspapers always

79

run of baseball players, like the one that shows Irv Noren staring at a shirt held by Pete Runnels, and the caption says he is admiring Runnels' new sportshirt.

The highlight of that summer was the discovery that a man who worked in my father's office lived right next door to Irv Noren. So one afternoon my father drove Diane and me over to meet the man in the flesh. As a bonus, we would also meet shortstop Gene Verble, who lived in the same apartment complex in Northwest Washington.

Irv Noren shook my hand, and I said something to him, and he smiled, and I was thrilled. But I remember that at the same time I was just a bit disappointed because the ballplayers, out of their striped uniforms and away from the Olympian fields of Griffith Stadium, were so ordinary.

They lived in ordinary apartments and drove ordinary cars and had ordinary wives and children. I am not sure what I expected. Perhaps I thought they might be surrounded by glowing light, like the saints on holy cards. It was an early lesson in the relative merits of fantasy and reality; reality can never compete. It is better to let heroes alone. Better to let them lope through the outfield of memory and imagination than to let them turn solid. On the ballfield, the players were gods—even the last-place, bedraggled Washington Senators were godlike, graceful in the windup, the swing, heroic to my eyes even in defeat. In uniform, Irv Noren was Galahad. Out of uniform, the son of a baker from Pasadena.

Clark Griffith broke my heart that summer when he traded Irv Noren to the New York Yankees. The last picture in my scrapbook shows Irv Noren smiling in a hated Yankee uniform, saying "The New York Club certainly went all out to get me and it is up to me to prove it made a wise move."

I continued to follow the Senators after that, but it was never quite the same. I tried to work up an enthusiasm for some other Senator, but it was always half-hearted. When Noren left, the glory was gone.

My husband mentioned to me recently that he had seen Irv Noren coaching third base for the Oakland A's in the World Series. I suppose he has jowls and a belly now. I'd rather not think about it. I will stay with fantasy. Irv Noren is immortal in the heavy beige pages of my scrapbook. There is a picture of him swinging for the fences, his clear eyes looking somewhere ahead into the future, his waist trim and tight under the uniform belt, his open, boyish Swedish face unsullied by time, a large W on his breast.

Around him I have lettered, carefully, in blue crayon: BEST; CENTERFIELDER; YEA NOREN!

It is not the worst sort of immortality one could hope for.

5
Rites of Passage

Colliding with puberty at mid-century was, in a word, embarrassing. I suppose it always was and perhaps it always will be; but I have a feeling that nature's onward march is less a mystery to today's kids than it was to us. I, for one, was not at all prepared for the inexplicable things that were happening to the sturdy, uncomplicated little body I had grown to know and love. Things bulged, grew, sprouted, started up without my permission. It was very unsettling.

My mother told me, as I was preparing to depart for Camp Mayflather in the summer of 1948, that she had some things to explain to me when I returned. (No, that was not a typographical error. It really was Camp Mayflather, named, so we were told, for a lady who was very active in the Girl Scouts. It was several acres in the Blue Ridge Mountains of Virginia, where I learned to build a latrine in the woods, make Indian bird calls, and got exiled from my cabin for leading a midnight frog hunt.)

Camp Mayflather beat my mother to the punch. Not officially, of course. The Girl Scouts might tell us about bird calls, but not the Birds and the Bees. The older girls filled us in on that. I thought the whole thing was revolting. Besides, who could be expected to work up any enthusiasm for a phenomenon generally referred to as "The Curse."

Since we took showers in the nude at Camp Mayflather, it was easy to see that puberty had already begun to work its chemistry on some of us. One plumpish camper had al-

ready developed a stylish thatch of pubic hair, at which
the rest of us stared in fascination. It must have been dis-
concerting for her, soaping herself up while twenty pairs of
eyes were riveted on her privates.

I hoped desperately that nature would bypass me in that
regard. I was rather fond of that nice little pink-white V
of skin I owned. To grow hair anyplace but where it properly belonged (i.e. on the head) was not quite decent.
Pubic hair was something to keep hidden, like a wart or
varicose veins, or some other disfigurement. All the pictures
I had ever seen of full grown ladies with no clothes on featured bare, pink patches of skin Down There. My bachelor
uncle had a picture in his bedroom in my grandmother's
house of a Naked Indian Lady standing on a rock in the
middle of Niagara Falls, wearing a headdress and a grim
expression. But maybe Indian ladies didn't grow hair There.
My uncle also had in his slide collection a series of pinups
from the 1939 World's Fair. I always liked to peer at them,
using a hand viewer; they had upswept hair and wore high
heels and carried umbrellas and didn't have pubic hair.
Neither did paintings and statues of Aphrodite that weren't
dirty because they were Art.

Nature, alas, did not pass me by. Beano, who was two
years younger, and thus slower to fall victim to the ravages
of puberty, did not hesitate to rub it in. I remember sitting
on a beach one day with her and arguing about whether I
Had Any or not. I kept my legs pressed tightly together
for the duration of the argument.

BEANO: You do too. I saw it. Under your bathing suit. It
sticks out.

ME: It does not. I don't have any.

BEANO: You do too.

ME: I do not.

BEANO: Yes you do.

ME: No I don't.

84

BEANO: I'll ask your mother.

ME: You do and you can't be in the Science Club.

Worse yet, wavy brown shafts of hair had started to appear on my legs. At least pubic hair could be kept hidden, but I couldn't go around wearing leggings all year. It wasn't a light, attractive peach fuzz like some girls got, but ugly, noticeable brown stuff. Ugh! It took me two years to work up the courage to shave it off. In the meantime I sat in school with my legs pulled up close to my desk so my uniform skirt would hang down to the tip of my socks. I once filched a tube of Nair from my mother's vanity, and slathered the blue-white goo all over my legs. To my horror, the stench of it wafted out of the room and filled the house. My mother came to find out what was going on and when she opened my door, she found me standing in the closet with only my head sticking out. I was mortified.

"What are you doing?"

"Nothing."

"Why are you standing in the closet?"

"I—ah—I just sort of felt like it."

"What's that awful smell?"

"Smell? What smell?"

And if that wasn't bad enough, I was also losing my Tarzan chest. I could still get out a healthy WAH-WAH-WAH-WAH-WAH, but there was less room for it now. I had to thump right in the middle between two small but noticeable hillocks.

My favorite outfit, on hot summer days, was a pair of green Girl Scout shorts and a cotton pullover, comfortable gear for either a fastball or a cartwheel. One day, in the middle of a baseball game, Ruthie—who lived at the bottom of the hill and was more sophisticated than I—told me that I "showed."

I immediately went home to look in the mirror. Horror of horrors, it was true. Two small but undeniable nipples

pushed out the light cotton fabric. Ruthie had advised me
what to do. She wore a slip under her shirt and shorts.

I tried it. I tucked the bottom half of the slip into my
underpants, but it bunched and wasn't very comfortable.
When I was pitching, a corner of it would come loose and
hang out the leg of my shorts. I would try to tuck it back
up again, pretending I was just leaning my glove on my hip
the way the Big Leaguers do.

I was much too embarrassed to ask my mother to buy me
a bra. I decided to try to make one out of my father's under-
shirt. I gave up after I had cut it up and made a few stitches
in it, and threw it in the rag bag in the cellar. Not long
afterwards, my mother bought me my first genuine bra. I
don't remember it as a particularly symbolic event, but it
was sort of funny-looking, with the little round holes and
the hook. It was also much better for baseball than the slip-
tucked-in-pants.

Puberty dissolved the old, easy camaraderie that had existed on the plains of childhood between boys and girls.
We still played baseball, but things weren't quite the same.
One day Beano and I went into David's house, where David
and Wayne Robey were playing in the cellar. David and
Wayne huddled in a corner, giggling, saying things just loud
enough for us to hear. They said, "A red dot on a white tennis ball" (we knew what *that* meant) and asked each other
if they had heard the new song: Blood on the saddle. They
hummed a song to the tune of "Old Smokey":

> On top of Stromboli
> All tattered and torn
> Lie the pants of poor Ingrid
> A new star is born.

Beano and I left in disgust.

But it was on the first day that my period arrived that the
weight of puberty came crashing down. Not only was there

the problem of what this might do to my Big League career, but it seemed unfair and ridiculous that this should have to happen to me. I asked my mother why this had to happen to girls, and she explained that it meant I could have babies some day. Who wanted babies? I said how come boys didn't have to get anything like it, and she said that boys had to shave every day when they grew up, and that was much more annoying than having a period. It didn't seem the same to me. I sat on my bed, wallowing in self-pity, chafing at the bulky Kotex and thinking Dark Thoughts. My mother had explained it all to me, very matter-of-factly, and had given me books that were filled with inexplicable diagrams of internal organs and that bored me completely. The sum total of sex education in school, was a Walt Disney cartoon about menstruation shown to the Girl Scouts, that featured Dancing Ovaries. But by then we knew all about it anyhow.

In school, the girls who were more sophisticated—and the ones with older sisters—liked to tell horror stories about "The Curse." The stories were told with a fiendish relish, the way an older child might terrorize his small siblings with Frankenstein. There were stories of girls carried moaning to hospitals with cramps; stories of girls bleeding to death before their stricken parents; stories of girls wearing white formals to proms and standing up to discover a large red stain on the back of a dress, A Fate Worse Than Death.

Menstruation was regarded as something to be spoken about in whispers; this rather ordinary fact of life was taboo in mixed company. We were always separated from the boys when we were to be told something about reproductive biology. Boys and girls never spoke of it to each other. One girl told a story of walking with her boy friend across a vacant lot on the way to the movies and coming across a soiled, discarded Kotex. We all sucked in our breath when the story was told, as if the cast away Kotex had betrayed some shameful secret.

When I had to go to the drugstore to buy a box of Kotex, it usually took me ten minutes to summon the courage to go and ask the clerk for it. I would say, in tones barely audible, "A-box-of-Kotex-please," and more often than not he would bellow to a fellow clerk, "Harry, toss me a box of Kotex, will'ya," and I would want to sink into the floor. I would ask him to wrap it in brown paper and I would hurry out with it, praying that I would not run into a boy I went to school with, because he would be able to guess by the shape of the box what it was I was carrying.

I was seized, at the time of puberty, with fits of excessive modesty. With all those unsettling things happening to my body, I wanted to keep it strictly to myself. I didn't even want my mother to come into my room when I was getting dressed. When I had to change at school, for a basketball game, or at a friend's house when I had stayed overnight, I figured out an elaborate system for getting from one set of clothes to another without Showing Anything. If I was wearing pajamas, I would first slide off the pajama top and hold it across my chest with one arm while I struggled to get my bra on with the other. Then I would slip on a shirt, and if it wasn't long enough to cover Down There, I would bend over double and pull my pants on lickety-split, exposing only a flash of buttocks. The worst tragedy, of course, would be to have a boy See You. One of the girls in school posed a riddle to us one day. What would we do if we were in a shower room and a man came in the foyer and said he was not going to leave and we had to go past him to get our clothes?

We considered. "Run with hands over breasts," suggested one girl.

Ah, but that left you-know-what exposed.

"Hands down there," suggested another.

That didn't really solve the problem.

We were perplexed.

The answer? Run out with hands over your face. Then he might see an anonymous body, but he wouldn't know it was You, and there would be no shame.

We sighed at the brilliance of it.

We never developed the easy familiarity with the bodies of our female classmates that the boys were to develop with each other. Girls' shower rooms always had curtains. The bathrooms always had doors. We read the message even in the architecture made for us. We were supposed to be ashamed of our bodies. It wasn't any Freudian *Angst* at not having penises; that is a male distortion of the female anatomy as something pathological, not normal. It was the message of a society whose mores were controlled by males; a society in which a deep-rooted male fear and suspicion of female sexuality stretching way back into the past of the species cropped up like weeds through the highway of our "enlightened" age. Things have changed since mid-century, but the weeds still grow. There is still controversy over sex education in schools and *Harper's Bazaar* drew its greatest barrage of protest mail from a picture of actress Faye Dunaway, armpits unshaven. We still seem to want to imagine that women are made of some nice, neat, practical material like polyurethane foam, and they don't sweat, or menstruate, or grow hair under the arms.

I am not sure exactly when or how I became aware of the complexities of the whole reproductive process. It must have been a combination of my mother's talks, the books she gave me to read, and the jokes I heard in the sixth grade.

I can state unequivocably that the filthiest, rottenest jokes I ever heard in my life I heard in the sixth grade. If I didn't know much about sex before then, I learned fast. We cackled with relish over the raunchiest of them, even if we didn't completely understand them. I walked home from school sometimes with Ruthie, who had a marvelous fund of jokes. (She had an older sister.) I remember one about oral sex and the communion fast and another about a lady who shaved off a nipple by mistake and somebody mistook it for a gumdrop. That gives you some idea of the level of wit involved in the sixth-grade specials.

I may have sniggered knowingly at the jokes; relations with the opposite sex were quite another thing. I went to my first boy-girl party in the sixth grade. Sally and her sister gave it, and I was invited. I wore one of my ruffled dresses with the sash. The rest of the guests played Post Office, but I was too shy. I sat on the steps and watched, until somebody came over and told me my underpants were showing, and I scrambled down, blushing the shade of a beet. By the time the party got around to Flashlight, I had grown a little bolder. (In Flashlight, the lights are out and the person who is It sits in the middle of the room and tries to catch couples kissing with a beam of light.) But there were more girls than boys, so I had to kiss Sally's sister, Marybee. It wasn't all that much fun, but with a shortage of boys, we had to improvise.

There were other boy-girl parties after that, and I heard stories about the kissing and giggling that went on, but I didn't go to them. I wasn't invited and I wasn't that keen on kissing, anyhow. On the whole, I would rather have played catch.

All the winding up, I did, and the sliding and the tackling and the swinging from trees like Tarzan may have been good for my muscle development, but they did not make me graceful. An imitation of Ewell Blackwell's curve ball is not exactly a picture of feminine beauty. My feet grew considerably before the rest of me did, and I was always tripping over them. My parents decided that dancing lessons might be helpful.

It was the era when middle-class children were obligated

to better themselves; one had to take lessons in Something. With David it was the clarinet, and he played the same song every summer night, going sour on precisely the same note each time, which drove several neighbors to the brink of insanity. Beano and I were trundled off to dancing school.

The toes that had so often waggled in the air in Famous Windups now took to the shuffle-step and the grand jeté, or reasonable facsimiles thereof. All over America little female toes (not so little, in my case) were being shoved into black patent-leather tap shoes or little furry toe caps to be placed inside pink point shoes. Dancing school staples were Toe and Tap, so we divided our time between being Pavlova and Bojangles Robinson.

Beano and I took our lessons in a house in Northwest Washington, in a room that had been meant as a dining room, but now was embellished with mirrors and a ballet bar. We practiced our steps under the critical eye of Mrs. Erlichman, the entrepreneur of the school. She was a formidable lady, with tightly curled steel-gray hair and a large bosom that heaved under a black Leotard top when she illustrated the steps we were to perform. I had a serious handicap, since I could not tell my right hand from my left hand without making the Sign of the Cross. Since the Sign of the Cross had become an instinct, I knew that the hand that leaped to my forehead had to be the right one. That was hardly practical in the middle of *Swan Lake*. Mrs. Erlichman tied a pink ribbon around my right foot, so that at least I stopped crashing into Beano when she was leaping left and I was leaping right.

We were taught ballet by a woman who held me in absolute thrall, a tall, big-boned but incredibly graceful girl with the musical name of Beaté. She had danced with an opera company in her native Vienna and had come to the U.S. as a war bride. When the marriage faltered, she took to teaching ballet to support herself. When she dipped in a plié or whirled in the converted dining room with her hair flying after her like a pack of wild birds, I began to consider giving up the big Leagues for the ballet. I saw Moira Shearer in *The Red Shoes* four times, and I imagined myself on the giant screen, moving across the blue, lacquered floor like a rippling stream, clad in white feathers. I fluttered about the house as The Dying Swan, knocking over ashtrays and running into chairs, prompting my parents to request the Swan to die in her own room, where she would do less harm.

The spirit of my passion for the dance was willing, but the flesh, alas, was weak. My toes, specifically. I had inherited exactly the wrong kind of feet for a prima ballerina. A toe dancer's toes should be short and even, like the slats of a picket fence. Mine started at the little toe and climbed upward, duplicating the slope of the Matterhorn. Beano, blessed with the right kind of feet, bounced around on tiptoes as easily as she did in her sneakers. I crammed my feet into two pairs of bunny furs and later special foam-rubber pads, and I was still in agony. In the recitals I whirled and dipped in my tutu, but from the expression on my face one might have guessed I had been clamped into thumbscrews.

The recitals were the culmination of the whole year's work in dancing school, and no expense was spared to make it a spectacle. When the spring began to break up the frozen gravel of the streets and push up the tulips the squirrels hadn't eaten during the winter, we began to dance in earnest. Now we had an accompanist, no longer did we merely dance to a phonograph. She was a cheerful, heavy-set woman, and I would mumble the steps of my numbers (and *one* and *two* and *step* and *turn*) while staring mesmerized at the folds of skin on her arms jouncing along with the music.

While we danced, our mothers kept busy buying the prescribed material for our costumes, fitting paper pattern sections to our torsos as we fidgeted, sewing up our costumes for the big night. My very favorite was a harem costume with billowing pants and a silver bodice, for a dance I did with six other girls to "Song of India." We were not exactly the tired businessman's dream of what harem girls should be, since we came into two basic shapes: one like the letter I, the other like the letter O.

For a tap number to "I'm a lonely little petunia in an onion patch" the patterns were wrong, and the striped satin costumes barely covered what chest expansion we could offer. We must have been a magnificent sight doing that number, six pairs of feet tapping away, and twelve arms clutched desperately to our sides to prevent the striped satin from tumbling down in a shuffling turn.

My big solo that year was a tap number to "Goofus" and I nearly wore grooves in the cement floor of our basement, with my phonograph piping away.

My costume for the big number was white satin slacks with red polka dots, a purple satin blazer, and a derby. On recital night, I stood backstage at the Masonic temple at Sixteenth Street and Kalorama Road, watching the violinist hired for the night, a short, bald man who dripped sweat as the pastel spotlights played on his shining head. I stood and squeezed my thighs together so I wouldn't go to the bathroom in my white satin slacks, saying over and over again, "Jesus, Mary, Joseph; Jesus, Mary, Joseph. Jesus, Mary, Joseph."

Then, as my stomach lurched, I heard the accompanist launch into the introduction to "Goofus." I had two choices: stumble out on stage or turn and run, and be disgraced forever. I pushed myself out on the stage.

I still remember the sensation of being on stage that night, the spots obliterating the sight of the audience. I could feel it, a great beast coiled just beyond the footlights. We had been taught by Mrs. Erlichman that a part of dancing was projecting our personality beyond the lights to the darkness beyond, so I clamped on the lower part of my face a smile as frozen as a refrigerated lamb chop. Halfway through "Goofus" it had solidified to the point where I felt my mouth would start to crack and fall on the stage in little tinkling pieces. All through the dance I kept saying the steps in my mind (and *one* and *two* and *step* and *turn*) and I felt a great stab of joy when I knew I was going to make it without forgetting the steps or falling on my face. All of a sudden "Goofus" was over and I took a bow and ran off the stage, shaking and wishing I could do it all over again.

Critical reaction was mixed, to put it charitably. In the audience my father turned to my mother and said with a sigh, "Well, we just threw another hundred dollars out in the street."

The recital continued for what must have seemed an interminable time to all the mothers and fathers sitting in the audience. Every group had to have its four minutes in the spotlight. Every child who took private lessons had to have her solo, no matter how gangly, how hopelessly uncoordinated she might be. I say "she" because there was only one boy in the recital. His name was Norman Leener and he was Mrs. Erlichman's pride. He danced very well. We all figured he was a fairy. We didn't know what a fairy was, specifically, but any boy who took ballet lessons had to be one.

The highlight of the recital each year was an acrobatic dance by another of Mrs. Erlichman's stars, Barbara Browning. The dance featured a huge jungle drum, and a single spotlight would snap on, recorded tom-toms would pulsate through the hall, and Barbara Browning came strutting on stage. The fathers, who had been dozing through such varied exotica as "Goofus" and "Song of India" sat up in their seats.

Barbara Browning was eighteen years old and she had long dark hair and the face and body of a movie star. For her number she wore a one-piece leopard-skin costume that left only the essentials to the imagination. She could twist her limber body into any position, twirling a baton at the same time. When she danced she projected that perfect combination of wholesomeness and sensuality that mid-century required of its ideal woman. She was the lead major-ette at the public high school, and I sat in the Masonic hall that night and watched her, knowing that being Barbara Browning, dancing on a jungle drum in a leopardskin had to be the most perfect state of existence in the universe. In-spired by her, I took baton lessons. I succeeded only in breaking a chip out of the good mahogany coffee table in the living room. Catholic schools didn't have majorettes— that was too lusty a phenomenon for us, so that particular skill wouldn't have done me much good anyhow.

Now and then Mrs. Erlichman had help in teaching a class from a former pupil of hers, a slim, pretty blond girl named Lorraine Leroy who had graduated to become a profes-sional dancer. She danced with the troupe that entertained between halves at the Redskin games, which was considered quite an honor. She seemed to me to be as sophisticated as the women I sat and watched in the darkness of the Silver Theater (I had outgrown the Seco), her black opera hose and bright red lipsticked mouth the tokens of mystery and maturity. Years later, when I was in college and hardly ever thought about dancing class any more, I went on a date with a law student from Georgetown to a local night club whose genteel shabbiness made it a chic place for college kids to go. After we had a drink and the required "intel-lectual" conversation, the emcee of the night club stepped to the center of the floor and announced that we were about to be entertained by the talented toes of Lorraine Leroy.

And suddenly, there she was, Lorraine, wearing a fringed miniskirt and the black opera hose, her hair blond and curly, tapping on the parquet squares of the night-club floor, look-

ing exactly as she had in the converted dining room. That
she had not aged surprised me. It shouldn't have, because
back in that dining room she had been only a few years
older than I despite the chasm I saw between her station
and mine.

Lorraine Leroy tapped, her red mouth curved up in a
smile ("Project! Project!" Mrs. Erlichman used to say) and
the people at the tables watched her idly as they kept on
chatting. She was a good dancer, I could see that now. She
was better than so many of the dancers who pranced endlessly through the movie musicals at the Silver. But the time
was not propitious for tap dancers. The art had fallen to a
neglected state. Even black people, who were so good at
it, had begun to shun it as a badge of servility, like shoe-
shine kits. Lorraine Leroy tapped and smiled and I sipped
a sloe gin fizz and felt sad that Lorraine Leroy should be
here in this shabby club dancing for people who didn't care.
She should have been dancing with Gene Kelly in some
MGM city, around a fountain that bubbled clear water,
and didn't have Schlitz cans or pigeon shit in it. I marveled
at how time changed things. Once I ached to be Lorraine
Leroy, glamorous woman. Now I could not suppress a superior twinge; how much better to be a college girl sitting
with a law student, respectable, upwardly mobile, the American version of a princess, than to be tap dancing at the
Club 1600.

I gave up going to dancing class the year I graduated
from parochial school. I had guessed by then that destiny
had not meant me to be a dancer, and trudging off to lessons
no longer held any excitement. Besides, Mrs. Erlichman
was a purist; toe and tap only, no ballroom dancing. What
I really needed at that time was somebody to show me how
to dance the two-step. A plié was not much help when a boy
asked me to dance.

By the time we had reached the eighth grade, the nuns

realized that we needed some sort of schooling in the way young ladies and gentlemen behave with one another. Dancing was considered a perfectly proper form of social intercourse, providing of course, that the partners did not show an excess of zeal in pressing the flesh together. My eighth-grade teacher, Sister Maria, would sometimes reward us for diligent work by calling off schoolwork for an afternoon and throwing a party. These affairs were generally a huge success, as evidenced by a critical review in my diary:

"Tues, Jan. 30: Sister Maria sure knows how to plan a party. Fun. Lunch first, then dancing. Got asked to dance by everybody."

That last notation is more a tribute to Sister Maria's zeal in propelling boys to the dance floor than to my girlish charms. To begin with, there were only three boys in the class who were as tall as I was. I could rest my chin on some of my dancing partners' heads. Most of the boys couldn't dance at all. They walked on my feet and mumbled excuses. After which, I walked on their feet and mumbled excuses. But the dance floor was always full. Any boy hovering on the sidelines ran the risk of being dragged over to a female classmate by Sister Maria.

Sister Maria was always vigilant to see that all of us shared in the gaiety of special occasions—even the strays, the nail-biters, the fat girls and the pimply boys, the stars and the bench warmers. On Valentine's day all the girls got white carnations, a gift from the boys (Sister Maria took up the collection.) When the girls made party lunches they were piled in an anonymous heap on her desk and the boys had to choose from the wrappings on the package, not the wrapping on the girl. Once a boy picked a basket, he claimed the girl who had made it as his lunch partner.

My lunch boxes were always old shoe boxes, scavenged from the back of my mother's closet. I would dump out the dust balls and put in the sandwiches and wrap up the shoe box in blue paper embroidered with red heart cutouts. My mother made the sandwiches, and they were specially good ones on party days. The conversation between me and my luncheon partner went like this:

"Hey, these are good sandwiches."

"Yeah, my mother makes real good sandwiches."

"Yeah, your mother sure makes good sandwiches."

LONG PAUSE. SOUND OF CHEWING.

"Turkey. I like turkey."

"Yeah, turkey. I like it too."

"I like lots of mayonnaise on it."

"I do too. Some people don't."

"I guess they don't."

"I like turkey best of anything. Roast beef is good too."

"Yeah, roast beef is good."

LONG PAUSE. MORE CHEWING.

"There's some cake here too."

"Oh, is there?"

"Yes, white cake with frosting on it."

"Oh, I like that."

"I do too."

"I bet your mother makes good cake."

"Yeah, she does."

"Yeah, well, she sure makes good sandwiches."

CHEW. CHEW. CHEW.

6
The Dream People

I did not deign to fall in love with any of the boys who asked me to dance under duress and the watchful eyes of Sister Maria. Not with Richard, who was a good pitcher and who did the box step over and over again in the same spot on the brown tile floor, or with John, who was very tall and so paralyzed with fear when he approached a girl that his stomach rumbled, or with Noel, who had dimples and wavy hair and was generally proclaimed to be "cute," or with Johnny, the football player.

I was in love with Irv Noren, of course, but there were others. I try to remember them all; there were more than a few, but foremost among them was Montgomery Clift in *Red River*.

I was not alone. All the girls in the eighth grade fell in love with Montgomery Clift. His face had the perfection of a fragile porcelain vase; his beauty was so sensual, and at the same time so vulnerable, it was almost blinding. I think every girl who saw him in the quiet dark of a movie theater of a Saturday afternoon fell in love with Montgomery Clift, his dark eyes like the deep water of a cavern pool, holding the promise of worlds of tenderness; the straight, perfect blade of a nose that should have been the work of some sculptor the equal of Michelangelo. There was something that happened with young girls and male movie stars, and it happened instantly, inexplicably, simultaneously to all of us, as if we were prompted by some unconscious race memory. A man who was to us no more than a flat shadow on an asbestos screen became the repository of all the dreams of all our summer nights, a tabernacle for all our unfulfilled wishes. Like our passion for the ballplayers, our love for the movie stars permitted the perfume of sexuality to drift about like a vapor, sniffed now and then but only half recognized. At the same time I was in love with Montgomery Clift I found the growing awareness of how people "did it" pretty revolting: all that touching and pinching and groping about. It seemed to me that if one had to "do it" after one got married, the best way was quick and efficient, sort of like the way the dogs in the neighborhood did it, only they had the execrable taste to do it in the street. With me and Montgomery it wasn't that sort of thing at all. Love with him would be long, langorous sighs, pressing close against his manly chest, and telling each other all the secrets we had never told anybody, and gazing eyeball-to-eyeball, and he wouldn't think of putting his hand on my thigh. (I liked my heroes pure as the driven snow. I had just graduated to adult books after reading all the horse books and dog books ever written. I thought that human heroes could at least possess the virtues ascribed to *Lad, a Dog* by Albert Payson Terhune. When a protagonist in an adventure novel fell from grace by so much as unhitching a bra I no longer admired him. I was a terrible prude.)

I was in love for a brief time with Robert Wagner. I went to see *With a Song in My Heart* primed to fall in love with him. Six other girls in the class saw the movie before I did and all they talked about was Robert Wagner, who had a part that lasted perhaps three minutes.

Susan Hayward was playing singer Jane Froman, and in one scene she is entertaining injured American GI's in a hospital. She comes up to a shell-shocked GI who can neither move nor talk. He just stares up at her with spaniel eyes and a face so all-American soap-and-water perfect it made you want to cry. I did. So did millions of others. That scene made Robert Wagner a movie star.

I fell in love with James Dean, of course. He mumbled, and he was sensitive and inarticulate and so in need of Someone to Love Him. I saw *East of Eden* four times, melting to a stickly little puddle of goo each time he kissed Julie Harris on the ferris wheel.

(The current that flowed in the movie houses from pubescent girls to the giant shadows of men was transmitted, somehow, from the shadows to the men themselves. It immobilized them, froze them into the prison of a million girlish dreams of what they should be, as if the dreams were the stinger of some huge female spider whose poison paralyzed its prey. Montgomery Clift was haunted by his beauty, or the memory of it, after an automobile accident scarred his face. He died young, tragically, as did James Dean, who seemed as if he was trying to outrace the venom in the stinger by driving his automobiles too fast. Others, not quite so electric, survived to try and struggle free. Tony Curtis, whom we swooned over in *The Prince Who Was a Thief* finally struggled free of bare-chested, boyish heroes with a few good roles like *The Sweet Smell of Success*. Robert Wagner still plays charming boys. Would anyone believe him as anything else?)

Who else did I fall in love with?

Richard Burton in *The Desert Rats*. I saw it seven times. I liked the way he talked.

Marlon Brando in *On the Waterfront*. We all fell in love with Marlon. By the time that one came out I was in high school, and we were stalking Georgetown Men. None of us would have given a longshoreman a passing glance. But Marlon, ah, that was something else! In one scene he came crashing into Eva Marie Saint's bedroom and all she had on was a slip. A SLIP! And she kissed him and they slid down the wall out of sight. Wow. WOW!

Ben Johnson as Sargent Tyree in *She Wore a Yellow Ribbon*. It boggles my mind to see him as a grizzled old-timer in *The Last Picture Show*. When did he get old?

Stewart Granger in *King Solomon's Mines*.

Richard Widmark in *Red Skies of Montana*.

Richard Todd in *Robin Hood*.

Alan Ladd in something about the Foreign Legion.

I wonder if anyone can—or ever will—master the arithmetic of The Movies' impact on my generation. They were a part of the constancy of my childhood. Since the day I went to see *They Died with Their Boots On* at the age of four, there was never a time when I didn't go to the movies. When I got too old for the Seco and the cowboy movies I went to the Silver, which housed under its unimposing façade a classic example of movie house baroque, with its red plush seats and velvet curtains and a ceiling that soared like a medieval cathedral. My generation's entire model of the universe came via just such places from the back lot at MGM. Ancient Rome was Robert Taylor's bare thighs, James Mason in a toga and lots of marble; the Orient was John Wayne in a droopy moustache as Attila the Hun or an evil yellow man torturing Alan Ladd and saying: "You will talk, Amelican Swine. We have ways to make you talk." Broadway was Dan Dailey drinking himself to Skid Row, then giving up the bottle and winning Stardom and Vera Ellen; The West was a main street and two men with drawn guns and theme music with lots of drums. The world of the movies was much more vibrant than anything reality could give us. On the screen, Elizabeth Taylor's face was so big that our family Plymouth would fit neatly in her right nostril. The colors were dazzling; the blue of a Texas sky or the red of Marilyn Monroe's lower lip had the intensity of Picasso's palette. It is a tribute to the impact the movies had on me that I remember Joseph McCarthy only dimly, as a gray picture on a TV screen, and the Korean War as only headlines and blurry newsreels. But I can remember the lyrics to every melody in "Pagan Love Song," songs where "skies" inevitably rhymes with "eyes."

The world the movies gave us was Never-Never Land; nothing could be as vast as the world that came to us in Technicolor and Cinemascope. I was struck by that when I went to Versailles on a college trip to Europe. I had seen Versailles in a hundred movies. I walked through the real thing, peering at the tiny, crowded rooms, the faded gilt on the chairs, the rococo angels on the wallpaper bleached out by time, the china pitchers looking like something from my grandmother's parlor, the chamber pots. Could this be the glittering palace of the Sun King? This faded, dreary, cluttered dustbox? No, I had seen Versailles in the movies, its arched ceiling hung with chandeliers the size of elephants, the gold of the upholstery glittering like the plunder of a thousand Cathays, the skin of its women the shade of skim milk. And there were no chamber pots. Would Robert Taylor use a chamber pot? Would Wanda Hendrix? Would Rhonda Fleming? (All stars in those days had to be Wanda or Rhonda or Tab or Rock or Kirk. If it was Herman it got changed to Kirk. Carrie Snodgrass would have been laughed off the soundstages.)

The women we saw on the screen on Saturdays at the Silver were goddesses. There is no other word for them. They stood at the very pinnacle of mid-century's altar of success. For a woman, no other triumph could equal Being a Movie Star. Nothing could compare—not getting elected as the first woman President, not writing a bestselling novel or winning the Nobel Prize. Now and then *Life* magazine would run a feature on a Movie Star Coming Home (Elaine Stewart Returns to New Jersey) and I would sit on the glider on our porch with *Life* on my knees, imagining how sweet it must be to be Elaine Stewart, coming home. It was the ultimate vengeance. It would erase every snub,

every social gaffe. Who would remember that your underpants showed at a party in the fifth grade or that you wore
braces and stepped on boys' toes when you danced? No one
could fault a movie star. No one could say a movie star
hadn't made it, even if she spoke her lines as though they
were kindergarten blocks falling out of her mouth or if the
films that carried her name before the title in scarlet letters
were juvenile sagas about Foreign Legionnaires and harem
girls.

I imagined me, coming home.

There would be a motorcade, of course, and it would
pass under a huge banner: SILVER SPRING WELCOMES CARYL
RIVERS. The *Life* caption would read, "Caryl Rivers, the
slender, beautiful blonde who is the hottest thing to hit
Hollywood in years, waves to fellow citizens of Silver Spring,
Maryland. She is the winner of this year's Academy Award
for her role as a nun with amnesia stranded on a desert island with an American flier. Her big scene, when she has
fallen in love with the flyer and finally remembers that she
is a sister of charity, brought out handkerchiefs all across
the nation. With Miss Rivers in the limousine is her co-star
and fiancé, Grant Truehart. The couple, both Catholics,
will be married in the Vatican next week in a ceremony that
has been billed as The Wedding of the Century." As the
limousine moves past the parochial school and then around
the corner past the high school, I see faces in the crowd;
there are the prettiest girls in the eighth grade, looking
dowdy now; the basketball player I had admired from afar,
struck dumb with admiration; the president of the freshman
class, the queen of the Winter Hop; I have peopled the line
of march with everybody I ever envied.

It was the movie stars that set the style for us. We had no
idea who the Paris designers were, or what the New York
socialites said and did and wore and looked like. We

wanted to be like the movie stars. It started for me with Esther Williams.

I saw every movie Esther Williams ever made, most of them at least twice; all of them had plot lines as substantial as a cobweb, and sumptuous pools filled with water as blue as a postcard of Nice and violins that played as Esther swam smile-to-smile with Ricardo Montalban in the Tahitian moonlight. She never had a hair out of place, her smile prevailed, even under water, her broad white teeth gleaming at the multicolored fish that swam by. To this day, Rich means only one thing to me: having a pool like the ones Esther Williams used to swim in.

At Mayo Beach I used to try to imagine that the green-brown water was the blue of a pool in Tahiti, and there were no beetles in it, and it was not Beano swimming beside me, but Ricardo Montalban. I would stroke along very carefully, dipping my arms into the water in that graceful way that Esther Williams did, smiling at the beetles and at the jellyfish across the net. I concentrated so hard on the arms and the smile that I neglected to stay afloat, and came up sputtering brackish water. I was not the only one. At times the rusty metal floats at Mayo Beach were surrounded by little girls grinning and dipping their hands into the water with elaborate formality. Beano and I sometimes had best Esther Williams contests, but at no time was either one of us even remotely convincing.

Later on, I would gaze with dismay at the class pictures we had taken in school—there I would be, puffed-sleeve blouse and an ear-to-ear grin with the photographer's lamplight glinting off my braces. That wasn't the kind of picture I wanted. I wanted the kind that I saw in movie magazines or billboards, the kind that featured The Look. The Look was standard for movie-star pictures, although the art reached its zenith with Marilyn Monroe. It was head raised above a daring decolletage, eyes vacant and lips moist and parted slightly, which was generally agreed to be looking sexy. I practiced The Look sometimes, making sure the bathroom door was locked before I did. I would slip off my bra and wrap a silk scarf under my shoulders, pulling it down as far as possible without exposing a nipple corner, and sit on the edge of the sink. If I hunched my shoulders I could even manage some cleavage, which looked OK from the front, my vantage point. From the side I must have looked like Quasimodo. I would unfocus my eyes, and let my lower lip droop slightly, but not enough to reveal the braces on my bottom teeth. I was quite pleased with my version of The Look, although I am convinced anyone who saw me would have believed me a victim of some rare nerve disease rather than a sex queen. Sometimes I would whisper dialogue into the mirror: "I love you, Armand, but I am a queen and I must stay with my people. You will be in my heart forever, my love!"

I tried to approximate the style of the movie stars. I had a Marilyn Monroe outfit—off-the-shoulder peasant blouse, black tight skirt and hoop earrings. What Marilyn Monroe put into the black skirt and the peasant blouse I did not, alas, possess. When Grace Kelly came along I swept my hair back and wore long white gloves to dances and practiced looking glacial. I got my hair cut in the Italian boy style like Audrey Hepburn. For a while I was fixated on lavender because I read that Kim Novak wore only lavender. And there was Debbie Reynolds.

I forget the name of the movie that made Debbie Reynolds a star, but I do remember that she did a song and dance number with Carleton Carpenter (I was in love with him too, for a while) about the courtship of two chimps. It was called "Aba Daba Honeymoon," and it was a smash. The style of the moment was pert, cute, girlish. Debbie Reynolds was carbon-copied in a hundred thousand Spring Follies, two hundred thousand junior proms, three hun-

dred thousand junior class plays. All across the continent
noses wrinkled cutely, curled heads bounced, clear little
voices piped "Aba Daba Honeymoon" in pastel spotlights.

I made a few half-hearted stabs at being Debbie, but I
knew in my soul it was a lost cause. As foolhardy as it might
have been to ape Kim's lazy freshness, or Marilyn's sultry
languor or Audrey's adorable grin, I knew I didn't have a
prayer when it came to being pert. Nobody who is five feet
eight inches tall, and who is the possessor of size ten feet,
braces, hairy legs and a CYO All-Star jacket is ever going
to make it as Pert.

Debbie Reynolds was a fixture in the musicals I saw on
weekends at the Silver. I must have seen six hundred
musicals. I saw Ann Miller and Cyd Charisse hoofing in
productions that cost millions to produce. My grandmother,
who lived with us at the time, had a full-length mirror in her
room, and when she was busy in the kitchen I would sneak
in with my first pair of heels and shorts, pose like Cyd and
admire my legs, which unlike my bosom, were filling out
nicely; and after the Nair I didn't have to keep them stuck
under my desk. I would do a shuffling turn, just as Mrs.
Erlichman had taught me, and imagined that five hundred extras with hats and canes were about to pop out from
behind the dresser. (I still cherish the notion that if I hadn't
given up on those dancing lessons, I could have been one of
the great ones, singing, dancing, stopping the show as the
patrons leap to their feet to cheer. I cherish this image despite one minor handicap: a gross lack of talent. I won the
male lead in a college musical, since it was an all-girl school
and I can sing both soprano and baritone. I do a great imitation of Jeanette MacDonald and Nelson Eddy singing
"Sweethearts." The college musical was supposed to start
off with the hero (me) and my horse (two other girls in a
horse costume) galloping up the center aisle to the stage
from the rear of the hall. The problem was that to get to

the back of the hall we had to go through the chapel, which was above it. Nobody had thought to put a light on in the chapel, which was as black as the pit. We kept stumbling through the chapel, bumping into pews, as the accompanist downstairs played our intro over and over and over. The rear end of the horse kept trying to keep her costume clutched in one hand and feel her way through the pews with the other. We kept saying "Shit!" when we tripped over each other, oblivious to the sacred presence. We finally made it to the stage, and the production was downhill from there on.)

Most of the movies that I went to see at the Silver ranged from fluff, at the top of the scale, to swill at the bottom. I saw a couple of them that I remembered from Saturday at the Silver on television recently. There was *Yankee Pasha* with Jeff Chandler pursuing Rhonda Fleming to someplace in the Near East where she has been abducted by a sultan for his harem. Mamie Van Doren was a harem girl who kept leaning her remarkable and ill-concealed breastworks against Chandler and panting audibly. He of course rebuffed her, since his heart beat faster only for Rhonda. The final scene shows Jeff and Rhonda on a clipper ship sailing into the sunset. Dialogue:

RHONDA: What a strange land, where women are the slaves of men.

JEFF: But my heart is your slave forever. (Clinch. Fadeout.)

Then there was *Zulu*, with Tyrone Power and Susan Hayward both showing a wide swath of chest. Sample dialogue:

POWER (To Hayward, who for some reason is wearing a satin gown in the middle of the African veldt): Imagine, you here in the jungle, fighting Zulus!

And *The World in His Arms* with Gregory Peck as a New

England sea captain and Ann Blyth as a Russian princess. (Anthony Quinn played a character called Portugee, and he smiled a lot and said things like, "Heh, Heh, Heh, someday I keel you, Boston Man." So much for Mediterranean civilization.) At the climax of this one, Gregory Peck raids a Russian stronghold in Alaska at the turn of the century to rescue Ann from marriage to an evil count. Sample dialogue:

FIRST MATE (To another seaman as the ship sails off into the sunset): Where's the Captain?

SECOND MATE: Don't bother him now. He's got (significant pause) The World in His Arms."

Pan to the bridge, where Gregory is steering the ship with Ann in his arms. She is wearing a strapless satin ballgown, but there is nary a goosepimple on her milky skin, despite the fact that this is supposed to be the Pacific Ocean off Alaska. Every curl in her long black hair looks as though it has been freshly done by Charles of the Ritz. She wears an expression on her face that can only be translated as Rapture.

They were dream people, the movie stars, and we knew them well. The inflection in Gregory Peck's voice will be remembered by the girls of my generation when they have forgotten the sound of their fathers' voices. Montgomery Clift is in his grave and I still see with perfect clarity in my mind's eye that way he had of looking up like a startled deer, poised for flight. Alan Ladd is gone and I can see his blond pompadour, waving gently like the ocean on a calm day, and the way his jaw muscles would clench when a crisis arose. Some of them have been familiar to us as far back as we can remember. We have followed Elizabeth Taylor from *National Velvet* through grandmotherhood, and she tickled our imaginations with every scandal along the way. We believed in them. We believed in the message of perfection they brought to us like missionaries bringing news of some distant, more powerful god.

The dream women told us, with their bodies and The Look and their shining hair and capped teeth that things ended well only for the Beautiful. Beauty got Gregory Peck, and Alan Ladd; if any woman who was less than perfect appeared, we knew she would be the heroine's best friend, or neighbor, but she would never stand at center stage and Jeff Chandler's heart would never beat for her. The perfection was not logical. How could Sally Forrest have only a rumpled forelock after a championship tennis match in *Hard, Fast and Beautiful* when after one set I was soaked with sweat and my hair frizzed (when I had a permanent) and drooped limply across my face (when I didn't). How could Denise Darcel's hair be so fresh and shining after three weeks on a wagon train when there wasn't enough water to drink, much less take a Lustre-Creme Shampoo? How did all the ladies in the jungle adventures capsize in a canoe in one scene, and have their page-boy bobs curving perfectly in the light of the campfire in the next?

Somewhere inside, I still believe in them, even though I know it was all done with make-up men and hairdressers and camera angles. I believe that somewhere there are women who wake up in the morning with their breath sweet as violets, who do not have to dash to the john to gargle with Listerine before talking to anyone when they get up; women whose hair curls by magic after immersion in water; women who could slog through the Okefenokee Swamp and wind up with only an adorable smudge of dirt on their cheek; women who don't get dandruff or thigh bulges or constipation.

I wonder what the dream people have done to our appetite for real things. After all that perfection, won't real people inevitably be a disappointment, like the real Versailles? How can men who loved Kim and Ava and Rhonda be content with women who wear rollers in their hair at night and get grouchy with menstrual cramps? How can women who loved Tony Curtis and Robert Wagner and Montgomery Clift be happy with insurance salesmen or bank tellers who snore at night and have bellies that hang over their belts and who lose their hair?

The movie people have been burned into our consciousness with all the power of Cinemascope. They gave us dreams made of cotton batting, silly, trivial little stories as Truth, calculated perfection as beauty, the shimmer without the deeps, and an indestructible model of a universe too simple to exist in real time. We needed bread, and they let us eat cake. We are still digesting it. I guess we always will be.

7
An Army of Youth

For my graduation from parochial school my parents bought me a white organdy dress and my first pair of heels, white linen pumps that lifted me a half-inch above five-eight. I clumped about in them like a newly shod horse, practicing so that I would not trip on the polished wood floor of the new gym of the convent high school where graduation ceremonies were to be held. My graduation outfit also included a little white organdy hat and an ersatz sterling silver anklet. Anklets were the fashion of the moment. You were supposed to get the name of your boy friend engraved on it, but since I didn't have a boy friend, I just had the man of the store etch the word CARYL on the little silver plate.

On a hot June night I tottered up to the stage of the gym to receive my diploma from Father Ziep, and I stood with the rest of the class and read from a card with a picture on it of Christ opening a door in his chest to reveal the Sacred Heart. We recited: "We do hereby dedicate ourselves to Thee. To Thy Sacred Heart, we consecrate our souls with all their faculties, our bodies with all their senses, our hearts and all their affections. We desire always to honor, love and glorify thy divine heart in everything we do."

I knew as I picked up the diploma with the blue-pebbled imitation leather cover on it, that I was leaving the sheltering roof of the parochial school. But I wasn't going far. I was already enrolled in the convent high school. Most of the girls in the eighth grade were going with me. It was assumed that we would go to a Catholic High School.

The county had an excellent public high school, but such secular institutions were frowned on. It was assumed that Temptations to the Faith swarmed through the corridors of Montgomery Blair High School, rapacious as an influenza virus. There were rumors, generally believed, that girls at the public school had a club called The Black Widows, for which the membership requirement was a ruptured hymen. Catholic parents were exhorted from the pulpit to send their children to Catholic schools to fulfill their sacred obligations to their offspring. Besides, I had a four-year scholarship to the convent school, and the school had a good basketball team. This latter fact carried more weight with me, I suspect, than the potential safe nurture of my Christian character.

The convent school was a complex of buildings nestled on a verdant acre of the town. The convent was a large white frame building half hidden by evergreens, and the school was a brand-new brick building that stood beside the convent.

I arrived for Freshman Day at the school with a special outfit that I had chosen with great care: a red corduroy skirt and a white angora sweater, with a purple scarf at the neck fastened with a huge gold pin I had won in a spelling bee, with the word "Excellence" on it in raised letters. Over the sweater I wore my All-Star jacket.

As the highlight of the day, a group of freshmen that included Sally and me put on a skit that was a takeoff on *Hamlet.* On the copy of the script in my scrapbook I have noted approvingly: "Get the jokes":

OPHELIA: All through the day my hands have trembled, my eyes are reddened, my brow scorched, my lips ache. Kiss me, Hamlet.

HAMLET: Wouldn't you rather have a Four-Way Cold Tablet?

OPHELIA: Hamlet, I wouldst have words with thee. Oh Hamlet, I am of all ladies most dejected, wretched, miserable, dejected. What sayest thou, Hamlet?!

HAMLET: I wish I'd stayed awake in high school English.

OPHELIA: Hamlet, the day will come when you will ascend the throne of Denmark and rule the Danes, for you are truly a Great Dane.

HAMLET: No wonder they gave me a can of Strongheart for breakfast.

Most of my friends from parochial school were with me on Freshman Day: Sally, still a blond tomboy; Alice, plump and friendly and possessed of a skin like ripe peaches; Mary Ann, a small, quicksilver girl who was not pretty in any conventional sense but who had a sly sense of humor; Diane, who I had met in dancing school and who had come to the convent school and was now my classmate; and Clare, who was trying to shed resistant baby fat and who was a year ahead of me, and already announcing an ambition to be the editor of the New York *Times*.

None of us knew, as we practiced our skit for Freshman Day, that with the initiation into our new school we were moving solidly into what the sociologists would call a subculture. Everything seemed so familiar; the nuns wore the familiar habits, since both schools were taught by the same Order, the same pictures of saints and martyrs graced the walls. But while we attended parochial school we were children, and we were not swept so completely into the womb of the Catholic Church. I never thought of myself as being much different from Beano and David; we went to different schools and different churches, but that was of no consequence when we galloped across the back yards and went prospecting for treasure. Now, my world would begin to narrow, and the center of it would no longer be the back yard and the neighborhood, but the school. Beano and I would remain friends, but we gradually began to draw apart as the nucleus of our activities shifted, so that by the time I was ready to graduate from high school we saw each other only infrequently. At the convent school I would become part of a society that was markedly different from the one that existed at Montgomery Blair High School, despite the many things we all had in common as high school students at mid-century. Anyone who passed through the Catholic schools of the fifties was in many ways as much a product of a ghetto as a Jew from the Lower East Side or a Black from inner-city Chicago. The borders we respected were not imposed on us from without, but from within—they were firm borders nonetheless. And all of us who shared the experience, whether we moved far beyond those borders or we did not, were marked by it. It is something we can never forget.

As my friends and I rehearsed *Hamlet,* none of us were aware that when we had graduated from parochial school we had left the peaceful glade of God's Kingdom, that enchanted swamp of miracles and mysteries presided over by the benevolent Father of us all. Indeed, the mysteries and the miracles remained, but a huge black cloud had begun to form in the ethereal, cloudless sky of God's kingdom. It had huge letters on it, spelling s-i-n, and on the darkening plain under the cloud we could hear the thunk and clamor of the clash of arms. We were no longer children. We were *soldiers.* Life was now to be one long struggle with the enemies of a sterner God than the one we had known. There was a distinct paramilitary cast to the religon to which we were now being introduced. Even our uniforms were martial. I was thrilled the first time I tried one on; eventually I came to loathe them. The uniform was a heavy blue serge dress with a sailor collar and cuffs and a thin red tie in which a precise square knot was supposed to be tied. It was hot and it got shiny in the seat and discolored at the armpits, the snaps fell off the cuffs and the ties got crappy. But the worst aspect of the uniform was the required brown oxfords. My feet, in brown oxfords, looked like gunboats. I bought a pair with crepe soles and I squeaked through the halls for two years.

I was introduced to the new martial spirit at one of the first assemblies we attended as freshmen. We were all herded into the gymnasium to hear a guest speaker who had just returned from the African missions. At the close of the program we all stood and sang the hymn of the Catholic Students Mission Crusade. It bounced along like a football fight song, and once I had learned the words, I sang it with great relish. It was written by a priest named Father Daniel Lord, S.J., whose picture appeared often in the school newspaper, the *Silver Quill.* He had a leprechaun face, silvered hair, and a twinkle in his eye. If he had chosen Tin Pan Alley instead of the Roman collar, he would have made a mint. The CSMC hymn was his masterpiece, and it was a lulu. (I sing it still, washing dishes, though I am careful to lower my voice if I see anyone walking by the open window. I do not want people to think I am some kind of New Left radical with a cache of arms in the cellar. The tone of the CSMC hymn is decidedly militant):

> An Army of Youth
> Flying the Standard of Truth
> We're fighting for Christ the Lord
> Heads lifted high
> Catholic Action our Cry
> And the Cross Our only sword;
> On Earth's battlefield
> Never a vantage we'll yield
> As dauntlessly on we swing;
> Comrades true
> Dare and do
> 'Neath the Queens White and Blue

117

For our Flag
For our Faith
For Christ the King.
Christ lifts his hands
The King commands
His challenge come and follow me;
From every side
With eager stride
We form in the ranks of victory.
Let foemen lurk
And laggards shirk
We throw our fortunes with the Lord
Mary's son
'Till the world is won
We have pledged you our loyal word.

And after the song, we recited the CSMC pledge: "I offer myself as a soldier in this Holy War, the conquest of the world for the Sacred Heart."

If this was a Holy War, there had to be an enemy. The Japs and the Jerries had gone down to inglorious defeat (and were still doing so in every third movie at the Silver) so they weren't the enemy any more. Who then? Who were we struggling against to win the world for the Sacred Heart?

The Communists!

Or, as we always put it, the Godless Atheistic Materialistic Communists. Even when the prefix wasn't articulated, it was understood.

In the Year of Our Lord nineteen hundred and fifty-one I was thirteen years old. The Republic of the United States of America was one hundred and seventy-five, and by official reckoning, the Catholic Church was the same age as the year, since the birth of Christ was regarded as the incorporation date of the Church. "The Church" of course meant Roman Catholic. All other denominations were accorded only lower-case letters.

I was a member of both institutions, the secular and the godly, and I was aware as I entered high school that this was double fortune. I understood that my soul wore a special insignia, which I perceived to be the word CATHOLIC stitched to the fabric of my soul the way my mother sewed name tags into my shorts for Camp Mayflather. It would shine like neon, giving me special distinction, if I made it to heaven, and it would be equally conspicuous if I went the other way. It was understandable that some pagan might find his way down there, or a Protestant. But a Catholic who wound up in Mephisto's parlor despite all the extra options God gave Catholics would rate at the very least an extra jab of the pitchfork.

There was no such indelible mark on me proclaiming my citizenship in the country that was the Last Best Hope of Mankind. But I knew in my bones that I was of the same breed that blasted Hitler and took care of the Japs in *Thirty Seconds Over Tokyo.*

I stood in 1951, in my blue serge dress with the white collar and cuffs and the red tie, on a sun-swept plain of absolute certainty. Clare and Alice and Diane and Sally and Mary Ann and I all knew that God was in his heaven and all was well with the world, except, of course, in those areas where the Godless Atheistic Materialistic Communists held sway. There was no question in my mind that Truth sat in residence, simultaneously, with the Catholic Church and the United States of America. These were the twin beacons of virtue that were to blink unremittingly through my high school years. There was no question about the fact that the great goals of the two institutions were synonymous. Church and state had, at mid-century, one all-encompassing bond. Nothing manufactures the warm tingle of camaraderie more effectively than hating the same people at the same time. In chanceries and the offices of Congress, of the K of C hall and in city hall, the same attitudes toward the Communists prevailed, and if there was a touch of paranoia in those attitudes, so much the better for détente.

The Communists hated God and Capitalist Democracy; it was apparent, therefore, that God was a Capitalist and a Democrat. (We took the further liberty of assuming He was also a Catholic. It was fortuitous that His philosophies were the same as ours.)

The rhetoric clanged from the two institutions, interchangeably. I heard it from the pulpit and from John Foster Dulles in *Newsweek* and from going to see *A Yank in Korea* with Lon McAllister at the Silver battling the Yellow (and Red) Peril.

Everything seemed so simple then; Good and Evil and Them and Us seemed so obvious, so inevitable, so eternal. But beneath the certainty ran the underground stream of doubt. I can see it now very clearly, from my distance in time. Did I sense it then? Perhaps, in an oblique way, I sensed that the country was perplexed and baffled because 1945 had not lasted forever. We had saved the world, washed the shores of insignificant little islands with odd names like Iwo Jima in American blood, destroyed the Nazis and the Japanese Imperial War Machine, given of our wealth to clear away the rubble of war and rebuild a continent. For a time, the world adored us. We were an adolescent glowing with health and muscles and dreams, pushed into a game of nations played for centuries by cynical old men. When the game resumed its brutal and uncaring course, we were not ready for it. We wanted a simple answer, and we found one. It was *their* fault. Joe Stalin killed 1945. It was a relief to have someone to blame. *The Commies did it.* We could say it and hate them and be protected from the complexities of the world beyond our oceans. Blocking the nation hunger of the Communists became something more than enlightened self-interest. It became a crusade. And if there was anyone who knew about crusades, it was the sponsor of the originals—the Catholic Church.

For the American church it was a pleasant, if novel, experience to be the loudest bleep in the cacophony of patriotism. After all, the jokes about Al Smith were still going around, like the one about the telegram he sent to the Pope after the 1928 election: UNPACK. The question of whether Catholics could serve both the Pope and the Stars and Stripes was still being debated in respectable forums by respectable men. In other lands, the ancient threads of Catholicism were woven into the fabric of the class that ruled. Archbishop and aristocrat stood jowl-to-jowl, privileged and sure. But the American church was the immigrants' church. It was for many years the only haven for people who heard such words as "Hunkie," "Polack," "Frog" hurled at them across city streets, and there were times when the church seemed to be the only place that did not hang out a sign: NO IRISH NEED APPLY.

There was none of this sort of harrassment of Catholics in Silver Spring, Maryland, in the year nineteen hundred and fifty-one, of course. If there were cattle-boat crossings in our family history, or potato famines, we were beyond the scars. The lines of anxiety in our parents' faces were riven by twenty-year mortgages, payments on wide-bodied Ford station wagons, tuition, slow-to-rise government salaries or the disillusion of settling-in middle age.

But if people forget, institutions remember. The Catholic Church in 1951 was rather like the first Jew in the country club. He looks at the faces smiling at him from the bar overlooking the eighteenth hole, but when he turns around the nerve ends in his ears tense, straining to catch a whispered: "Kike."

We spend a good deal of time in religion class talking about Persecution. Sister Daniel, who taught the class, spoke about Persecution as if it were as inevitable as the Junior

Prom. She assigned us to go and see *The Cardinal Mind-zenty Story* at the Silver, and we were given a composition to write on the theme: Persecution of Catholics.

The Communists were the likely persecutors, of course, but Sister Daniel hinted that there were Others who might like to see us hanging by our thumbs. We weren't exactly sure who these Others were, but we cast a wary eye at the Baptists up the street. They looked nice enough, the men in blue suits and the women in flowered bonnets, but who knew what anti-Papist fury broiled beneath?

I was very keen on fighting communism. I signed up for journalism class so I could put my pen to the service of Stopping the Red Tide. I was an immediate success.

I entered the "My Greatest Gratitude" contest sponsored by a national magazine for Catholic students called *The Queen's Work* (For the Queen's Teens). The contest rules stipulated that the entrant must, in twenty-five words or less, describe the event that would call forth his or her greatest gratitude.

I wrote: MARY KEEPS PROMISE OF FATIMA. ON THANKSGIVING DAY RUSSIA LIFTS THE IRON CURTAIN AND RESTORES RELIGIOUS FREEDOM TO COMMUNIST DOMINATED COUNTRIES.

Fame and wealth followed. I won the contest. Not only did I get my name and my winning entry printed in the magazine, but I also received a check for twenty-five dollars. My professional career as a writer had begun!

Sally, who was also taking journalism, interviewed me for the school paper. After considerable giggling, I came up with a memorable quote for her story in the *Silver Quill:*

"When Caryl was asked what she thought about winning the contest, she said: 'I'm glad the school has solid floors because when I saw that check I almost fell through!'"

I was fired by early success to greater heights of patriotic fervor. I assaulted the Red Menace in editorials for the paper, essays for the American Legion, term papers. I wrote a composition titled, "A Tale of Two Cities." It was about one urban center where people walked freely in the sunlight and birds sang, and another that was all Orwellian chill and midnight door knocks. I built up the suspense to the very end where I dramatically revealed that the cities were (fanfare!) New York and Moscow! (All I had seen of New York was the Polo Grounds, Grant's Tomb, Radio City and Bedloe's Island; I knew nothing about Moscow except that a lot of Commies lived there. That did not hinder my prose, and I got an A for the composition.)

I have saved all those papers, and I look back at them now, blowing off the dust and smoothing down the curling yellow edges of the erasable bond typing paper, and I am appalled at the bloody little female fascist the pages reveal.

One stirring editorial I wrote was headed: TO COMMUNISTS! and I said: "You won't like this! We're starting a fight! Against You!"

I then went on to reveal that this great new effort to battle communism was getting out the vote for the '52 election. It must have made knees knock in the Kremlin when the *Silver Quill* pointed out that the Boy Scouts were giving out 28 million Liberty Bell cutouts, and that the Motion Picture Owners Association had placed signs in every theater lobby urging people to vote.

And if the Politburo wasn't overwhelmed by my prose up to this point, I saved a flourish for the end:

"To those of you who aren't communists, and are reading this editorial out of curiosity, our congratulations are offered. By fighting you have proved that you love your country and what it stands for: True Freedom. But get down on your knees, especially on election day. God has blessed America with Fighting Americans. May God Always so bless America."

God was foremost in the supporters of the fight against communism, as the *Silver Quill* was careful to point out.

Catholics did not have a monopoly on anti-communism, of course. In 1951 everybody had started to see pink provocateurs behind bushes and in public libraries. It had become the conventional wisdom by the time I graduated. When *Time* chose John Foster Dulles as its man of the year for 1955, it headlined: HE REINFORCED THE OUTPOSTS.

Time raved: "Much of the world was being lulled by new and gentle tones from Moscow. Did Malenkov's Russia really want peace? In trying to get an answer all the world would understand, Secretary Dulles at Berlin pressed Malenkov with greater skill than any diplomat has shown in dealing with the Russians. With one sharp stroke after another, he stripped the Communists bare of any pretense that they wanted peace at anything but their own outrageous price. If millions remained deluded by the soft Moscow line, it was not the fault of Dulles, who rescued millions from gullibility."

The Red Menace was as likely to be the sermon topic at the First Presbyterian Church as it was to be the talk at twelve o'clock mass. But other religious denominations did not seem to link their special symbols with the rhetoric of patriotism the way we did. I do not recall that the Lutherans were given to sketching Martin Luther wearing the flag as a sarong or that the Jews pictured Moses with the Ten Commandments in one hand and the great seal of the United States with the other. But the *Silver Quill* decked out the Blessed Mother in more patriotic finery than the head matron at a DAR convention.

A special issue of the paper dedicated to Mary featured a huge pen-and-ink drawing of the Virgin standing atop the globe, and behind her furled the Stars and Stripes. Above the drawing was the headline: GUARD WELL THAT FLAG: FOR FAITH AND HOPE AND BETTER DAYS TO BE!

Elsewhere on the page was an interview with George Washington, Patrick Henry, and Benjamin Franklin, all of whom are pictured sitting on a cloud in heaven peering down at a Marian Year rally on the grounds of the Washington Monument.

Washington says gloomily, "I must admit, our teenagers aren't as interested in spreading truth as a lot of communist youth are in spreading lies."

Franklin nods and says, "What a glorious future our country would have if they stopped trusting themselves so much and put Mary behind the Constitution. With those two guarding our land, we'd be invincible!"

(Interviewing heavenly celebrities was a favorite device in the *Silver Quill* when we ran short of news. When we were low on copy, we would dredge up—down in this case —saint, seraphim, or departed patriot. My favorite example of the genre is this one, from the sports page:

"'It's good to have a high batting average in baseball, but it's even better to be up in the .400's with God,' emphasized the Blessed Virgin Mary, mother of God, in an interview Nov. 2.

"Seated on a large cumulus cloud in the middle of seventh heaven, Mary remarked that she was glad the Catholic Youth Organization sports programs were helping to bring Catholic Youth all over the country closer to God.")

I was indeed correct when I said in my editorial that America was blessed with Fighting Americans in the fifties: There was Senator Joseph McCarthy, Louis Budenz, Herbert (*I Led Three Lives*) Philbrick, J. Edgar Hoover, and Sister Francis Marie.

It is just possible that you do not recognize that last name. Sister Francis, alas, was not as illustrious as her compatriots. But she was no less a Fighting American. She taught us history, and it was her misfortune to expend her anti-Communist zeal on a group of Catholic teen-agers who were about as likely to be seduced by Karl Marx as they were by Groucho, Harpo, or Chico.

Still, as Mr. Hoover pointed out, the Red Tide insinuated itself in unlikely places. It was just possible that one of us, one day, might be swept into a plot to sell atomic secrets, or duped into helping get socialist books in the county library, or at the very least be silent when the Communists tried to outlaw prayer in the schools.

So Sister Francis did not spare herself. She could not have battled harder if she had been the lone nun at the Stalin school in downtown Minsk. She was small and eagle-nosed, and she had a glass eye that made it impossible to tell if she was looking at you or not. It helped her image as a red-baiter.

Sister Francis had somehow chanced on an organization called Christiantern (opposite of Comintern) and it was understood that if we wanted to get a good grade in American history we would be wise to do volunteer work for Christiantern.

The organization was headquartered in a grubby basement room in Northwest Washington, and was presided over by a handsome and (so I thought) sinister man who insisted we address him as colonel. A group of White Russians were somehow involved in the group, and we often heard references to Prince somebody-or-other as we stuffed envelopes with petitions against the admission of Red China to the UN.

I always felt a shiver of delicious apprehension on entering Christiantern's underground headquarters. That was probably romantic fantasy. The grubby basement was undoubtedly more a sign of poverty than of clandestine purpose. Christiantern must have been one of the swarm of little committees with such diverse aims as ending vivisection or promoting the marigold as national flower that grind away in basements throughout the republic. We were given pins to wear that were flimsy tin under the gilt. They were tiny slingshots, representing the victory of little David over the giant.

Suddenly, however, our connections with Christiantern were severed. It was whispered in the halls that somebody in the organization had run afoul of the Subversive Activities Control Board. Could Christiantern be a Commie front?

The idea delighted us. We never did know the facts in the case, nor did we try very hard to discover them. But we painted our little slingshots red with nail polish and shuffled around ostentatiously in the halls, chanting, "Reddy-red-red, Red red Red." It did not endear us to Sister Francis.

With all this anti-communism to occupy our time in American history class, it was May before we got to the battle of Saratoga. There, for all we knew, American history ended. Sister Francis passed out to us copies of five New York State Regents exams and dictated the answers to all the questions. We were told to memorize them, and Sister Francis gave us one of them as our final exam. We dutifully wrote down the correct numbers, matching up Woodrow Wilson with Open Covenants, when for all we knew an open covenant was an uncovered sewer.

We did examine, in the course of the year, some of the contributions of Catholicism in America, with the result that it was a long time before we realized that Lord Calvert and his Act of Toleration in Catholic Maryland did not outshine the Declaration of Independence, and that Cardinal Gibbons, John Barry, and Roger Brooke Taney were not on everybody's list of Greatest Americans. Senator McCarthy was singled out for special praise by Sister Francis as a Good Catholic Citizen.

We had few ringing phrases to memorize in the Catholic chapters; unfortunately, Great Catholic Patriots didn't seem to say much of significance. Pulaski and Kosciusko fought in the Revolution, but if they said anything great it was probably in Polish and nobody understood. I thought for many years that John Barry had said "We have met the enemy and they are ours" at some naval battle or other, but I checked with the public library and that was Oliver Hazard Perry (a Protestant).

Our textbooks, undaunted, managed to dig up quotes from Great Catholic Americans that illustrated the inextricable linkage between God and country. Justice Taney was a prime example. The text skimmed over the fact that he delivered the Dred Scott decision, which proclaimed the Negro to be a piece of property and not a person. But it elaborated on this anecdote about him: Justice Taney, it seems, often went to confession to a priest who was a prison chaplin.

When Taney entered the box, the priest addressed him as Mr. Chief Justice.

To which Taney replied: "No father, just another prisoner at the bar."

The story was probably apocryphal, but it was typical of the pithy aphorisms that Great Catholic Americans—the few of them—were always spouting.

8
Our Crowd

We used to tell a joke in the halls of the convent school. It went like this:

Sister Mary asks her first-graders what they want to be when they grow up.

Johnny says a fireman.

Mary says a nurse.

"And what do you want to be, Sally," asks Sister Mary.

"A prostitute."

Sister Mary faints dead away. She is revived and when she recovers she asks Sally: "Now, dear, what did you say?"

"I want to be a prostitute," says Sally.

Sister Mary lets out a sigh of relief. "For a moment there I thought you said Protestant."

We were given to understand that we lived in a world irrevocably divided into separate spheres, like the globes that sat in each classroom. One sphere was labeled CATHO-LIC and the other NON-CATHOLIC. In the latter category were lumped the pagan hordes of Asia, rabbinical scholars, pleasant Episcopal ladies in print dresses, and my mother (Lutheran).

The nuns made it clear that prolonged exposure to non-Catholics was not healthy. They gave off a subversive perfume; unseen, like radiation, but deadly. We all chuckled over the joke about Sister Mary with perfect appreciation. It was not so far-fetched to think that the Church was more kindly disposed toward the oldest profession than toward our rivals for the hearts and minds of men. That was how

Protestants were regarded, not as brothers in a great Christian fellowship, but as followers of heresy, no matter how well-intentioned.

At mid-century, ecumenism was only a dissident itch in the chambers of some Catholic minds. The subject was summed up for us in a sentence:

It is a sin to attend a non-Catholic service.

By attending a non-Catholic service, one was giving tacit approval to Error; and Protestanism was Error, no question about that.

(The nuns didn't say much about the Jews, except to mention that one sure sign of the end of the world would be the conversion of all the Jews. It was a foregone conclusion that they would one day see the light, just as at some future date the Russian leaders would feel the weight of the prayers of Catholic schoolchildren and run to church beating their breasts and singing "Ave Maria.")

The notion was so ingrained in me, despite my mother's contention that it was nonsense, that on the rare occasions that I went to church with her, even the high-pitched tremor of "Rock of Ages" from the choir dripped with alien fascination. Where were the statues of Mary and the stations of the cross and the little flickering candles?

(My mother's mother, a member of the United Brethren Church, was an ecumenist before her time. Sometimes she went to church with my mother, and sometimes to Mass with my father and me. She was in her eighties then, and quite deaf. She mortified my mother as the congregation rose to sing one day by announcing in what she assumed to be a whisper: "Up and down! Up and down! This is worse than the Catholic church!")

We were never taught in school to hate non-Catholics. There were no stories of evil Jews eating babies or Baptists worshiping the devil in unspeakable rites. The proper attitude toward non-Catholics was a combination of pity and suspicion. They were nice people, but you wouldn't want your daughter to marry one.

Everyone who was not Catholic was to be pitied because they had not received the Gift of Faith. God poured his bounties over Catholic heads and gave us a system of insurance as wide-ranging as the Travelers' umbrella. Sister Daniel outlined all the benefits in detail in Freshman religion. Going to Mass and Communion for the First Fridays of nine consecutive months was a positive guarantee of dying in the state of Grace. The wearing of the miraculous medal, attending novenas at church, even simply carrying a rosary in your pocket—all these carried guarantees of a lesser degree but helpful nonetheless. Various indulgences were available on a sliding scale for heroic efforts like fasting during Lent to quickie efforts like genuflecting and muttering "Sacred Heart of Jesus, I Adore Thee." Grace, it seemed, was a fluid commodity that could be stored up in jars and hoarded away for some future time when it might be needed. Non-Catholics did not have such easy access to the Grace-tap. All they could do was lead Good Lives, a commendable but clearly inferior way to get to heaven.

Sister Daniel was careful to point out to us that with all the Grace we were getting, we were obligated to behave in an exemplary fashion. We were supposed to put mere public school students to shame by our actions; no hanging around Peoples Drug Store after school, flirting with boys, no gum-chewing in uniform, no unladylike giggling or horsing around. Our attitude was expressed by an editorial in the *Silver Quill* that concluded:

"It is often possible to single a Catholic Youth out of a crowd and say he or she is living what he believes. Non-Catholics at times wonder what makes non-Catholics different. The answer is simple. We have Mary at our side."

Mary was Catholic property, another indication of our superiority. I used to walk home from school, wearing my uniform, and as I passed groups of students from the public high school I waited for them to look at me in admiration, to notice my good posture and the aura of superior Catholicity that surrounded me; the nuns assured us that people always watched Catholics very closely and were edified by their conduct. But the public high school students never gave me more than a passing glance, and if they commented about me at all to each other, it must have been to say something like: "Would you look at the fruity uniform that kid has on!"

In religion class, Sister Daniel outlined the entrance requirements for heaven with all the precision of the membership chairman of a country club instructing prospective applicants.

Catholics who died in the state of Grace went to a privileged place in heaven, if they didn't have any sins to work off in purgatory first. The Catholics got the box seats. Protestants and other people who had been baptized and had lived good lives could go to heaven, but they had to sit more toward the rear of the hall. Jews and other unbaptized people couldn't get into heaven proper. For them, God had set aside a porch that was tacked onto the main heaven where they could enjoy a state of natural happiness but could not view the Celestial Presence.

I always felt, rather treasonably, that the porch was a better deal than heaven proper. On the porch I visualized people running naked through the grass, swimming in crystal pools just like the ones Esther Williams swam in, and eating cheeseburgers and ice cream sodas. All that people in heaven seemed to get to do was sit around and stare at the throne. This, we were assured, was bliss, but it sounded pretty dull to me. I thought it must give God the heebie-jeebies to have all those people—rows and rows and rows of them—just sitting there staring at him.

Heroic, if corny, baptism stories were a staple in the convent school. They usually centered around the Brave Catholic Girl or Boy who is at the scene of an accident or a drowning. Before the Catholic youth called for the rescue squad, he or she dripped water across the victim's head and said: "I baptize thee in the name of the Father, Son, and the Holy Ghost."

(When I first learned about baptism in parochial school I was intrigued. I went around one day pouring water on the heads of ants, thereby dispatching them to ant-heaven in a flood. But they went in the state of Grace. I baptized the dog, who did not like having water dripped on his muzzle, even in the name of such an august Person as the Trinity. When I heard stories about people who believed they had been baptized, but really hadn't, I panicked. Maybe the priest who baptized me wasn't really a priest but an imposter; a Communist agent who did not have the Right Intention and whose job was to mis-baptize Catholics to keep them out of heaven. I immediately went to the bathroom and baptized myself.)

The nuns encouraged us to pray for the conversion of any non-Catholic relatives, and they inspired us with happy conversion stories, which went like this:

Mrs. Brown was a Catholic. Mr. Brown was not. But he was a good man and he permitted the children (three boys, three girls) to be raised Catholic. The children had pleaded with Mr. Brown to become a Catholic, but he had always said he was happy in his own religion. The Browns began to pray. All of them. They prayed for five years, but they had begun to give up hope. But one Sunday morning, when Mrs. Brown and the children were getting dressed, Mr. Brown came into the living room, dressed in his good suit, and he said: "Let's all go to Mass together. I want to become a Catholic!"

The nuns told us that any non-Catholic who believed in his heart that the Catholic Church was the One True Faith and still refused to convert was doomed to hell for eternity. Sister Daniel had a story about that, too:

A young man was born into a very wealthy Episcopal family. They lived in an area where Catholics were hated. The son met a priest one day who gave him some Catholic books to read. After reading them, the young man was convinced the Catholic Church was the true faith. But his father threatened to disinherit him if he became a Catholic. The son did not convert and saved his inheritance, but when he died, guess where he went?

My friend Clare, whose mother was Roman Catholic and whose father had taken up Yoga (a very exotic thing to do at mid-century) asked the same question every year in religion class. What about a Catholic who believed in his heart that Presbyterianism was the true religion. Wouldn't *he* go to hell if he didn't convert to Presbyterianism?

The reaction was always the same; the nun's mouth tightened at the corners and she paled visibly, and she said that such a thing couldn't happen.

"Why not?"

"Because the Catholic Church is the true faith."

"But what if the man believes it isn't? He really believes it isn't."

"That just couldn't happen."

Clare never did get an answer.

I was probably less susceptible than most to the general suspicion of Protestants because of my mother. I broached the subject of conversion a few times to her, but I knew in my heart she was not going to appear in our hallway one morning in a flowered pillbox, beaming at my father and me and cooing: "Let's all go to Mass. I want to become a Catholic."

I liked her the way she was, anyhow, and it didn't seem to me that being able to say the Hail Mary or the Agnus Dei in Latin would really improve her. She was an active worker at the schools I attended, both the parochial school and the high school. In fact, many people thought that *she* was the Catholic and it was my father who was the Protestant. She was even the co-chairman of a fund drive to raise money for a new novitiate for the nuns.

Her relationship with the nuns in parochial school was more than cordial. There were several of the nuns, including Sister Eugene, the principal, and Sister Maria, my eighth-grade teacher, whom she admired as teachers and as human beings. But it was a different story at the convent school.

Together with a small group of other women, my mother had been the driving force behind the revitalization of the convent school PTA. She and my father ran an intramural basketball program, sponsored by the high school for young girls in the parish. Every Saturday morning my mother and my father and I would come to the gym and referee and coach the intramural games. My mother also helped to set up dances at the school with boys from Catholic schools in Washington. She was nominated to be the president of the PTA for the year that would be my senior year at the school. But another woman in the organization, Mrs. G., had other ideas. Mrs. G., who belonged to a different parish than we did, asked the Sister Superior, Sister Anna: Should a *non-*Catholic be president of the PTA?

Sister Superior called my mother on the telephone and asked my mother to come and see her.

Sister Superior began with a smile, saying that perhaps it was not a good idea that the PTA be dominated by people from our parish, since there were girls from other parishes attending the school as well. And she added, "And of course we would like to have a *Catholic* parent as president of the PTA."

My mother got the message and walked out. My father was furious. He and my mother went to see Sister Maria, who was now the principal of the grade school. They said that they were resigning from both the parish PTA and the convent school PTA (my brother was now attending the parish school).

"I expected that my wife might run into discrimination from bigoted Catholics. But in all the years she had worked in the parish, the only place we found it is from a nun," my father said.

Sister Maria said she could hardly believe that Sister Anna had meant to discriminate. At that moment, into the office walked Father O'Connor, one of the parish priests who had often come to poker games at our house, slipping off his black jacket to reveal a shirt that said WAIKIKI HULA! HULA! on it.

"It's no use talking to Sister Anna," he said. "I've just been there for an hour. She's made up her mind. It's a waste of time to talk to her any more."

And he turned to my mother and said, "I apologize, Helen. This is not what Catholicism is all about."

My mother decided simply to withdraw. She did not want to get her friends at the school embroiled in a donnybrook, and she knew that some of them would be terribly uncomfortable about taking issue with a sister superior. She also did not want to ruin my last year at the school. Afterward, several of the nuns came to her privately and said they believed that the superior's decision had been unfair. The new president of the parish PTA called her and asked her to rejoin.

"Ask God to help you make a decision," he said.

"I already asked God," my mother said. "He told me to stay the hell away from there."

I will always be grateful to Sister Superior; I can still see her with my mind's eye, that broad face with eyes that were always cool when her apple cheeks puffed up in a smile. Behind the steel-rimmed glasses a sugared piety congealed in her pale blue eyes. I have seen that smile many times since on the faces of small-souled people who have been given a modicum of power, and I have learned to distrust it. I know, as Hamlet says, that one may "smile, and smile, and be a villain." Sister Anna gave me an early lesson in the nature of bigotry; an understanding that it can just as easily be evil as good that parades under the banner of religion.

The chauvinism that permeated our attitudes toward non-Catholics at mid-century leaked into every aspect of our life. We were urged to have Catholic friends, to attend none other than Catholic schools, to date Catholic boys, and if we married one, to live in Catholic neighborhoods. We were to huddle together in catacombs of our own construction like the early Christians, as if, like them, we were being hunted by some malevolent power who wanted to amuse the Saturday afternoon sports fans by throwing us to the lions. It was assumed that the non-Catholic world spent its time hatching plots to dismember the Mystical Body of Christ, when in fact nobody really cared what we did in our churches as long as we didn't do it in the street and frighten the automobiles. There was nobody to persecute us in Silver Spring, Maryland. The Presbyterians were worrying about dandelions in the lawns, the Baptists were worrying about the mortgage, and if any Lutherans wanted to seduce us, it had nothing to do with Free Will and the Pope; they were male and under twenty, and their concerns were with biology, not theology.

Still, the siege mentality endured. We were soldiers, even if the enemy displayed a deceptive lethargy about combat. Soldiers must be battle-ready, even in the summers, those long hot lazy Maryland summers when even a lion wouldn't have the energy to take a bite out of a plump, juicy Christian. Special convocations like the Summer School of Catholic Action reminded us that we had a world to win.

I signed up for the summer school, along with Alice and Diane, in my sophomore year. The "SSCA" was to be held on the campus of Boston College, and I must confess that my motives had more to do with a chance to see New England than with any great zeal for Catholic Action. The school delegation boarded the train for Boston, some twenty strong. Our chaperone, Sister Mary Victor, had instructed us carefully that our behavior must be at all times that of Good Catholic Girls. We were each given a copy of the convention Blue Book, which contained all the information about the courses to be given at the school. The Blue Book echoed Sister Mary Victor's warning:

"Delegates to the convention must behave at all times like Catholic ladies and gentlemen. Their behavior should be calculated to show the power of Catholic teaching on our personal lives. It should be a good example to all and not cause the slightest scandal to anyone. Anyone who does not intend to act at all times in public and private in a way to give example, to represent the Catholic Church in the best light, will be asked to leave immediately."

Taboo activities included:

Talking across the light shafts.

Leaving the blinds open when dressing.

Boys going to girls' rooms—and vice versa.

Running up bills on room service.

"Noise, dirt, inconsiderate or ungentlemanly conduct brands the offender and his school and family as common and ignorant and unfit to be represented at a gathering like ours."

We were staying at the Hotel Touraine, across from the Boston Common, and the first evening we were there, we gathered in one of the rooms for a gab session. Somebody broke out a pack of cigarettes—definitely not Good Catholic Girl behavior. I was wearing dungarees, definitely not Good Catholic Girl attire. There was a knock on the door.

"Who is it?" asked Alice.

"Sister Mary Victor."

I was the last one left who had a cigarette going when Sister Mary Victor knocked, since for every puff I took I coughed six times. The windows had been opened to draw off the smoke, so I threw my Kool out the window. I looked down at my dungarees. There was only one answer. I dived under the bed.

The door was opened and Sister Mary Victor entered. She smiled on her brood. "Where is Caryl?"

"I think she's taking a nap," somebody lied.

Sister Mary Victor sat down on the bed. I could see the heels of her black shoes as I lay on my stomach under the bed. All the smoke I had inhaled from the cigarette was floating about in my lungs; I clutched at my throat, massaging it desperately to keep the cough back. Sister Mary Victor's heels tapped on the floor. She was chatting merrily about the trip and the plans for the next day. She was in no hurry to leave. Under the bed, I was dying.

She finally said good night, and I emerged, gasping like a beached whale. I gave up smoking for the duration of the Summer School of Catholic Action.

The next day I trotted dutifully off to the campus of Boston College, Blue Book in hand. I thumbed through it, trying to select a session to attend. I decided to pass up "Helps in Making Converts," even though it promised, "Your particular problem with a non-Catholic friend, relative or parent will be discussed first."

I flipped past "One Hundred Million Protestants": "More Protestants came into the church last year than ever before in history. What is the typical American Protestant thinking about? What does he want? How does he live? You can help him in more ways than you realize!"

I considered several self-improvement-through-religion

courses that presented a Christ tailor-made for the America of the fifties: The Dale Carnegie Christ.

"With Christ We Do All Things Well" promised to describe how to do a good job, have success in life, how to converse with others, and how to dress.

"Develop Your Personality" pointed out that imitating Christ was a short cut to a healthy personality. Christ, the Blue Book said, has Enthusiasm, Energy, Courage, Strength and Poise.

The Macho Christ appeared in another course, "Christ the Manly Man": "If He was a perfect Man, he certainly was a masculine man. It was from among a group of calloused, muscled fishermen that he chose his friends. He preached a strong, manly uncompromising doctrine. He was a man with steel in his face!" (Mid-century was the time when Men had to be Men, and they couldn't cry and they had to like football and not the ballet; so of course Christ had to be the sort of guy who would be happy in the locker room, wearing a jockstrap. Never mind that He said something about turning the other cheek, or "Blessed are the Meek" or "Suffer the little children to come unto me." Ignore all that; you want people to think he was a faggot?)

Those courses were tempting, but not quite what I wanted.

I glanced at "Courtship and Marriage." It promised to deal with the differences between men and women. The Blue Book announced: "The souls of men and women differ, just as their bodies do. Women like lettuce, men hamburger. These bodily or somatic differences are paralleled by psyche differences."

(In all my later reading of psychology, I never hit on the hamburger-lettuce gap. Could Freud have missed something Big?)

I turned the page to "Workshop in Social Recreation."

It promised to teach such party games as Merry-Go-Round and Human Frog Pond.

(If somebody today asked me at a party if I wanted to play Merry-Go-Round or Human Frog Pond I would grab my coat and my husband and run, lacking the guts for such exotic-sounding perversions. But those were more innocent times. I am sure that the priest who conducted the workshop would have assumed that fellatio was some obscure office in the Vatican, and I am equally sure that Human Frog Pond was less risqué than Post Office!)

The workshop looked like fun, but hardly serious enough to justify my 500-mile trip to the SSCA. Another workshop called "Have I a Vocation?" I avoided like the Plague. I thumbed some more, and then I found it. Just the thing. "The Red Menace."

I marched off to "The Red Menace," ready to get more ammunition for resounding editorials in the *Silver Quill*. What I got, for the first time, was an understanding of what communism was all about. As the title implies, the course was not exactly an objective presentation, but it did avoid the hysteria that always accompanied any discussion of the subject in the pulpit or in school. I learned about Hegel, about Marx's theories of class warfare. Few of the nuns who taught in the convent school could have spoken with any understanding of the Marxist view of history. All they were expected to know and to communicate was that communism was evil.

I saved the Blue Book, the way I saved the gardenias from every formal dance I ever went to, and when I flip through it now, I see it as a morass of trivia: the middle-class pieties, the Christ with Poise, the endless talk of converting Protestants, the courses on editing the sodality newspaper and raising money for the missions. But glittering among it all, like a new-minted silver dollar in a waste bin, was a page that bore the heading "The Catholic Answer to Race Relations."

The Blue Book said it was a course taught by Father Lewis Toomey, S.J., and this is what it said:

"The gigantic struggle to establish peace and justice in the world may not be won by solving the problem of race relations, but it will not be won without it. The acceptance of a Christian Democratic solution of race relations is the moral price of survival. Such an acceptance is the price America must pay in order to join its undoubted leadership in economic and military affairs with moral leadership. And America will establish a claim to moral leadership only when it finds the courage to resolve the contradictory situation of a nation divided by un-Democratic, un-Christian practices in race relations."

This was two years before Brown versus the Board of Education, which outlawed segregation in schools; thirteen years before Watts.

The entire time I was in Catholic school I never heard a nun or a priest say anything but that the souls of men were equal before God, and that it was sinful to hate another person because of his color. There was even a painful tokenism in my high school, one black girl imported from nearby Washington. She was dark and big-boned and adolescent-awkward. She must have been miserable. Perhaps if she had been small and dainty and paler, she would have been courted by the other girls as exotic.

But there was no connection made between believing in the equality of man and doing much about it. We were continually being exhorted to Catholic Action. "You Can Change the World," we were told. But Catholic Action was interpreted as forming a living J for Jesus and M for Mary and saying the Rosary; or trying to convert Episcopalians; or going to the Summer School of Catholic Action and learning to play Human Frog Pond.

A mission speaker at the school left us pamphlets describing the work of an order of priests in the South. It lamented the fact that while two out of three Negroes in some parts of Africa were Catholic, only 2 per cent of American Blacks shared the True Faith. The pamphlet did not mention that many of these American blacks were desperately poor, ill-fed, ill-clothed, that they lived in tenements where rats danced in the walls, or they lived in tarpaper shanties on hardscrabble, unyielding land; that they were not allowed into colleges or white toilets or movies or restaurants or unions or swimming pools, that they were discriminated against by the Great American Christian Society our textbooks paid homage to. The only problem mentioned by the mission pamphlet was that not enough black people were Catholics.

The missions were the focus of most of our fund-raising activities in high school. It did not occur to us that misery as appalling as the squalor of Far East villages could be found seven miles away in the shadow of the Capitol; or that sprawling to the south of us in Appalachia was a region as dispossessed as stretches of the Indian subcontinent; or that in our own county the facilities for the retarded, the poor, the elderly, the maimed, were hopelessly inadequate.

We had picnic lunches for the missions and film showings and card games and fashion shows, raffles and contests. Each Lent we were given little purple boxes called mite boxes (after the biblical parable of the widow's mite) which were to be filled with money from such sacrifices as giving up movies or candy. Sister Mary Victor wanted more than a mite from us. She passed out the mite boxes and said when they came back she didn't want them to jingle. She wanted them to *rustle*.

The missions gave me a chance to go on another summer junket. The Catholic Students Mission Crusade (the one that had the glorious fight song) was holding its convention.

I signed up (and so did Diane and Alice) because the convention was going to be held on the South Bend campus of Notre Dame University, the Valhalla of Catholic education. Notre Dame was the home of the Fighting Irish, and Rockne-Pat O'Brien, a place where dwelt handsome Catholic fullbacks wearing miraculous medals under their jerseys. I saw myself walking along a path next to an ivy-covered building, talking seriously to a handsome Catholic fullback about the Problems of the Missions.

It didn't turn out exactly that way. The Catholic football players were all on vacation with the rest of the college boys, and the girl delegates to the crusade far outnumbered the boy delegates. On the overnight train to South Bend, the boys had their pick of girls; they were not going to choose one with size-ten feet and braces. I remember sitting in the vista-dome car of the train, alone in a seat for two, looking up at the stars through the blue-tinted glass, while the prettiest girls paired off with the available boys. Diane, who had long curls and the face of an amiable doll, got one. I was smitten with a young man from St. John's High School who looked like Carleton Carpenter, but he was sitting next to a girl from Georgetown Visitation Convent who had dainty size-four loafers, white teeth, and, as Fitzgerald put it, money in her smile.

I sat listening to someone play "Down by the Old Mill Stream" on a banjo, feeling unwanted and alone, watching boy-girl heads slipping silently together, soaking myself in self-pity and not caring a fig about the missions.

When we arrived at the Notre Dame campus, we were given copies of the convention bulletin (published at Crusade Castle, Cincinnati 26, Ohio), which announced: "We are supposed to be living in an age of progress, and yet half the world is closed off from the other by an Iron Curtain, and Christians are being persecuted more ferociously than in the age of Nero. Priests and Religious who only a few

1. Texas Ranger—Age Five

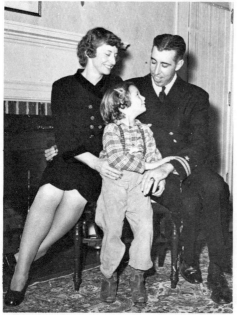

2. My Parents and Me

3. The American Beauty—
   Camp Mayflather

4. Family Portrait

5. Easter 1947

6. First Communion

7. I Enter High School

8. Saint Michael's Girls Basketball Team, 1950

9. Saint Michael Plays Blessed Sacrament

10. Victory Prayers at Half-time

11. Summer School of Catholic Action, Boston College

12. Notre Dame Convention

13. Junior Prom, High School

14. High School Graduation, Diane and Me

15. Off to Europe—1958

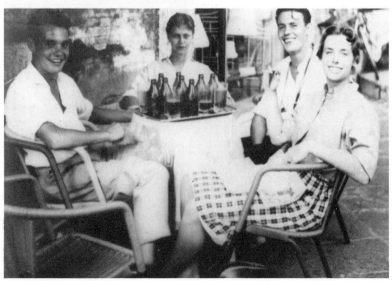

years ago were students in your schools are dying in communist prisons."

I wandered through the gymnasium at the university which was devoted entirely to a mission exhibit. It resembled nothing so much as the trade fairs that periodically inhabit Grange halls and municipal auditoriums to hustle tractors, prefabricated houses, or pleasure boats. There were fifty-two exhibits, each offering printed material and gimmicks. I picked up a piggy bank from the Salesians and a Dixie Box bank from the Trinitarians. There was no shortage of takers for the material, for, as the convention manager gushed in the bulletin: "It looks like this will be an all time record-breaker for the CSMC!"

Another auditorium featured movies; and since I was big on movies I spent a lot of time there. I saw, *Pearl of the Orient* and *The World of Juan Mateo,* and *Christ in Korea,* and *Splendid Italy,* and *Mid Sweat and Toil in Dixie* and in none of them did boy-meet-girl. It was more like missionary-meets-soul. The endings were happy.

Several times I got a chance to gawk at the undisputed star celebrity of the convention, Bishop Fulton J. Sheen, in the flesh. An aura of pure charisma surrounded his handsome, silvered head like the halo of an angel on a Holy Card. And I heard the keynote speaker of the convention say: "All the problems of the world are in some way mission problems."

There was, of course, no question in the mind of anyone at the CSMC convention about the fact that it was the Will Of God that everybody in the world ought to be Catholic, and that converting them was the noblest way of doing God's will here on earth. And no doubt the missionaries did much good in their far-flung posts. No doubt they taught children and gave them food and shelter and eased pain. But the reason for it all, as presented to us, was so detached from human compassion as to be almost mathematically

abstract. All those people who were served by the missionaries for whom we saved our nickels and dimes were only
silver fish in the sea of possible salvation. They were souls,
as indistinguishable from one another as the numbers in a
giant computer that might have been sitting in a corner of
the office of the Society for the Propagation of the Faith
and tabulating them on IBM cards.

One convention speaker said scornfully that missionaries
were not social workers. Had he forgotten that Christ said,
"I was hungry and you gave me to eat; I was naked and you
clothed me." Were these acts meaningless unless a few souls
got scooped up for the Catholic Church in the process? It
is not surprising that various unconverted peoples looked
on the missionaries with the same suspicion with which a
steer eyes a branding iron. Incredible as it may have seemed
to us, there were a great many people in the nations of
the world, who—despite our invitation—did not really want
to be part of Our Crowd.

9
Saints, Censors, and the BVM

The convent school was a new building, plain and square, bare of any architectural distinction except a Greek-style pediment and pillars at the front door topped by a cross, which were absurdly out of style with the plain, institutional lines of the rest of the building. A few shrubs stood like sentries around the building, but they only served to accentuate the new, raw look of the building. It looked exactly like any new school in any suburb in an era when the population was exploding and schools were popping out of the ground like garden weeds. Unlike the weeds, which were generally well constructed, the schools had pipes that froze and walls that cracked and windows that wouldn't close right, but by the time the flaws were discovered the contractor was somewhere else, building a shopping center with pipes that would freeze and walls that would crack.

But if the façade of the building gave little hint as to what sort of activities went on within, there was no such anonymity inside. The icons of Catholicism were not restricted to the chapel; Saints and angels and Virgins and Christs abounded. The bulletin board in each classroom displayed a religious sentiment appropriate to the season; the blackboards were often so full of religious symbols there was little room for anything else. In one classroom we did our geometry problems under a picture of a dove, an altar and chalked-in Gothic letters: COME HOLY SPIRIT. In another we declined Latin verbs around a huge rose and the words O ROSA MYSTICA, ORA PRO NOBIS (Mystical Rose, pray for us), and in a third we hardly had room to get a sentence in French under a Star of Bethlehem, a crib, an Angel, and the command: COME AND ADORE HIM.

(Another classroom featured a favorite duo of pictures that graced many Catholic schools. They were St. Joan of Arc and Sir Galahad, both done in what can only be described as a neo-medieval style. We had had the same two pictures on the wall of the sixth-grade classroom in parochial school. One boy, asked by the nun to identify them, stared at them for a long time. Then he said, "Joan of Arc there—and the other one—" he paused, then inspiration struck—"Kid Gavilan!" We all roared. Kid Gavilan, a contender for the middleweight title, was not exactly seeking the Holy Grail.)

The idea of all the artwork in the halls of the convent school was to help us to remember, at all times, that we were Catholics. We could hardly forget it; we couldn't turn around without bumping into a crucifix or a haloed saint, or more often than not, Mother Marie Claire: Mother Marie wasn't a saint, but she was, like Kid Gavilan, a contender.

Mother Marie was the founder of the order of nuns who taught at the school. She may indeed have been a kindly woman and a saintly soul, but in the pictures of her that adorned the hallways and the bookmarks that the nuns gave out, she had an expression that looked as though she had just bitten into a sour pickle.

(In the *Quill* room, the lair of the newspaper staff, we had two pictures of Mother Marie and a stack of bookmarks. We regarded ourselves as the school's version of the Algonquin wits, and one of our favorite pastimes was writing captions for Mother Marie bookmarks, such as:

"I Dreamed I Became A Saint in my Maidenform Bra!" or "She's lovely! She's engaged! She Uses Holy Water!" or "Wanted For Arson!")

The nuns were lobbying to get Mother Marie declared a

saint. To have a founder who was a saint would mean a big boost in status for the order. Our assemblies often dramatized the Life of Mother Marie, which meant a skit with a student dressed as Mother Marie kneeling and praying, and suddenly seeing a vision of the Madonna (another student on a platform behind a transparent curtain.) Mother Marie would cry aloud: "I shall found a new order of Sisters!"

We always knew how it was going to end, so the Life of Mother Marie skits got a little tedious after four years. We wrote new endings to the drama in the *Quill* room, in which Mother Marie did not go on to found a new order of nuns, but in fact became a dancing girl and led a life of sin. We thought the new ending would perk up "The Life of Mother Marie" considerably. However, we did not suggest the changes to the moderator of the newspaper. We thought she might not see the humor of it.

Mother Marie's problem in the sainthood derby seemed to be her miracle quota. There are precise and rigid requirements for sainthood, among them the sort of miracles that one has caused to happen.

Mother Marie's main talent in the miracle field seemed to be an ability to stop fires. The *Quill* staff had an idea for hastening the process of beatification. We suggested that it would be a good idea to set the school on fire, wait until a good blaze worked up, and then toss into the flames the school's entire supply of Mother Marie bookmarks. If the fire stopped, the nuns would have a dandy miracle. If not, those were the breaks, and maybe Mother Marie wasn't cut out to be a saint.

(Perhaps nowhere in the world does more breezy sacrilege occur than in Catholic schools. I can recall jokes about the saints and even God himself that are so blasphemous that I blanch on remembering them. It did not seem strange to us that we could kneel in a chapel and be brought to the verge of tears by the awful spectacle of the Crucifixion, and a minute later outside the chapel chuckle to a line about the successor to "Rock Around the Clock": "Rock Around the Crucifix" by Pontius Pilate and his Nail Drivin' Five. There was another one about Christ teaching the Disciples to walk on the water. When St. Peter started to sink he cried out for help, Christ turned around and said, "Dummy, walk on the rocks like the rest of us." It never occurred to us that God would be offended. He and His miracles and His minions were so much a part of our daily life that it would have seemed unnatural to exempt him from our adolescent humor.)

Another saint who was mentioned often at the convent school was Maria Goretti. She was a twelve-year-old girl who had lived in Italy at the turn of the century. One day, when the rest of her family was at work in the fields, a handyman approached and said that if she would submit to him, he would not harm her. She refused and he raped her and stabbed her repeatedly while she called out the names of the Holy Family. She died of her wounds and he went to prison. He later repented and joined a monastery, where he had a visitation from her and she said that she forgave him.

It was a horrible and Gothic story, but these qualities were somehow lost when the story was dramatized and put on a record. The nuns played the record over the PA system in the cafeteria during Lent. (Since Lent was the penitential season, we were supposed to be somber and reflective at lunch.) I remember sitting in the cafeteria, my brown lunch bag perched on one of the white Formica-topped tables, chewing my egg-salad sandwich and listening to the Maria Goretti story:

"No, no, it's a sin!"

PANT. PANT. PANT. "You must do as I say."

"It's a sin! A sin!"

PANT. PANT. PANT.
"Jesus, Mary, Joseph. *Jesus Mary Joseph!*"
PANT PANT. PANT PANT. PANT PANT.

Visitations, like the one Maria Goretti paid to her murderer, were the subjects of the stories we were told in religion class by Sister Daniel. There was no symbolism to any of the stories; Sister Daniel was presenting us with events as real as the ones John Cameron Swayze described on the TV news when he was Hopscotching the World for Headlines. It did not seem at all surprising to us that the Blessed Mother or various saints should be popping up from behind rocks to confront Mexican laborers or Belgian nuns. These appearances usually resulted in a request to get something built. Our Lady of Guadaloupe wanted a cathedral; Our Lady of Lourdes a grotto. The Blessed Mother may have kept more people employed than the average department of public works. But Our Lady of Fatima was the favorite. When she appeared to three children in Portugal early in the century she said she wanted the conversion of Russia, and that was generally assumed to be an anti-Communist statement.

(A favorite story that we told in the halls of the school was that one of the Portuguese children wrote a letter about something the Blessed Mother had told her. The letter was to be opened and its contents revealed to the world at some future date—either 1960 or 1970—the date varied with the teller. It was said that the Pope had been allowed to see the letter in advance and its contents had been so horrible that he fainted. We listened to the story with the same delicious shiver of terror we got from "Inner Sanctum" on the radio.)

Our Lady of Fatima was the big dramatic production at the school one year, and I had a part in it. My role as a peasant woman required me to bow my head in fear when the sun spun in the heavens and to kneel when Our Lady appeared. The Blessed Mother, a thin, blond senior, stood atop a cloud suspended between two trees. The apparition was a stunning climax to the show. It had a Ziegfeldian grandeur to it, and it drew prolonged Ooooooohs from the crowd. The Oooooooohs were a vindication of weeks of work by the stage crew.

When the Religion that Sister Daniel taught us at the convent school was not a parade of miracles and saints, it was catechism, only slightly more advanced than the little green book we used in parochial school, or it was a set of rules to help us stay on the straight and narrow. Moral Guidance was a course that was designed to help us meet the challenges of life with a right conscience.

Sister Philomena taught us Moral Guidance, and she did it strictly by the book; a burgundy volume that was also titled *Moral Guidance*. It was indeed helpful for a teen-ager growing up in a suburb of what was then Eisenhower's America. Moral Guidance set up hypothetical moral crises for us, and then proceeded to solve them in the correct manner for our edification. It took a stretch of the imagination for me to put myself in some of the predicaments M.G.'s cast of characters got themselves into:

Convict Z is chained to a wall in prison. The wall catches fire. May convict Z cut off his chained hand to escape the fire, or would it be a mortal sin of self-mutilation?

Catholic aviator Alphonse (most of the characters in M.G. had the prefix Catholic before their name) is flying his airplane. His plane is hit, and he knows he cannot escape. May he crash-dive his plane into the enemy aircraft?

Catholic girl Maria lives in a country that has been occupied by an enemy force. May she slice up her face so she will not be sexually attractive to them?

I remember that Alphonse might crash and Z might hack; I do not remember the verdict on Catholic girl Maria, though

I assume that Maria also might slice, given the fact that Impurity ranks much higher than mere self-mutilation in the hierarchy of sin in the convent school.

The Catholicism that we were taught by Sister Daniel and Sister Philomena was the same thing that was being taught in most of the parochial high schools in the country in the nineteen-fifties, and though we did not know it at the time, it was a peculiar hybrid; a solid base of a peasant religion of miracle and mystery with a sprinkling of poorly articulated concepts from a more intellectual plane.

But we, in our sailor uniforms and our oxfords, we were not peasant women struggling to survive in a hostile land. We were teen-agers coming of age in an America that faced all the complex problems of a world power in the technological era. The simple faith that served our grandparents would not suffice for us. It was not enough that we should be devoted to Our Lady of Fatima and pray for the conversion of Russia. As citizens of the Republic we would be asked to choose leaders who offered us complicated policies on anti-ballistic missile systems and nuclear disarmament and trade agreements. We could not say the rosary and wait for Mary to send us an inspiration on how we should stand on de facto segregation. We were part of a species that unlocked the secret of the atom and used it to burn hundreds of thousands of human beings to a tangle of melted flesh and bone. Did Mother Marie Claire have any answers for us about the morality of dropping the Bomb? Moral Guidance never mentioned it. I cannot remember that the subject of Hiroshima and Nagasaki ever even arose in that convent school. Hitler had incinerated six million Jews in the recent war, and nobody ever mentioned that, either. Persecution of Catholics was the only kind that counted. The technological, complex, terrifying world was barred from the halls of that convent school. There were no daily papers, no news magazines, no periodicals except for the lowbrow Catholic ones devoted to the sodality and the missions, no current events. Maria Goretti was more real than Dag Hammarskjöld. Safety was to be found in the shadow of the school, the church, the parish. It was not safe to bundle our intellectual curiosity in some kind of magical dangerous, they were impertinent. Good Catholic girls didn't ask too many questions.

It is perhaps the greatest indictment of Catholic popular education at mid-century that its aim often seemed to be to bundle our intellectual curiosity in some kind of magical Saran Wrap that would let only the rays of the Church's truth filter through while shriveling the rays of everybody else's truth before they could penetrate. The irony of it was that while we rattled our rhetorical sabers at the Communists, we were paying them the ultimate tribute of being just like them. The same impulse that led the Communists to keep a tight rein on what appeared in *Pravda* was precisely the same one that led the archbishop to ban the movie *Martin Luther*. (Guess who the Bad Guys were in that one?)

Our minds were kept innocent of anything but praise for the Church. Sister Daniel did not mention the Inquisition, the political avarice of some of the popes, the power struggles, the wealth, the whole incredible pageant of a magnificent institution that housed both sanctity and depravity, the cruelest of repression and the deepest compassion. The Catholic Church nurtured both Torquemada the Inquisitor and Damien the Leper, but all we ever heard about was the latter.

We did not hear the names of Kant or Descartes; we did not read the poetry of Byron; Thomas Paine was an atheist, that was all we were told of him. We did not hear the name of Darwin in biology class. One day, Clare (who like me had the dangerous habit of reading books that were not in the school library) asked Sister Mary Xavier in biology 101 to explain Darwin's theory of evolution.

Sister Mary Xavier looked up, annoyed.

"Well, Clare, if you want to believe *your* grandmother swung through trees by her tail like a monkey, that is certainly all right with me."

That was the end of the question of evolution, as far as Sister Mary Xavier was concerned.

One classmate of mine, a pretty, dark-haired girl named Mary Frances, asked a priest who had come to give us a marriage course a question about artificial insemination. He barked at her to sit down, and reported her question to Sister Superior. She was called in and chastised for "insolence." The subject was not fit for the minds of good Catholic girls.

Censorship at the school ran the gamut from the sublime to the ridiculous. I was denied permission to use Gibbon's *Decline and Fall of the Roman Empire* for a term paper, and was given a stern lecture for even suggesting it. Clare brought the popular novel *Prince of Foxes* to school and it was confiscated. The school paper was ordered not to run a cartoon of a senior on a horse unless the cartoon could be changed to show her riding sidesaddle. No lady rode astride. Even the lyrics of the Spring Follies had to be changed. The finale was to be the entire cast in a rousing rendition of "Spring Is Bustin' Out All Over," a direct steal from "June Is Bustin' Out All Over," from *Carousel.* Sister Superior decreed that "Bustin'" was vulgar. So we all stood on the stage at the finale and sang: "Spring is *bursting* out all over—"

Temptation, it seemed, lurked everywhere, even in the lyrics of Oscar Hammerstein. But in no place did it lurk with such a vengeance, no place was temptation more infectious, than on the silver screen. The Legion of Decency kept on the alert.

The Legion was in the business of rating movies long before the Motion Picture Association did so. Copies of the Legion's monthly pronouncements were tacked on the bulletin boards in the school, and we were expected to abide by its decision.

The movies on the C list were condemned. It was a mortal sin to see them. Most of the C movies were French and Italian films with the word Love or Passion in the title somewhere. Very few American movies were immoral enough to get a C rating; Jane Russell's cleavage did it for *The Outlaw* and that, plus her navel did it for *The French Line*. The word "virgin" brought down the wrath of the Legion on *The Moon Is Blue*. (They weren't talking about the Virgin Mary.)

On the B list were most American movies. B-1 movies were morally unobjectionable for adults. B-2 movies were morally objectionable in part for adults. The A movies were O.K. for everybody, and they were usually Walt Disney cartoons or travelogues. Critic Walter Kerr, a graduate of Catholic University, complained that if he followed all the Catholic movie and theater guides, the only production he would have been able to see one year was the *Ice Follies*.

Each year, at an assembly, we had to stand, right hands raised as if we were being inducted into the Army, and take the Legion of Decency pledge. We knew of course, what it was that bugged the Legion. Sex. We saw plenty of movies in which people were garroted, bayoneted, shot, strangled, and otherwise dispatched from life in a violent manner. That did not seem to disturb the Legion. It was cleavage that was the great threat to the moral fiber of America. But now and then a film appeared that earned the full approval of the Legion. Why couldn't every movie be like *The Song of Bernadette*.

The nuns held a special showing of *The Song of Bernadette* in the gymnasium. Jennifer Jones was Bernadette.

That was frowned on because she was divorced, but since the content of the film was so commendable the transgressions of Miss Jones could be overlooked.

We all got weepy when Bernadette left the young man who loved her to go into the convent; and an apparition of the Blessed Virgin Mary at Lourdes was inspiring as done by Hollywood. They did it with so much more style than we did.

(In the *Quill* room we thought the whole thing should have been done as a musical. We even thought up some production numbers. One, to the tune of "Lady of Spain," a big hit by Eddie Fisher, was to be sung and danced by Bernadette and the chorus of nuns:

> Lady of Lourdes I adore you
> Right from the day I first saw you
> My soul has been yearning for You
> What else could a Catholic soul do—)

If there was one thing about the Catholic popular religion of the fifties that seemed to mystify most non-Catholics, it was our attachment to Mary. To someone looking in from outside, I can well imagine that the spectacle of the May procession, with all the children dressed in white marching through the streets of Silver Spring with the Virgin carried aloft, must have smacked a bit of the spring festival to Aphrodite in suburban Rome around 202 B.C. It must have seemed idolatrous to those whose worship was of a more austere cast, and I suppose it was. But it was marvelous all the same. There was all the excitement of a parade as we formed into ranks and waited for the procession to start. The smell of incense floated on the air, and as we walked with our rosaries in our hands we chanted the "Hail Mary" in cadence or we sang: "Bring Flowers of the Fairest." It was joyous, tuneful, and it filled us with the wonder of being alive on a fine spring day, and part of a faith that offered such marvelous entertainments.

Our devotion to Mary did at times seem to overshadow all else in our theology. When I was a young child, I remember praying to Mary at night, and feeling her become a presence in my room, hovering above the bed, gentle and sheltering. She was both disembodied and faceless; a vapor only. Sometimes Jesus was there with her and sometimes God the Father, kindly, omnipotent grownups who would keep the demons of the night away from me. When I reached high school, Mary had become the pre-eminent person of the heavenly cast. God the Father receded into a vague omnipresence. The Holy Ghost made cameo appearances now and then as a dove; even Christ got fewer column inches in the *Silver Quill* than the Blessed Mother. Mary was no longer a floating presence in my room. I had grown too old for that. I still said the prayers, but I had begun to wonder whom I was praying to.

The grand finale at the close of all the meetings of the Sodality of Our Lady, an organization to which we all belonged, was a tableau of the Blessed Mother. One of the nuns would begin to play a hymn on the piano ("Mother Beloved, of God and of Men") and as we sang, the curtains would sweep open to reveal Mary, standing on the top of the globe with her hands outstretched to give grace to the world. It was considered an honor to get to be Mary in a tableau. I wanted to be Mary, like everybody else, but did Mary have size-ten feet and braces? (Now that I think about it, no homely girl ever got to be Mary.)

If we could find a way to link Mary with the great events in our history textbooks, we did it. The highlight of a Columbus Day pageant, as reported by the *Silver Quill*, featured "The Blessed Mother appearing in the background of a tableau depicting Columbus and Queen Isabella, signifying her approval of the mission of Columbus."

(Did the Blessed Mother also approve the wholesale slaughter and enslavement of the Indians by men from Catholic Spain, carrying the Crucifix in their bloody pilgrimage for gold and Glory? The *Silver Quill* did not mention that.)

A smattering of headlines from the *Silver Quill* gives an indication of our number-one newsmaker:

SODALITY PREFECT CROWNS VIRGIN

PUPILS STAGE LIVING ROSARY AT GROTTO

MARY AIDS SODALISTS IN LENT

LEGISLATOR PROPOSES
STAMP HONORING MARY

SENIORS DEMONSTRATE VISION OF OUR LADY

AREA RESIDENTS HONOR GOD'S MOTHER

This journalistic focus on the BVM culminated in one issue which was to be called the Marian Year issue. The whole inside section of the paper would deal with nothing but the Blessed Virgin Mary. The staff of the newspaper objected to the idea; not that we had anything against Mary, but we figured we couldn't get enough decent copy to fill all that space. We argued, to no avail. Authority prevailed and the Marian Year appeared on schedule. It vacillated from sentimental slop ("Mary is the raindrop, Mary is the morning dew") to cornball verse:

> Put not your hopes in isotopes
> In neutrons nor in wishin'
> For Peace is brought by Mary
> And not atomic Fission.

We exalted Mary as the co-redemptrix of mankind, the finest flower of womanhood; and at the same time we dehumanized her. She became a plaster statue standing on top of a globe. She was sinless, flawless, sanitized, deodorized to the point it was not possible to recognize in her anything of the species God had created from the dust of the earth. Even Christ was allowed to be human, to throw the moneylenders out of the temple in a rage, to sweat blood before Calvary. We saw nothing of Mary but plastic serenity. In the dozens of pictures we saw of her at the foot of the Cross she was never old enough to be the mother of a thirty-three-year-old man. She always had the face of an ethereal nineteen-year-old. The expression on her face was one of slight melancholy, never of agony. She was beautiful, of course. We were living in a society that demanded physical beauty of its ideal women. Listen to the *Silver Quill* editorializing in the Marian Year issue:

"In the truest and deepest sense Mary was wonderfully beautiful. Since Christ derived his own body from her we may be assured her own features were exquisite perfection."

Christ, we assumed, would never have the bad taste to choose an ugly woman for his mother. Exquisite Mary was just right for Christ, the man with steel in his face. The images were right out of the billboard art department at Warner Brothers.

So many of society's attitudes toward women were grafted onto Mary. She was totally passive, as she was presented to us. God chose her, she accepted. She became a vessel for God's will.

From the Marian Year issue: "She gave no public manifestation of cleverness or intellectual power. (How did we know that?) She poured all her intellectual strength into the developing mind of the child that God had entrusted to her. Mary couldn't be a *brain*. Horrors!

And the last paragraph of that article neatly sums up the feminist case against the image of Mary:

"Mary's sanctity was measured by how many clothes she

washed, how many meals she prepared, how many kindly little offices she performed on behalf of her family and neighbors. In her greatness, Mary never rose above the little things done by slaves, servants—and mothers!"

How could we identify with the Mary that was proffered to us? This perfect, patient, smiling, sinless paragon. She shared with the rest of womankind the physical act of birth, but she did not share the universal human act that for all other women made birth possible. She was the Blessed *Virgin.* Her virginity was stressed to an extraordinary degree. If she was perfection, and she was Virgin, were not all women who did not share her condition soiled to some degree? It did not occur to us that this emphasis on the virginity of Mary was part of a legacy of medieval ascetics who saw women as low creatures, temptations placed in the middle of the road to heaven. We were told that it was through Mary that God raised womanhood. Raised us from what? We never thought to ask. But we knew that the nuns regarded human sexuality as a baser part of our nature, rather than as a normal part of the human personality. The Madonna-whore view of women prevailed, though it was never said quite that way. So we prayed to this shining symbol, this moon of perfect womanhood who floated in the heavenly ether beyond our reach forever. Like some character from Greek mythology, she was hurled from the common clay of earth, from the sweating, vile crowds, into the firmament to become a star to light the way of men forever. But was it exaltation—or exile?

10 *True-hearted Girls*

The nun who taught us music would attack the keyboard with a vengeance. The piano by the side of the stage rumbled as if it were about to break into a rousing version of one of those bouncy, heroic "we're-all-men-together" numbers from an operetta by Sigmund Romberg. Which, in fact, it was.

The school song borrowed the music to "Stout-hearted Men" and most of the words as well. It was impossible to sing, though we gave it a valiant try. We squeaked on the high notes and growled on the low ones, but we did it with spirit:

> GIRLS!
> We have dreams!
> If we act!
> They will come true.
> TO!
> Turn our dreams
> To a fact it's up to you.
> If you love the school and its spirit
> Never fear it
> It will come true!
>
> CHORUS
>
> Let us be girls who are true hearted girls
> Who'll bring honor to our dear school
> Playing or working our duty ne'er shirking
> We'll stand by our school till the end—!

If you listened closely to the words of the song, you might assume that we were all about to rush up to the roof of the school to pour boiling oil on some pagan hordes about to storm the biology lab. The martial tone was echoed in the prose of the school yearbook:

"In its faithful ministers, The Catholic Church has the cohesive strength that gives unity and keeps the spirit alive. So also, at the school, this power manifests itself in the underclassmen. In the first year, the Freshman learns the ideals of a good Christian life and the spirit of the school. In sophomore and junior year, the student strives to perfect these ideals, and in senior year she prepares to go out and propagate this Christ-truth in years to come."

The yearbook conjures up the images of a tide of girls in sailor uniforms, marching off with rosaries in hand, spreading the word like female Elmer Gantrys. It is not exactly an accurate picture; for while we were indeed expected to propagate the Christ-truth, we were to do it in a ladylike way. We were not to be loud or vulgar or tough or pushy or impolite. We were to be refined, even in beating back the advances of Satan.

Despite the songs and the rhetoric, we were aware that the virtues that were expected of us were not the martial ones. The president of the senior council in my junior year expressed it perfectly in an open letter to her schoolmates:

"We as students have a duty to God and our parents to do our very best in learning and forming our character through obedience and co-operation."

And the yearbook pointed out that we were learning "Whether leader or follower, she must be at all times dependable, efficient, and co-operative."

We were expected to be, in a word, docile. Like well-broken riding mares, we were to do what we were told, quietly and with the least amount of trouble for our handlers. To insure our correct behavior, we were given a set of rules that governed our behavior in public and even in the privacy of the bathrooms.

The nun who was assigned as Sister Superior during my first two years at the convent school brought with her a mechanism for insuring that the rules we were to live by would be more than guidelines for us. They would be The Law. The demerit system would see to that.

We were all given handbooks, courtesy of Sister Christina, a tall reed of a woman with all the charm of an iced mackerel. The handbooks spelled out in detail all violations of the law: Talking in the halls, late assignments, dirty uniform ties, unladylike behavior, and standing in front of the Hairline.

The Hairline was the nuns' version of the Maginot line—only they kept a sharper eye on it than the French did on the original. The unpredictability of the plumbing in the school being what it was, the nuns endeavored to protect it. They shuddered at the idea of four hundred girls, all standing in the bathrooms, combing their tresses over the basins. So lines were drawn on the floors in the johns, some three feet back from the mirror over the basins, and we had to stand behind it when we combed our hair.

We were given positive incentives to observe the Hairline meticulously, because we never knew when the doors of the bathroom were going to fly open, and a nun would fly in like a commando raider, her eyes sweeping the room for infractions of the Hairline.

I had a problem with the Hairline, because I was slightly nearsighted and I refused to wear glasses. (Braces *and* glasses? I preferred to squint. At least when I kept my mouth shut the braces didn't show.) So if I didn't stand in front of the Hairline I might wind up parting my ear instead of my hair. But every time I flung caution to the winds and stuck my face up to the mirror, I found two faces staring back at me. Mine and Sister Angela's. Triumph would glitter in her eyes and she would waggle the demerit slip in her long, bony hand.

Sister Angela was the school's champion disciplinarian; the best Hairline-watcher, cigarette-smoke-sniffer, and all-around sleuth of the various sins enumerated in the handbook. She was a tall, thin, pale woman with skin the shade of ice milk and pale blue eyes that came to life behind the ovals of her steel-rimmed glasses only when she caught somebody *in flagrante delicto*. Her manner of propulsion could only be guessed at. It seemed inconceivable that she walked like other mere mortals. She seemed to glide along the corridors like some silent black ghost. She made no sound at all, except for the barely audible rustle of a skirt now and then. She was always materializing behind us, demerit slip in hand.

She always got me for talking in the halls. It was considered evil. I am not sure why it was that we were not allowed to converse as we moved from the classrooms to the gym for assemblies, unless the nuns figured the decibel level might unhinge the cinderblocks in the hallways. Class officers were impressed into service as prefects. (Screws, they are called in prison parlance.) The prefects had to stand at each landing on the stairways and along the corridors with pen and pencil, writing down names of talkers on demerit slips to hand in to the office.

Smoking was among the more heinous crimes at the school. We were not allowed to smoke on the school premises, or on the way to and from school. Smoking was unladylike behavior for good Catholic girls. Not only did it look "cheap," it could lead to all kinds of unspeakable behavior. Cigarette smoke was some sort of scent of the devil, sent to unbutton the stays of our moral fiber. Sister Angela had smoke-sensitive nerve endings in her nostrils, and if even the most delicate tracery of smoke coiled from behind a bathroom door she would charge in, eyes glittering like a

hawk circling for the kill. When any girl was apprehended
smoking in the john, the crime would initiate a frisk party
that would go through the entire school. We were ordered
to open our pocketbooks and the contents were inspected.
Possession of tobacco was clear evidence of guilt. Sister
Angela carried the hunt for the evil weed even further.
After dances were held in the school gym, she would be
out early the next morning, searching the grounds for cigarette butts with lipstick on them. If she found any, cigarette
security would be tightened all during the following week.

The demerit system was generally unpopular in the
school. The students hated it, and many of the nuns regarded it as a nuisance. Since each demerit had to be
worked off by staying twelve minutes after school, the nuns
had to take turns as overseers of "demerit hall." We were
not allowed to do homework in demerit hall, so the over-
seer had to think up algebra problems or Latin verbs to
decline to keep us occupied. I was in demerit hall a good
deal of the time, since I couldn't keep my mouth shut. Sally,
who had a similar problem, was usually there with me.

Despite the rules, despite the lectures and the letters
from the student council president and the prose of the
yearbook, docility never took very well on most of the members of my class in the convent school. I realize now that
we were rather doggedly anti-establishment, though if
someone had used the word to us we would have stared at
him blankly. We had no intention of being the bland, docile,
and inoffensive Good Catholic Girl of the nuns' fables. She
was such a little prick, that good Catholic Girl, always saying, "I am a child of Mary" and sniffing disapproval of anything that looked like fun. When it became apparent that
there was no way we could avoid demerits, except by behavior so exemplary as to be unnatural, we started to make
a sport of it. Demerits became status symbols. Demerit hall
had to be expanded, overflowing from one classroom into

two or more. We employed stratagems to disrupt demerit hall, especially when Sister Mary John was in charge. She was a small, pleasant woman who seemed to move about in a fog of confusion. Each time she left the room we would set the clock ahead fifteen minutes, so that when Sister Mary John announced that it was four-thirty and demerit hall was shut for the day, it would really be only three-thirty. The demerit system was abandoned a short time after it was instituted, to the relief of everyone except Sister Christina and Sister Angela.

Sister Angela was well known for taking immediate and irrational dislikes to certain students. Both Clare and I, unfortunately, fell into that category. At one point in the school year she simply refused to talk to Clare at all. Clare would go up to her desk and say, "Sister, I have a dentist's appointment, can I leave now?" and Sister Angela would stare right through her. The next day Sister Angela would say to her, "You left class without permission yesterday. Go to the principal's office."

After a half-year of this, Clare's mother came up to confront Sister Angela. She walked into the classroom and sat down in a chair opposite Sister Angela's desk, crossing her legs as she usually did when she sat.

Sister Angela stared at her coldly, without a word of greeting.

"Ladies never sit with their legs crossed," she said.

Another girl that Sister Angela couldn't stand was Connie, a dark-haired, irrepressible girl. Connie kept complaining to Sister Angela that the desk she had been assigned to was broken. Sister Angela paid no heed. One day she sent Connie to the board to do an algebra problem, and as Connie drew the trapezoid, Sister Angela flew down the aisle to inspect Connie's desk. Connie had a reputation as a smoker.

Just as Sister Angela opened the desk to begin her inspection the entire desk collapsed and fell on her foot. Sister Angela gave a howl of rage and screamed at Connie: "You did it! I know you did it!"

"But, Sister, I was at the board all the time," Connie protested.

I incurred Sister Angela's wrath by watering her beloved African violets from the top instead of the bottom. She had pots and pots of violets sitting on the window sills of the classroom, and we all took turns with classroom chores, which included washing blackboards, freshening up the drawing of the Holy Ghost as Dove that fluttered in the center of the board, and watering the violets.

When it was my turn, I took the watering can and started to rain a little shower down on the delicate purple blooms. Sister Angela saw me and gave a whoop and after a very fast glide she grabbed the watering can away from me. She glared at me like a mother hen protecting her chicks from a weasel. She said I must have known that African violets are watered from the little pans at the bottom of the pots, not the top.

I said I didn't know that.

She said I did.

I said I didn't.

She said I did and to stop being impertinent. She accused me of harboring violeticide in my heart. She blackballed me from the National Honor Society even though my marks were among the highest in the class. She never left me alone with the African violets again.

Perhaps it was the rules, and the expectations of the nuns, or just adolescent high spirits, but we developed an esprit de corps that flourished in my class at the convent school and propelled us to rowdy and forbidden—if always innocent—things. We delighted in all-girl forays to a bar called Phil's, where we would drink beer and smoke and giggle, clad in Bermuda shorts and matching knee socks and shirts. (It was the outfit of the moment. It was termed "collegiate," a word that expressed the apex of fashion.)

All-girl slumber parties were great social events, and the high point of one of them was when we scaled the fence at Indian Springs Country Club in our underwear for a dip in the pool. We had to scramble out and hightail it across the golf course when a watchman appeared, clutching dripping panties and pajama bottoms. But the great event of my senior year, which was to live on in legend at the convent school and was to cause the nuns to heave great sighs of despair over us, was the Mission Party.

It began, innocently enough, with a proposal that our class hold a fund-raising party for the missions. After some discussion, it was decided that a costume party would be the proper vehicle. One of the girls had a relative who worked at the Franciscan monastery in Washington, so we were able to secure a function room at the monastery. It was to be an all-girl affair, and given the dedication to chastity of the monks and the fact that they went to bed early, it seemed an agreeable arrangement.

The night the party was to be held, I rummaged around in my father's closet for my costume. I pulled out his riding boots, navy pith helmet and a khaki shirt from his navy uniform, which I wore with my Bermuda shorts. I decided I would go as Stanley, an appropriate costume for a journalist, and to give a clue to my identity I said often throughout the evening, to no one in particular, "Dr. Livingstone, I presume." I thought it was quite witty.

Six cases of beer were smuggled into the hall and the merriment and the noise level increased with the consumption. It was obligatory to get drunk on such occasions. If you couldn't consume enough beer to produce the real condition (and I couldn't), you had to simulate a tipsy haze. I remember running around a balcony at the monastery raining Schlitz down on my fellow partygoers, shouting

"Take that, Dr. Livingstone!" which gives you an idea of the tone of the whole affair. When the party finally started to run down, I had to drag Sally out of the john; she had developed an incredible talent for getting blotto on moderate amounts of alcohol. She was in a stupor on the toilet, her seat where it should be and her head and her arms dangling to her toes.

I got Sally into my parents' car, which I was using for the evening, and five other girls piled in too. Halfway home Sally said she had to go again, so I stopped the car and she hopped out and squatted down by the side of the road, grinning drunkenly all the while, as the headlights of astonished motorists swept over her.

The inevitable happened, of course. The nuns found out about the Mission Party. Sister Superior walked into the classroom one day, and said in the same tones that Alan Ladd used announcing a suicide mission to his men that we were all to assemble in recital hall.

We were marched to the hall in silence, glancing at each other and at the matching grim expressions on the faces of the nuns. When we had assembled and were permitted to sit down, Sister Superior walked up on the stage, on her round face the look of offended Jehovah.

She knew, she told us, about the shameful orgy we had staged. And (shudder!) in the name of the missions! And (double shudder!) at the Holy Monastery. We had disgraced ourselves, the school, our families, the nuns, the archdiocese, the Church, the Pope, and God—the entire chain of command.

And then she said, her moon face as serious as a saint on a holy card, that the Holy Ghost had told her about the mission party.

(We already had the informer pegged—a convent-bound girl who had been shocked by the depravity of the whole affair. So we knew the Holy Ghost had an accomplice. Afterward we made clandestine drawings on the blackboards of a dove, perched on a stool and wearing a striped convict's hat. The Holy Ghost as Stool Pigeon was an innovation in liturgical art.)

Sister Superior then asked how many girls had not had anything to drink at the Mission Party. A few hands shot up.

"Go to the chapel and pray for your classmates," Sister Superior said, and the non-drinkers dutifully trooped out.

"How many girls drank for the first time at the mission party?" Sister Superior asked.

The new drinkers were sent to one side of the room. The hardened drinkers stayed where they were.

Sister Superior gave us a lecture that vibrated with fire and brimstone and dire threats. She hinted at the summoning of parents to the school, and mass expulsions. Nothing ever came of it. It would have been bad public relations to expel practically the entire senior class. Besides, the nuns would be rid of us soon, a prospect that they must have welcomed. The juniors showed much more potential for shaping up as Good Catholic Girls.

11
Brides of Christ Meet the Marriage Act

They were a category of being unto themselves. It was as if God had created three strains of Homo sapiens: men, women, and nuns.

Priests were clearly identifiable as men. They wore clothes that set them apart somewhat, but their black suits and turned-around collars were not so different from the clothes our fathers wore to work. Priests were celibate, but they did many of the ordinary things men do. They smoked cigars and they drove cars, they tossed footballs around, they paid bills and ate in restaurants. Nuns were not recognizable as women. Anatomically they consisted of faces and hands. Now and then we saw the outlines of mounds when the sweaters were buttoned against the cold. The mounds seemed strangely non-functional, as propellers on our parents' cars might be. Their bodies were swathed in yards and yards of black material, so that only the extreme anatomical distinctions could be observed: tall or short, fat or thin.

But the thing that set them apart even more, perhaps, was that they moved differently. Under the black material they seemed to be constructed of a stiffer material than flesh. They sat straight in their chairs and they never crossed their legs or slumped in an easy chair. They did not reach out to touch other adults, as if there were some impropriety in doing so, and when we reached adolescence we slipped into the untouchable sector of the population.

As we grew older, our relationship with the nuns

changed, subtly but surely. They were often marvelous with young children; I was hugged and petted and fondled more than a few times as a child. Freed from the chores of an independent life, the nuns could pour their attentions and affection onto the children in their care. The constraints of their training seemed to sluff off in a schoolyard of noisy first-graders. They lost the stiffness, and the consciousness of self that so often marked their relationships with adults.

I did not know, nor did my classmates, that when we walked up to the stage of the gym in the convent school that we were moving past some invisible equator that stretched between the land of childhood and the province of adults. But I did perceive as I went into high school that the old easiness that had existed between nuns and pupils at the parochial school had vanished. I thought that it was the nuns who changed, but it wasn't. It was us. We grew up.

I observed the way nuns behaved in high school: how they moved, how they incorporated pious phrases into their speech, how they spoke to each other with an elaborate formality. I saw how they changed when confronted with priests or with the fathers of girls, some of them turning distant and very proper, others fluttering, sychophantic, almost girlish and coy. I had no idea how they got that way. I supposed it happened miraculously, the way St. Paul got knocked off his horse by a bolt of lightning and, zap! he was a Christian. It was not until later that I realized that it was all a product of elaborate and rigid instruction; that nuns were taught to walk with eyes cast down, to sit like robots made of tin and wire, to choke off any spontaneous gesture and replace it with a wooden movement proper to saintly women. There were always a few nuns who never quite made it, of course; the weight of the muslin and the rules of the order could not destroy some compulsion in them to reach out and touch other human beings in a natural way.

Sister Maria with her skirts tucked up, kicking a football was not a pose one might find on a holy card. But that was in parochial school, and then we were children, not Young Catholic Ladies.

For so many of the nuns, the habit choked off the precious avenue of access to their fellow human beings. "Nun's behavior" was not born in them, they had to learn it, the way Chinese women used to learn to hobble by having their feet bound. My friend Mary Ann went into the convent the summer we graduated from the convent school, and the following summer she came back to the convent in Silver Spring. I went to visit her, and I sat uncomfortably in the parlor waiting for her to come in. It was a "parlor," not a living room. It was filled with Good Furniture, the kind that is obviously meant to be sat in lightly, for brief periods of time, a place free of dust or litter or the clutter of activity. I sat straight in the chair; I had the feeling that to lean back on the brocade upholstery of the sofa would be an impropriety. When Mary Ann came in, dressed in the habit, she walked stiffly to a chair and sat down. We looked at each other. A moment of awkward silence followed. I did not know what to call her. I would have felt strange calling her "sister." And yet to call her Mary Ann seemed not correct, now that the habit covered all but her face and hands.

"Hi," I said.

"Hello," she said. She was as uncomfortable as I was. In the old days we would have traded wisecracks and been easy with each other. I wanted to say one of the funny, irreverent things I used to be able to say to her. She had chortled with me over "Rock Around the Crucifix" and "Walk on the rocks, dummy, with the rest of us." But I could sense that she could no longer laugh at such things. She spoke differently than I remembered; her sentences more carefully chosen, as if she had taken elocution lessons. She seemed subdued, sitting in the chair with the habit on, smaller. She was a small girl, but there had been a vibrancy about her that obscured her smallness. I saw the smallness now. We chatted, like strangers, for a few minutes, and then I left, knowing the Church had gained a nun and I had lost a friend.

I never saw her again. I hope she was one of the ones who beat the system; who refused to let the convent press her into a lump of jellied sanctity, who did not have the laughter wrung out of her. I cannot see her as a pale woman in black with eyes as cold as frozen cubes of holy water, walking with downcast eyes through life. She deserved better than that.

In the convent school, the nuns made an elaborate ritual of referring to everything they used in the plural: Our Desk, Our Books, Our Blackboard. It was intended as a sign of humility but it came out just the opposite. It became a badge of superior sacrifice. They never said, "We are better than you," but, "Our station in life is higher than yours." Everything about their life cut them off from us—their dress, their manners, their isolation from the commonplace things of our daily lives. We were both the losers. They did not understand us and we did not understand them. I never had a friendship with a nun during the entire time I spent in the convent school. It did not ever occur to me that I could have a nun for a friend. Nuns didn't have friends. I could not conceive of a relationship between us other than the formal, structured one that already existed.

One of the barriers that stood between us was that the nuns had no past. They were no longer magical creatures who appeared with the morning and vanished into mist at night, the way we had assumed they did when we were younger. We knew something of their lives, but in a general, not a particular way. We never saw the rooms they slept in, we never knew what they liked to eat or what books they liked to read. If they had mothers and fathers or brothers and sisters, they never spoke of them. It was as though they wished us to think they had materialized out of the air the day their final vows were taken. One nun who taught us chemistry, Sister Edwina John, once let it slip that she had attended another school run by the order in Florida. Since we knew Sister Edwina had entered the convent a short time ago and that this was her first year of teaching, we went to the library and got out the yearbook of the Florida school from two years back. All the schools run by the order exchanged yearbooks. We found a picture of Sister Edwina John when she was playing basketball for the Florida school, a pretty, smiling girl with curly brown hair, holding a basketball and wearing a gym suit.

One of the girls took the picture to Sister Edwina John, expecting her to be pleased. Instead, she was flustered and embarrassed. It was as if we had discovered some shameful secret about her as if the fact that she had curly brown hair and legs and a last name was tantamount to wearing a scarlet A on her breast. The yearbook was confiscated, and it was never replaced in the library.

We were fond of some of the nuns that taught us, of course. I remember that we gave our freshman teacher, Sister Ann Bernadette, a Teddy bear and a stuffed bunny. They were the gifts that girls gave to nuns. It was a peculiar gift, though it did not seem so at the time. Fuzzy bears and stuffed bunnies are gifts one gives to children, and they are symbolic of the ambivalent feelings we had toward the nuns. We stood in awe of the curtained world behind the convent doors, but at the same time we felt a protective condescension toward them. They had to have help in even the simplest things. They could not leave the convent alone, even to walk two blocks to the dentist's office. They could not go to movies, or to restaurants, or to a store, without asking permission like children. If they wanted to take a trip to see the White House or Skyline Drive in Virginia, parents of students would have to drive and chaperone them.

(There were always certain people on hand to be of service to the nuns, to drive them and arrange trips for them. A nun who is now living in the freer lifestyle most of the orders have adopted said to me recently that the nun's new freedom seems to anger the people who always used to help them. She says with a wry smile, "They're mad at us," and she wonders at the real motive for their former eager service. It is not surprising that they are angry. They have lost their surrogate children.)

Even we, as rather sheltered teen-agers in suburbia, knew many things about life that we did not speak of to the nuns. The pale eggshells of their sensibilities would be shattered, we assumed, by the knowledge that there was a red-haired stripper in the Coral Room in Southwest Washington who did bumps and grinds, and that good Catholic girls thought it was a terribly chic place to go. We were protective of the nun's innocence, and embarrassed for them when they had to confront any evidence that people did not enter the world carried in the bill of a stork.

It was generally agreed that nuns, who were celibate, should not only be protected from the fact of sexuality, but from any knowledge of it. Like Victorian ladies, the knowledge might stain them, or cause them to faint. I know now that the nuns were pathetically ill-equipped, through no fault of their own, to deal with the peculiar stirrings we were feeling. Some of them had never been on a date with a boy before they entered the convent. Some had no understanding of human sexuality beyond the sketchiest knowledge of the facts of intercourse. I remember being shocked by Sister Angela, giving us a lecture on low-cut gowns:

"The dresses some girls wear would make a baby cry," she said.

There was almost a leer on her face, if nuns could be

said to leer. She made the whole thing seem dirty. It was clear that babies and bosoms and sex and reproduction were all low and disgusting, the sort of things hogs did in a trough.

Sister Angela was zealous in pointing out the evils of sins against the sixth and ninth commandments. "Thou shalt not commit adultery" covered a multitude of sins, including kissing. (Clare once went to confession in the sixth grade and told the priest, "Bless me Father. I have sinned. I committed adultery."

"Just what did you do?" the priest asked her.

"Me and Mary Murphy talked about where babies come from.")

Sister Angela never used the words "sexual intercourse." Neither did any of the other nuns. They talked about "the Marriage Act." They said it quickly, as if the words might soil their tongues if held against it too long.

The Marriage Act was for the purpose of creating children. Period. One was not supposed to enjoy it. The nuns said that of course the Marriage Act in Christian Marriage was a sacred thing, but more often than not their eyes spoke only of revulsion and relief. We got the message that they were glad to be Brides of Christ and thereby escaped the nastiness that human love sometimes entailed.

Moral lessons about the sixth and ninth commandments were coated in little homilies. Sister Bernadette Ann liked the ones with happy endings:

A good Catholic girl went out with a handsome, Catholic West Point cadet. She fell immediately in love with him. He asked her for a kiss at the door. She wanted to kiss him, but drew back.

"I am a child of Mary," she said.

The young man went away and she didn't hear from him again for two years. She thought she had lost him forever. Then one day he reappeared on her doorstep and asked her to go out with him again, and she fell even more deeply in love than before.

Again, he asked her for a kiss at the door. She leaned up to kiss him, but a shadow passed between them. It was the shadow of the Holy Ghost. She drew away.

"I am a child of Mary," she said.

The young man was overjoyed. "I knew you would not fail me," he said. "I want to marry a pure woman. You are the one I choose to be my wife and the mother of my children."

(I wasn't exactly a sophisticate, but even *I* knew that this little drama was several notches down on the reality scale from the musicals at the Silver, with Debbie Reynolds kissing Gene Kelly in the haze of pink clouds blown by the MGM wind machine. I liked my heroes pure, but not *that* pure.)

Sister Angela preferred the grimmer fables, the ones with the scent of brimstone wafting about them. This was one of her favorites:

A sodality member, a girl who was generous and kind and good to her parents, fell in love with a good Catholic boy. They parked in his father's car one night. She knew she should avoid the near occasion of sin. (A near occasion of sin was anything—a parked car, a book, a movie—that could lead to sin. We were morally obliged to avoid them.) But she was not strong enough. She French-kissed her boy friend. A tree fell on the car and killed her. The boy lived, but spent the rest of his life in agony knowing the good, kind, cheerful girl was roasting in flames through all the corridors of eternity.

Just to let the full impact of the story soak in, Sister Angela described eternity for us: Imagine a mountain, and once every million years a swallow flew by and brushed the mountain top with his beak. The time it took the swallow to wear away the mountain would only be an instant in eternity; and *that* was how long the girl who kissed her boy friend would be cooking away in hell.

Sister Ann Viola, who taught us Citizenship, threw in gratis some helpful advice about how one should behave with male Citizens. First, we should not wear patent leather shoes; they would reflect our underwear. Secondly, a sodalist should take on a date the following items: a rosary, a pin, and a newspaper. The newspaper was to put on a boy's lap if you had to sit on it, the pin was to defend yourself if he tried to rape you, and the rosary, I presume, was to give you something to do if he succeeded, so you wouldn't have to think about it.

Third, it was a good idea for a sodalist to sprinkle talcum powder in the bathwater so she wouldn't be tempted to bad thoughts by her own naked body.

A great deal of attention was paid to our clothing by the nuns. We were not allowed to wear sleeveless dresses to school, even on hot May afternoons. I once forgot and threw on a sleeveless dress one day that we did not have to wear uniforms. Sister Angela made me borrow a sweater from a classmate and keep it draped over my shoulders. Did she think that the sight of my bare white shoulders would drive a classmate to lustful, unnatural daydreams? Strapless evening dresses were utterly forbidden. They were near occasions of sin for boys. It was assumed that the sight of one of us with no straps would turn a good Catholic boy into a steaming caldron of lust.

In the unlikely instance that one of my dates was ever so overwhelmed, he was doomed to frustration, straps or no. First of all, under the ball gown I always wore a Merry Widow, the favored undergarment of the day. It covered me from hips to bosom; it was padded with foam at the top (Diane, who was even flatter than I, added Kleenex as well) and wired at the bottom. Over the Merry Widow I wore four layers of stiff crinolines to make the skirt stick

out, and the dress that I deposited over it all was made of
tulle, a stiff, fishnet sort of material that has the consistency
of barbed wire. I used to get red chafe marks on my arms
where they brushed against the tulle. I was better fortified
than the Alcazar. Any boy who got fresh with me would
be lucky to get a handful of foam or wire.)

We got around the strapless dress prohibition by buying
them and then having our mothers sew up little velvet jackets that could come off when the nuns retired for the evening. They were always on hand to see that our Temples of
the Holy Spirit (as they urged us to think of our bodies)
were sufficiently veiled.

At the Valentine Formal one year, a photographer from
the Washington *Post* came to take pictures for the newspaper. He was a father of one of the girls. The following day
the *Post* ran a full-page spread on the dance. The nuns took
one look at it, and the fat hit the fan.

One of the girls, a classmate of mine named Marian, who
was blessed with generous frontage, unfortunately leaned
the wrong way at the wrong time. A half-inch of cleavage
was revealed to the world. Sister Angela held the offending
picture up for all of us to see. Marian, quaking in her brown
oxfords, was sent to the office. There she was practically
told by the principal that she was a whore. Poor Marian,
who was sweet and virginal and whose only lapse was a
moment's bad posture, was reduced to tears. We were told
to look upon her as a scarlet woman, who had disgraced
the school, the nuns, the archdiocese, the Church, etc. No
more *Post* photographers came to our dances.

"Modesty" was one of the virtues we as Good Catholic
girls were supposed to possess. But it was not enough for
us to be modest. We were supposed to shove our idea of
modesty down the throats of everybody else. There was
even an organization dedicated to that end—SDS (Supply-
Demand-Supply).

Brides of Christ Meet the Marriage Act

Our SDS didn't take over buildings—just retail stores. It was started by some priest in New Jersey who decided that his particular brand of Catholic action would be to dash in to dress shops with a group of his followers and drag the dresses off the racks. The ones that were approved as sufficiently "Marylike" (i.e. covered up), were tagged with cards that read: WHATEVER OUR BLESSED MOTHER APPROVES. Catholic buyers were supposed to purchase only those clothes with the Marylike tag on them.

The *Silver Quill* featured editorials about modesty and sketches of Marylike dresses, and the nuns urged us to purchase our gowns at a store run by Catholics called the Marian Shop. It featured Marylike dresses—which inevitably were icky, juvenile creations with puffed sleeves and mother-of-pearl buttons. We avoided the Marian Shop, preferring to do business with the Hecht Company. Their merchandise may not have been modest, but at least it had some style.

Sister Angela used the analogy of Hecht Company wares in one of her little parables. Virginity was, of course, the only acceptable condition for a Catholic girl; she should be unkissed until the wedding, after which the Marriage Act and all pertaining to it were O.K.—for the purpose of procreation.

Sister Angela asked us if we wanted to be "soiled goods." If we went to the Hecht Company, and we saw a blouse, clean and neat in a cellophane bag, and next to it we saw a blouse all smudged and wrinkled, which one would we buy? She did not have to spell out its meaning.

But marriage, simply the legal contract, was not enough. It had to be a Catholic contract. If you didn't get married by a priest, you were living in sin, and if you died, off you went to hell. I remember walking with Clare one day through the Hecht Company, and she stopped to talk with a girl she saw walking along the aisle. The girl had left school to get married by a justice of the peace. I stared at her the way I would have stared at Mary Magdalene. How could she be walking through the Hecht Company, unconcerned, as if her soul were not in mortal jeopardy? Why was she not rushing off to confession? I was in awe of her.

Once you were married—in a church, by a priest, you settled down and waited for the children to come. If they came and came and came, that was God's Will. You were not supposed to do anything about it; not even the rhythm method (total abstinence on what were believed to be fertile days). That was frowned upon, except in dire circumstances. It was a woman's duty to be a brood mare, even if it destroyed her health, her marriage, her family life, and kept them all in bleakest poverty. A classmate asked Sister Angela what a woman should do if she were very poor, and her husband had no job, and she had six children and the doctor told her not to get pregnant again because it would surely kill her.

"Pray," was Sister Angela's answer.

Could she use contraceptives?

"It would be a mortal sin. Better to die in the state of grace than to commit a mortal sin."

What did Sister Angela know about men and women, and their love for each other, or children, and their need for a parent? What did Sister Angela know of the despair and the ruin caused by too many children, too fast? Had she any conception—even the smallest glimmer of understanding—of the human misery caused by the doctrine she was so blithely and so ignorantly laying before us? Did she have any understanding that the origins of the Church's traditional teaching on birth control lay in the mists of a pre-Freudian past, when men did not understand their own sexuality and surrounded it in taboos to ventilate their fear? Did she know that it was a rule made by old men who elevated an obscure passage in the Old Testament to a moral imperative? Did she understand the nature of the male celibate power structure of the Church that had a sick, distorted, perverted view of women and their place in the universe? She did not comprehend any of these things, I am certain. It was not her business to understand. She was not expected to understand. She was expected to obey, not to think. There will be a time when the Church's traditional view on birth control will seem as peculiar as the ban on Galileo, who had the temerity to put forth the heresy that the earth is not the center of the solar system. A great many priests now say it, loud and clear; it is said by papal advisers with the most impeccable theological credentials. But at mid-century, nobody questioned the ban on contraception in public. In private, in the sanctity of their own bedrooms, they rebelled. The parents of most of my classmates were not so different from their protestant neighbors in producing the two or three children that were the national average. They knew, even if they did not speak of it, that the rules made by men and the Rule of God are not always the same thing.

It is easy now to look back and retell the stories and the silly fables, and laugh at them, but I can only wonder at the guilts planted in the seeds of adolescent psyches that would bear an evil fruit long after adolescence had passed. I was lucky; after the usual teen-age bouts with the scent of brimstone I came to understand the absurdity of it all. But I know others whose struggles with the guilt-weed were murderous. A woman who went through Catholic school at mid-century said to me, "I would love to see the data on how many female alcoholics and frigid wives evolved out of that crazy indoctrination."

My brother, Hugh, seven years younger than I, went to a school run by an order of brothers, and the memory of those years still brings a bitter taste to his mouth. A psychiatrist to whom he spoke of his high school years told my brother he had never seen such a job of ego destruction as the brothers worked on him. My parents wanted to take him out of the school because he seemed so unhappy. But he refused, and suffered on in silence. Years later he said to my mother, "Didn't you know what they were doing to me? They were trying to destroy me!" and my mother shook her head.

"You covered too well," she said.

The brothers were symbols of authority in a way that the nuns were not. They were male, powerful father figures. It was easier to discount things the nuns said, if only because their lack of comprehension about how the world worked was so transparent. And still, some of it took root. Clare said to me one day not long ago, "There were two kinds of kids in the school. Most of you listened to all the lectures, and all the stories, and you took in some of it and you shrugged off the rest. 'That's just crazy nun's talk,' you said. But then there were people like Hugh and me. We believed it all. All of it. It took us a long time to get over it."

But the nuns never wanted to harm us. The last thing in the world they wanted to do was hurt anyone. They did not shape the rules of the Church, or its mores. They did what they were supposed to do, and if they had questions, they kept them to themselves.

"It was an unreal life we led," one nun I know says in retrospect about her old way of convent life. And perhaps that is the best verdict on it. The sad irony about the nuns who taught in that convent school was that they wanted to devote their lives to helping people—to teaching—and yet the minutiae of their way of life stole from them the tools they needed for the job. Most of them were good women, many were kind and sincerely interested in the welfare of the girls they taught. But as teachers they were shackled to their sheltered world. They could teach us facts, but except for that rare nun who was both a natural teacher and a curious intellect, they could not convey any understanding of the world from which they had been cut off.

They could not console us in a time of trouble, because they were so far removed from the problems of everyday life that they could comprehend them only from a distance. Their strictly governed existence robbed them of one of the stanchions of the mature personality: the ability to make decisions about one's destiny and to accept the responsibility for them. Perhaps that is why so many of them seemed so childlike, so absurdly innocent. Innocence is a quality that may be charming in a girl of seventeen, but it is a grotesque anachronism in a woman of forty.

I remember the face of Sister Bernadette Ann, because it was so much like a nun's face. Her pale face was not young, but it showed none of the stress of living. Her face was void of lines, as if it had stopped making expressions years ago. I have often wondered if she was one of the ones who took the easy way out, who drifted through life buoyed up by rules that kept her afloat as if they were pontoons stitched to the hem of her habit. Hundreds of rules, that kept from her the burden—and the right—of decision.

The convent and its lifestyle was a medieval institution that had long outlived its time. It was like one of the Brontosauri I had written reports on in the Science Club, a relic of the past thrashing about in the modern age. The time for women to wear skirts to their feet and keep their eyes cast down was lost in the mists of the past along with crusaders and popes who ordered kings about. And yet, there was an aura about it to those outside the sheltered world. Perhaps it was the scent of the past; not the real past, but a storied one, in which a Galahad could say, "My strength is as the strength of ten because my heart is pure" and sainted heroines forsook human lust for love of God, and great dramas played out in sunlight that seemed filtered through the stained-glass figures of the great cathedral windows.

There was a haze as romantic as those pink clouds in the movie musicals drifting about the ideal of a life of Sacrifice for Christ. The same instinct that leads today's young people to the Peace Corps or SDS or the McGovern campaign was a part of the rush to the convent walls. Each summer brought girls like golden grains of wheat to be harvested by the religious orders. I watched the girls who left for the convent each year. While the rest of us sighed over Montgomery Clift in *Red River,* they dreamed instead of a pale, handsome Christ summoning them with open arms. They were swept away, some of them, by the romance of the Catholic Church, and, knowing little of life, believed themselves in love with Christ. I remember Therese, whose body was as round as a ball and whose movements were childlike; the chemistry of adolescence had barely started its work on her when she entered. She clung to the nuns as a child would cling to a mother's skirt, always staying after school to help with the chores. There was Jeanne, the girl who ratted on us after the mission party. Her expression always seemed to be one of disapproval; I rarely saw her smile. At sixteen, she had the chilled look about her of a woman of forty-five for whom life has turned sour. And there was my friend Alice, who was planning to enter the convent until her Catholic mother, a woman of good sense, said absolutely not. Alice argued, the nuns talked to her mother of the wonderful opportunity of giving a child to God. Alice's mother held firm. Her daughter had to attend one year of college. After that, if she chose to enter the convent, she could.

So Alice, who was pretty and sweet, but too plump to lure the eyes of adolescent males, went off to college. She lost thirty pounds and her desire to be a nun. The last I heard, she was married and living in the Far East someplace, having escaped a chance to be a miserable and maladjusted nun.

There were always a few girls who were normal teen-agers who opted for the convent. They had dated boys and taken part in school activities, and I had the feeling about them that despite their youth, they had the capacity to make a mature decision. But there were so many others who obviously did not. The school did not exactly encourage realism in its stories about How Vocations Happen. Here is a "news story" from the *Silver Quill* that is head-lined: GRADUATE DISCOVERS FUTURE LIFE BY SURRENDERING HEART TO LOVE.

"Kathy was a senior in high school when she finally discovered the course of her future life. And, as in most cases, it turned out to be loving someone. She had known him as long as she could remember. But it just dawned on her that it was he who she loved beyond her wildest dreams. Never in her wildest fantasy did she dream that anyone could be so completely perfect. He was more than just wonderfully kind, tender, strong, trustworthy, one whom she wanted as a companion forever. And to think that he returned a love deeper than her own! His very presence filled Kathy's heart with a warm glow and enkindled a flame that made the world and all its people seem especially precious. She gave no thought to her own wishes, for she longed only to serve and please her Beloved.

"So Kathy entered a convent, where she and Jesus could share a love more beautiful than life."

It was a glorious ideal, a soul burning for Christ, sharing glory in heaven and reaping souls for God. The orders welcomed the girls who were swept in starry-eyed with beams from heaven. While the obviously unfit were quickly weeded out, there was no serious attempt to probe the motivations of the aspiring nuns. Psychological testing was unknown in most orders. I wonder how many girls stayed despite serious doubts, because they could not face the stigma of leaving a failure? A girl who left the convent was in a peculiar position. I remember Julia, who departed for the convent with the same excitement she might have worked up for a big football weekend. She left quietly some months later, and when she saw any of her former classmates walking on the street in Silver Spring she would turn her head and hurry away. She knew we whispered about her behind her back. Since "The Call" was such a mystical thing, we did not understand how anybody could be Called and then Uncalled again.

"The Call" to the convent was some mysterious telegraph message directly from God to your own particular soul, and you ignored it at your peril. We were told by Sister Angela and Sister Bernadette Ann and Sister Mary Victor that God had marked certain people for religious vocations. The mark had been made at the moment of conception and it was a draft call from which there were no deferrals. Anyone who ignored The Call would live a life of misery and struggle and probably wouldn't even make it to heaven.

The Call was not defined precisely. We were told, rather ominously, it seemed to me, that we would *know* when it came. I am convinced that every child who went to Catholic school believed at some time or other that he or she had The Call. The Catholic Church at mid-century had a recruitment drive that made the Selling of the Pentagon look bush-league.

We were endlessly bombarded with propaganda about the religious life. We were marched off to symposiums on vocations, assembled to hear speakers pitch for their particular orders, assigned book reports on tomes about nuns and priests and ordered to say the rosary for more vocations for the Church.

The archdiocese of Washington had a priest who was in charge of vocations. Like a recruiting sergeant, he went from school to school in search of enlistments. His name was Father Millenbager, and I can see him now in my mind's eye, standing on the stage at the school, his arms folded, rocking back and forth on his heels, going into his spiel. He would begin with the soft sell: romance.

For some peculiar reason, all I can remember of the romance part of his talk is pink and blue washcloths. He told us about an order of nuns who got to use pink and blue washcloths instead of white ones. I'm not sure why that was such a big deal, but it was clear he thought it was a real zinger.

If romance didn't get us, Father Millenbager reached for the old standby: guilt.

He started to talk about the call, and that if you had The Call and you rejected it . . .

And in the audience, sitting there watching him rock back and forth, I would start to feel The Call. It was a palpitation of the heart or a hopping in the stomach, or a direct beam of light right from the heavenly throne to where I sat. I would begin to pray desperately for Vocations. Anybody's but mine. I would spot a likely looking classmate and try to steer God's light beam over to her chair. "Her, God, not me! Please God, not me! I don't want to be a nun!"

There was Father Millenbager, facing me with an invitation to join God's harvest. I shut my eyes. If I kept them shut, maybe The Call would just go away. I hung in there, waiting until The Call would, like General MacArthur's old soldier, just fade away.

12

Tender Is the Night

By the time I had finished my freshman year at the convent school I had an idea of the rudiments of how babies get born, despite the fact that Biology I concentrated on amoebas reproducing and ignored similar activities in people. Those sixth-grade jokes had given me a vivid—if distorted—mental picture. But I remember once that Clare related to me a dirty parody of a popular song, and she felt quite sophisticated as she sang the ditty in which "Bust of Venus" rhymed with "King Kong's Blank."

She nudged me when she came to the "Blank" and I chuckled with what I hoped was worldly hauteur. Later, I sat and puzzled over it. What rhymed with "Venus?"

It seems incredible to me now that I didn't know, but I distinctly remember my bafflement. It wasn't that I didn't know about the organ, having seen a number of them in the Peter Showing Club, but we never used proper names for genitals. Even the clinical words had the ring of shame to them. If we wanted to refer to the erogenous zone of the male, we simple called it his "you-know-what."

(Once, in the eighth grade, we had to read *The Skeleton in Armor*, by Longfellow. One stanza read:

> Under her loosened vest
> Fluttered her little breast
> Like birds within their nest
> By the hawk frighted.

I sat and prayed, "Oh God, dear God, please don't let me

have to read "Fluttered her little breast." One of the boys had to read it, and when he said the Word, everybody in the class tittered and he turned the shade of an aggravated beet.)

But it was my fondness for reading that was my real education. I read everything I could get my hands on, including the popular novels my parents brought home from the public library or bought in paperback. The more I read, the more I began to think that all the touching and groping I used to find so revolting just might not be so horrible after all.

I noted, as I read a particularly purple passage, a certain tingly, melty feeling you-know-where that was decidedly pleasant.

The books I was reading were a far cry from today's exotica. They were downright pure by comparison. There were no exotic positions, no tangles of five bodies at a time, no velvet whips or oral sex. But, since mid-century was a big era for bosoms, there was more print devoted to the touching, feeling, and handling of bosoms than to any other subject of the day, including the Communist menace. I thought the removal of a bra and the activities that followed must indeed be the sexiest thing in the world.

No flourish was spared in the description of these particular female properties. I remember reading one book in which a girl invites a boy to study with her, and since her parents are away, the subject turns out to be anatomy. He stares in fascination at her "Hot Velvet Lobes."

I went into the bathroom and took a look at mine. They seemed unremarkable. Alas, no one would ever think they were Hot Velvet Lobes.

Stored in my memory-bank are a series of classic breast-feeling sequences. *Peyton Place* offered nipples hard as diamonds and such dialogue as "Do it hard, honey! Hurt me! Bite me!" But my very favorite was from *The Viking* by Edison Marshall.

The Viking was a paperback with a cover that featured a handsome blond man wearing a double-horned helmet, and standing behind him is a nubile maiden popping out of a flimsy dress. *The Viking* offered about eighty pages of gore and derring-do before the hero got his hand under the lady's blouse. The dialogue was marvelously baroque.

"I think these must be the first wild strawberries of Spring," I said as her breasts burst into my eager hands.
"I misdoubt if you can tell so soon," she said.

The feeling and the sighing went on for about two pages, with the lady suggesting, as I recall, that they imagine that the Viking's busy fingers were five enchanted stallions at play in a fairy garden.

I read that passage so many times it was almost as familiar as the Pledge of Allegiance. But if the dialogue is not exact, there is a reason. I went to the public library recently to get the exact words, and I discovered that it did not exist in the hardcover version. Breast-feeling, it seems, was O.K. for paperbacks but unseemly for the shelves of such august institutions as public libraries. Instead of getting to play in a fairy garden, the hardcover Viking only gets an open-mouth kiss; however, Mr. Marshall managed to give the same ornate flavor to the lesser achievement:

Once, she could not keep her lips from opening on mine, and it was as though tongues of lightening, shot from opposite horizons, collided in the sky. I fed as a wanderer in a wasteland, I drank as an Arab lost in the endless sands. This was the barest sampling that she could spread before her lover, only the ready dishes instead of the spiced viands, the table wine instead of the perfumed nectars in unbreached casks sealed with magic rites, but was there a king who would not envy me?

And then there was Frank Yerby.

My grandmother, who had come to live with us when I was twelve, had a passion for books by Frank Yerby. She hardly seemed the type, since she was a very proper woman who knelt by her bed to say her prayers each night and I often saw her poring over an Evangelical magazine called *The Upper Room.* But she doted on Frank Yerby, and so did I. His specialty was southern epics that featured much description of cream-colored bosoms and the virile hands of men with names like Court Beaureguard sliding along same; or silken-belly-golden-thigh adventures like *The Saracen Blade:*

> He felt her lips opening under his like the petals of some great flower exotic and sweet, then they flamed quite suddenly on his, reaching, searching, clinging, until all the drums in his veins rolled in one prolonged gigantic thunder.
> He drew back. Released her wrists.
> "My lady," he whispered, "still has her Saracen Blade."
> "Oh damn you!" she cried. "May all the fiends in hell destroy your soul!"
> Then her arms swept up and her hands locked behind his head. He heard, far off and faint, the clatter that the dagger made when it struck the floor.

When I wasn't borrowing Frank Yerby tomes from my grandmother's bookcases, I rummaged around in my father's shelf for the war novels. War, as defined by the popular novels, was one long chain of carnage, interrupted frequently by shore leaves or furloughs in which noble American fighting men bedded down with native girls, titled British ladies, Italian peasant girls, Red Cross nurses, housewives, whores, cabaret singers, WACS, or anybody else available. The war novels were more explicit than the swashbuckling adventures, and they proceeded from breast-feeling (although there was a lot of *that* too) to the Real

Thing. The Real Thing, I was to understand, was like a tidal wave or an earthquake, or more commonly, the roar of an airplane engine, the most popular metaphor. Blood pounded, loins roared. ("Loins" was a big word in all the novels. Loins were always making like jet engines. It was a word that sounded heroic, like something a character from a Norse Epic might have. Somehow, a "roaring penis" doesn't have quite the same ring. At any rate, I was convinced that the Real Thing was noisier than a B-47 taking off and twice as earth-shaking. I must confess it is only in recent years that I have noticed that there *is* a similarity. It may be because our house is at the end of runway 33-15 at Logan International Airport, and since somebody takes off every two minutes, it is inevitable that we coincide with Pan Am to London, Northeast to Miami or Allegheny to Wilkes-Barre-Scranton.)

I was aware, of course, that all this racy literature wasn't at all the sort of thing young Catholic ladies should be reading. It was clear that despite the acres of purple-tinged print I was digesting, I was not going to be doing much of anything except in my creamy-breasted daydreams. But danger lurked even in daydreams. The nuns' lectures made that clear. The devil could zap you even with your thoughts. Now *that* was a problem.

Just having a Bad Thought pop into your mind was not necessarily a sin. The devil even sent Bad Thoughts to saints to tempt them. Only if you Gave In was it a sin. The perplexing theological question was: When was it Giving In?

I had a good idea. When I picked up a copy of *I, the Jury*, by Mickey Spillane, from my parents' nighttable, that was a near occasion of sin right there. *I, the Jury* was not exactly calculated to make one think of St. Theresa, the Little Flower, or the Sacrifice of the Mass.

When I read: "No, Charlotte, I'm the jury now and the judge and I have a promise to keep. Beautiful as you are, and as much as I almost loved you, I sentence you to death," I was on the verge.

But I read on.

> Her fingers were sliding the zipper on her skirt. The zipper and a button. Then the skirt fell in a heap around her legs. Before she stepped out of it she pushed the half-slip down. Slowly, so I could get the entire effect. Then, together, she pushed them away with a toe. Long, graceful, tanned legs. Gorgeous legs. Legs that were all curves and strength and made me see pictures I shouldn't see anymore. Legs of a golden color that needed no stockings to enhance. Lovely legs that started from a flat stomach and rounded themselves into thighs that belonged more in imagination than in reality. Beautiful calves. Heavier than you see in the movies. Passionate legs. All that were left were the transparent panties. And she was a real blonde.

Advantage, Satan.

> Her thumbs hooked in the fragile silk of the panties and pulled them down. She stepped out of them as delicately as one coming from a bathtub. She was completely naked now, a sun-tanned goddess giving herself to her lover. With arms outstretched she walked towards me. Lightly, her tongue ran over her lips, making them glisten with passion. The smell of her was like an exhilarating perfume. Slowly, a sigh escaped from her, making the hemispheres of her breasts quiver. She leaned forward to kiss me, her arms going out to encircle my neck.

Point, set, match Satan. I read all the way onto the end, where the sun-tanned goddess picked up a gun to blow Mike Hammer's brains out, but he got her in the gut instead.

> Her eyes had pain in them now. Pain preceding death. Pain and unbelief.

"How c-could you!" she gasped.

I had only a minute before talking to a corpse. But I got it in.

"It was easy," I said.

So, I had Given In. And once you Gave In, you had to do something about it, quick. Such a horrible sin had to be mortal, the sort that could plunge you into hellfire forever. An Act of Contrition was required.

The Act of Contrition was a prayer in which you said that you were sorry for what you had done and would not do it again. If you made a perfect Act of Contrition, the slate was wiped clean without the absolution of a priest in confession.

But there was a catch.

The word *perfect*.

To make a perfect Act of Contrition, you had to be contrite simply because you were sorry you offended God and *not* because you were terrified of going to hell.

And the reason you were saying the Act of Contrition in the first place was because you were terrified of going to hell.

I wish I had a dollar for every time I said the Act of Contrition.

The safest thing to do was to go to confession. I got to know very quickly which priests were in which booths. One did not go to a priest who had a loud voice or who was zealous about the whole question of Impurity. The best priest was one who was slightly deaf, very bored or rushing to get out of the box and home for supper. The best time to go to confession was just at the end of the scheduled time, because by then the priests were most likely to have achieved one of the two conditions.

I developed a confession technique. I would list all my minor offenses first, enunciating clearly:

I cheated on my algebra test once.

I argued with my parents six times.

I talked uncharitably about someone two times.

I was insolent to my teacher one time.

(If I didn't have enough minor offenses I made them up, padding it a little so I wouldn't get to the Major Offense too fast.)

Then I just sort of slipped it in, in a half-whisper: "IHadImpureThoughtsTwenty-ThreeTimes."

The whole time my palms were sweating and my throat was dry and the constant fear nagged at me that the priest had forgotten to close the little door that sealed off the other side of the confessional. What if he hadn't? What if somebody heard? *What if it was a boy? A boy I knew?*

The world would know that IHadImpureThoughts Twenty-ThreeTimes. I should have to run away, to sea or to a sultan's harem, disgraced. Please, *please* don't let the priest forget to close the door.

Then there was the desperate hope that the priest wouldn't ask any questions. How did you explain about "Her thumbs hooked in the fragile silk of her panties and pulled them down" to a priest? It was different for a boy. Boys were expected to have bad thoughts, to fall prey sometimes to ungovernable lust. But I was supposed to be a Temple of the Holy Spirit. The kind of thoughts that went on sometimes in my temple, it was like showing skinflicks in the church sanctuary.

I kept falling and repenting, falling and repenting. I emerged from confession each time, having said my five Hail Marys for penance, bathed in purity. Like Galahad, my strength was as the strength of ten because my heart was pure. Never again would I sin by Impurity. Waves of sanctity radiated from me, rippling the very air around me as I walked home from church. No more Frank Yerby, no more quivering lobes and roaring loins, no more "She pulled down her beige lace panties," no more Hot Velvet Lobes, no more hummy, tingly feeling you-know-where. I was pure, fortified with grace. I would read *The Imitation of Christ* and *The Life of Maria Goretti* and I would not fall again.

Purity lasted, on the average, 1.27 days. Then it was back to Hot Velvet Lobes.

While all this lasciviousness was going on in my head, what was happening in the real world was quite a different story. In my daydreams, dashing Gaylord de Frontenac, the handsome riverboat gambler, might put his virile hand on my creamy bosom while I sighed and panted, but any real live kid who tried to touch anything below the collarbone would get a karate chop.

My karate chop didn't get used much. For a long time, nobody even tried anything *above* the collarbone.

It took me an hour and a half, bolstered by Clare's encouragement, to get up the courage to ask a boy to the first dance at the convent school. He said yes, to my immense relief.

On the big night, he showed up at the door, corsage in hand. Etiquette demanded that a boy who was taking a girl to a dance had to bring a corsage.

My father opened the door and let him in. The boy's name was Jimmy Smith, and he had been one of my classmates at the parochial school.

"How are you, Jimmy?" my father asked politely.

He looked up at my father, with stricken eyes.

"Mr. Rivers, I'm scared."

And there was the time I worked up the nerve to have a party and went to Mass for three straight mornings in a row to insure that people (boy people) would come. The most dramatic entrance to the party (held in the rec room, which was painted for the occasion and Tonto banished to the other part of the cellar) was made by a freshman at

Georgetown University named "Ace" Kane. He came in with a toilet seat around his neck. It was by just such sophisticated and witty gambits that he had earned his nickname.

I danced a lot with a boy named Billy Jarboe, to "Your Lips Tell Me No No But There's Yes Yes in Your Eyes!" but nothing came of it, since he departed shortly for the seminary.

Some of my friends were going steady, but I didn't have anybody to go steady with. And from what I saw of going steady, I wasn't too impressed. Going Steady seemed to mean arguing a lot. Beano was going steady with Howard, who lived down the street and delivered the morning paper. She wore a friendship ring that he gave her and every time she had a fight with Howard she would throw it in our driveway, declaring she never wanted to see him again. Then she would repent of her action, and I had to help her grub about in the loose gravel of the driveway to find it. Sally was going steady with Jimmy Carey, and I could never figure out when she was speaking to him and when she wasn't.

One night, when my parents had gone to an early movie, Sally and Jimmy came over to my house with Jimmy's friend Ross. It was a near occasion of sin, just the sort of situation the nuns warned us against. Two pubescent boys and two nubile girls, alone together. In a house. Where there were beds.

What did we do with this golden opportunity? The scene in the living room that greeted my parents when they returned home from the movie made them gape with astonishment.

There was Ross, standing on the edge of a brocade chair, his arm covered with flour to the elbow, his fingers curled as if they were paralyzed. He was about to leap to the living room rug.

Ross, it seems, had seen *The Greatest Show on Earth*, a circus movie, six times, and was very much taken with it.

He suggested that we re-enact the whole thing in the living room. He played the Cornel Wilde part, the high flyer who falls and cripples his hand and cannot fly again. To give the proper dramatic emphasis to the crippled arm, Ross dragged out the flour tin and coated his arm. He was pleased with the sickly, withered look the floured arm achieved.

Where the action was, if that term can be applied loosely (very, very loosely) was at the parish teen canteen.

The canteen was, I suspect, exactly like every other such institution at mid-century, a time when stories on Juvenile Delinquency graced the covers of magazines, and adults worried about what to do with idle teen-age minds and hands. It was generally concluded that the solution was to give the kids Wholesome Entertainment (the character-building properties of football were given the same validity as Sacred Writ). Teen canteens were part of this theory, and the one sponsored by the parish was held in the basement of the parochial school, the same place we had munched on our hot lunches at the school. On Friday nights the long wooden tables would be cleared away, the dull brown tile floor swept of all movable grit, and the metal chairs lined up on two sides of the room.

By some sort of unspoken tradition, the girls lined up on the wall by the sixth-grade classroom, and the boys took positions across the room by the fifth grade. We came in groups, the girls like Sally and Alice and Diane and Clare and Mary Ann and I usually driven and picked up by a parent. The boys, who also came in groups, would insist on alighting a block away from the school if they were driven by parents. That way they could saunter to the school building in an independent, manly fashion.

One of the parish priests and one or more of the fathers were always on hand to chaperone. The rules were inflexible; gentlemanly—and ladylike—behavior at all times, propriety on the dance floor (the Dirty Boogie was forbidden), and most important—no alcoholic beverages in the hall, the parking lot, or on the breath. Violation of the latter statute meant immediate expulsion from the canteen.

The crowd that frequented the canteen was almost entirely composed of boys and girls from the Catholic schools in the area. Others were permitted as long as they obeyed the rules. On occasion, a strange group of boys would walk in, and the scene was like something from Westerns where the Bad Guy walks into the bar and the honky-tonk piano stops playing. Repressed excitement would shiver through the hall as the boys walked in, emulating the swagger of New York street gangs much admired in *Blackboard Jungle*. The boys walked close together, to ward off the menace of the alien environment, trying to maintain a facial set of icy-cool indifference. The priest and the fathers would look at them with eyes full of suspicion.

They were usually the sort of boys we referred to as "rocks" or sometimes "drakes," their hair combed back into a knife-edged ducktail and larded with grease, pink "Mr. B" collars resplendent at their necks, and string ties. Other times they were less stylish boys sloppily dressed in jackets and old pants, out helling around in somebody's father's car. They always stood close together in the darkness of a corner, staring morosely out of the fortress of their togetherness. Now and then one would come over and ask a girl to dance, and the girl would giggle at her friends at the adventure of it, and when the dance was over he would mumble something and return to his friends in the corner.

Now and then one or two of the boys would leave to go outside, and in a few minutes they would return. The priest and the fathers would watch carefully. Another boy would leave. The priest and the fathers would decide to take action.

"If you boys are drinking out there you have to leave right now. We don't allow that kind of thing here."

The boys would make some show of indifference or bravado.

"Let's get out of this creepy place," one would say, with manufactured disdain, and then turn to shuffle out. Once I saw a boy shove a father, and the father shoved back, but that was the extent of it. Usually the alien boys were glad to go. They were out seeking adventure in the streets of Silver Spring, not an easy task. It must have been obvious that the parish teen canteen was not to be the place to find it.

Aside from the intermittent excitement of the interlopers, the routine at the canteen never varied. The girls would arrive first, having spent considerable time deciding on appropriate outfits. My favorite consisted of a fuzzy brown turtle-neck sweater and my wide red corduroy skirt. For accessories I chose a rope of fake pearls, each one big enough to choke a pig, knotted right at the breastbone, and hanging to just above the crotch. Somewhere on my sweater I would stick my beloved "Excellence" pin, and of course I wore my saddle oxfords and triple-roll bobby socks. I believed myself quite chic.

I would cluster with the other girls by the sixth-grade classroom and we would talk aimlessly and eye the boys discreetly as they came in. Often, our discussion centered on the relative merits of the boys sauntering to their posts by the fifth-grade classroom. The supreme accolade accorded to a boy was "cute." Noel with his dimples was cute, as was Johnny the football player and Tony, with his blond hair and toothsome smile.

No one danced for a long, long time. The lights were dimmed, and the record player turntable revolved in the corner. Eddie Fisher crooned "Lady of Spain" and Frankie Laine boomed "Mule Train" and the fathers or the priest would go up to the boys and say, "Hey, how about you guys asking the girls to dance, huh?"

Finally, one of the most self-assured boys would come over and ask one of the prettiest girls to dance, and gradually one or two others would stray over. The Four Aces would sing "Garden in the Rain" on the phonograph.

Sitting on a hard metal chair, or standing with my back against the sixth-grade wall, I would try to mold my features into the proper expression; one I would strive to perfect through years of canteens and college mixers and "tea fights" (mixers) at the Naval Academy. It was a wistful romantic melancholy, the sort of look Audrey Hepburn was so good at. I imagined it might happen the way it happened in the movies. *He* would walk by and all of a sudden he would see my face. He would focus on it the way the camera zoomed in on Audrey in *Roman Holiday* and he would see in my face the answer to all his wildest dreams. He would see the vulnerability and the tenderness and the intelligence and the loyalty, the character, the breeding, that lack of artifice, the honesty, the One Woman Who Would Never Betray Him—all that he would see if I could just get the right expression on my face.

I guess I never did it right. Nobody ever saw what they were supposed to see. I was never in the first wave of girls asked to dance, rarely in the second. I usually made it in the third or fourth wave, and the boys who asked me were not the "cute" boys. They were the ones who were shy or fat or graceless, or who had braces on their teeth that were a match to mine. When I think of them now it is with a curious tenderness, because I imagine they were dreaming their dreams too, dancing with me, wincing as I deposited my size tens on their feet or my rope of pearls clanked against their groin, watching another girl over my shoulder as she danced with one of the "cute" boys, wrinkling her nose prettily, her bobbed hair glinting when she moved under one of the dim lights.

Most of my best friends in the convent schools—except

for Diane—were, like me, part of the third or fourth wave in the asked-to-dance derby; Clare and I shared that category—and more. We were co-workers on the *Silver Quill*, and she was always blackmailing me to go to the cafeteria and get her Cokes or I wouldn't get to be the editor when she graduated. She was always talking of the day she would be editor of the New York *Times* and I would be the assistant editor and I said I bloody well wouldn't go get her Cokes in the New York *Times* cafeteria. Of all my friends, it was only the two of us who squinted ahead into the mists of the future to see the outlines of forms other than the expected destiny of all girls of the fifties: a house, a man, a car, children. Nobody took us very seriously, except our parents; when we said we wanted to be journalists people smiled at us the way one smiles at a child who says he wants to be a fireman. They assumed that this was merely a girlhood dream that would fade before the reality of fraternity pins and little sparkly diamonds and white dresses with seed pearls and bouquets of stephanotis and carnations. So we reinforced our ambitions, one against the other, and kept on trying to see a separate shape for our tomorrows.

We could not ignore what the world expected of us, of course, nor could we dismiss as lightly as we pretended our shortcomings in that department. Diane was a living reminder.

Both Clare's and Diane's families lived in a red brick apartment complex across a highway from the winding, polluted Sligo Creek. They were old buildings then, as old as anything in Silver Spring could be, which meant two decades. The buildings were square and innocent of an architect's care, and the grounds around them were tended with indifference. Today they are in the shade of a twenty-story high-rise, and all around them are luxury apartments with doormen and swimming pools. But in those days Silver Spring had no skyline—unless one counts the four stories of the Hecht Company—and apartment living was not part of an affluent lifestyle, but something for people who couldn't quite afford a house and a mortgage.

Clare's father was a retired naval officer who had abandoned the sea to drive a cab and take up Yoga; he was sometimes to be found in a corner standing on his head when Clare's friends dropped by. He would be admired today as an individualist, but mid-century was not happy with unorthodoxy. Diane's father worked for the government and her mother worked too, for the telephone company.

Diane was one of those girls who bloom early, opening as perfectly as a morning glory while the rest of us struggled with pimples or baby fat or crooked teeth. Even as a freshman in the convent school she was possessed of a remarkable prettiness of the sort that was much in vogue at the time: wide-set blue eyes nestled in a round face, a smallish nose that turned up slightly, and long brown hair that tended to roll naturally into corkscrew curls about her face. She was tall and rather flat chested, but graceful, since she continued her dancing lessons long after I had given up in disgust.

Diane always seemed remarkably unself-conscious of her beauty, and she was a good-natured and generous girl. I don't ever remember hearing Diane say an unkind word about anyone. There was an innocence about her that seemed to shine from her fresh-scrubbed face; she seemed to exist in a different world from the one Clare and I inhabited, a world that was akin to a Walt Disney movie, where mornings were always clear and bright and birds chirped as a princess waited for the inevitable handsome prince to gallop by and see her and sweep her away. Her beauty and her innocent charm congealed into a wall around her, keeping the meanness of the world away from her. It seemed that only good things happened to Diane. She was always elected class president; her sweetness dissipated any envy other girls might have felt toward her. She was constantly being chosen queen of the St. John's summer carnival, or of some other school's senior prom, always getting asked up to West Point or to June Week at the Naval Academy. Boys were drawn irresistibly to her; Alice's brother, three years older than we were, carried a torch for her for years.

She was, it seems to me now, like the heroines in the books by F. Scott Fitzgerald I read long after I knew Diane. They seem always to be seen through the tender gauze of a young man's memory; belles of first blooming, made not really of flesh but of the smell of early summer nights and the flicker of fireflies and the half-forgotten sound of sweet, sweet music. They are creatures whose perfection brings a catch to the throat. Their perfection exists only in a brief web of time, an enchanted moment. Like some beautiful insect who dies at first mating, young males are drawn to them by some force deeper than understanding. All the midnight dreams of young men seem solidified for a moment in the curve of a throat or the bend of a curl. Fitzgerald expresses it in *Tender Is the Night* when Dick Diver meets Nicole:

> Whenever he turned towards her she was smiling a little, her face lighting up like an angel's when they came into the radiance of a roadside arc. She thanked him for everything, rather as if he had taken her to some party, and as Dick became less and less certain of his relation to her, her confidence increased—there was that excitement about her that seemed to reflect all the excitement of the world. Her hair, drawn back at the ears, brushed her shoulders in such a way that the face seemed to have just emerged from it, as if this were the exact moment when she was coming from a wood into clear moonlight. The unknown yielded her up. Dick wished that she had no background, that she was just a girl with no address save the night from which she had come.

Diane's mother basked, glowed, luxuriated, in her daughter's triumphs. It was her main topic of conversation, and at times this must have been wearing and painful to mothers whose daughters were not going to June Week or the senior prom. But it was hard to begrudge her her joy; her delight bubbled like Alka-Seltzer, and like her daughter, she was clear of the stringy tentacles of malice. She was clearly delighted with Diane and assumed everyone else must be too. In the cheerful ruin of her face were traces of what must have been the same sort of beauty that Diane possessed. She had auburn hair, streaked with gray, and she wore it long, as Diane did, though it usually hung in an indifferent manner, and she clapped a pillbox on the top of her head like an afterthought. There was no vanity in her for herself. Sometimes she wore Diane's outworn clothes, and her teeth were in need of repair, but she would prefer buying a white satin ballgown for Diane to caps for her teeth. Diane had a closet full of gowns: white tulle with a cowl neck for the Naval Academy, russet taffeta for the St. John's Regimental, blue satin for West Point. Whenever Clare and I were in need of a formal on short notice Diane cheerfully dipped into her closet and pulled out one of hers (though Clare had some difficulty in getting them to fit across the bust).

I was often in and out of Diane's apartment; her mother always seemed genuinely glad to see me, and I felt comfortable there, as Diane did at my house. I remember Diane's father, a tall, homely, large-boned man who always had a warm hello for me before he retreated to his newspaper and his cigar. I think of them grouped as if for a painting: Diane and her mother together, and her father on another side of the canvas, alone with his newspaper and his cigar. He seemed outside the closed circle of Diane and her mother—almost superfluous. I am sure he was proud of his daughter, but he could not share so completely in her life the way his wife did.

It was Diane who unwittingly set the standard for the girls who lived in the apartment complex. There were a few girls there who also went to the convent school, and the mothers all knew each other. The competition flowed like wine. Each girl's achievement—a weekend at Annapolis, dinner with a Georgetown Man—was grasped in the teeth of a mother, the way a dog grabs a bone he had found, carried back to the other mothers and shared, triumphantly. Each morsel was reassuring; it was proof that a daughter was Popular.

Popular. It was a big word at mid-century. *Popular.* As Webster defines it: "Regarded with favor or approval by associates." The word smells of success, a word that contained in three short syllables a distillation of the ambition of high school girls in the fifties. It meant to be *valued;* not exactly to be liked, because liking implies some real human commitment that was not necessary to popularity. There were popular girls who were sweet, like Diane, and popular girls who were spiteful and cruel but had an instinct for leadership that could not be ignored, and girls who were popular because they dressed well and had style, and girls who were popular simply because they had skin like new peaches or soft round eyes.

My mother, wisely, withdrew me from the competition. She told me that it did not matter if I was popular or not, that the girls who dated early got bored by twenty, that if I would just be patient my time for fun would come. I listened to her, because, young as I was, I could sense that she had no need to live through me. She was so clearly a separate person, and I thought her something special, because she knew of a world that other girls' mothers did not dream of. She had been a lawyer, and though she had given up her practice when I was very young the fact of it was still important to her definition of herself. If she had her frustrations and her disappointments, she worked them out in the field of her own soul, not in mine.

So I listened to Sigmund Romberg records in the solitude of my room and dreamed of a tender faceless love, or fell in love with ballplayers and movie stars. Clare, with characteristic energy, set out on a frenzied pursuit of the grail. Both of us would have given our eye teeth for the sort of popularity Diane had, but we didn't have a prayer. I hadn't read Fitzgerald yet, but if I had, I would have known immediately that I was not "The Last of the Belles." I would be part of the crowd of anonymous girls around her, the ones that go fuzzy and out of focus when the camera zooms in on the heroine.

I have since come to understand that being part of the fuzzy crowd was a stroke of luck; that my big feet and my braces might have been the gift of some fairy godmother wiser than I, though at the time I would have throttled any fairy godmother who stuck me with the damn things. They bought me time; time to discover who I was, to find the joy in tasks that could set my brain singing, to be alone, to look at the world while it did not look at me; to know an amount of pain and rejection, not enough to twist my insides, just enough to know it hurt, but I could survive it. The boys left me alone, except for the few of them I dated now and then, nice boys who did not press me, who went to movies and dances with me and probably had a nice time, but did not invest in me any of their dreams. Too much beauty, too soon is a dreadful thing for a girl. I know it now, though I did not know it then. People smile on it—the beauty, not the person inside it—and the person inside does not know the difference until the beauty starts to go, and that is a terrible time to be introduced to pain. Things come too easily to beautiful girls, and it takes more wisdom than a fifteen-year-old has to know that the easy things are rarely worth the having, that the sting of failure is as necessary to growth as rain to a plant. But the beautiful ones, the ones whose early bloom is dazzling, are carried along by a current of approval that can cause their own means of propulsion to atrophy.

But there was a worse legacy of early beauty for girls of mid-century, and I suspect it is not much different today. It robs a young girl of the ownership of herself. The young men see it, and they want to own it. They are protective of it, as with a fragile flower, and they invest its owner with their dreams. Before she knows it, their dreams may come to take the place of hers. She may have affixed her destiny to another, to be carried, as a male sea horse carries its young. Her future is decided for her before she has any understanding of what *she* wants the future to be—not what her mother or her young man or society wants her to be. She cannot know that the young men use her as a movie screen; that they project onto her so many things that are not there. Like Dick Diver looking at Nicole, they see in her "all the excitement there is in the world," and no one can possess that. The beautiful young girl, never knowing what it was she was supposed to give, is baffled and guilty, when, in the end, she disappoints.

The popularity derby that swirled about me in the convent school had its rules, its mores, its status symbols carefully ranked. Getting asked to a dance or a weekend at a college—Annapolis or West Point or Georgetown, had much more status than getting asked to a prom at one of the Catholic boy's high schools—unless you got elected queen or went with the captain of the football team. In my freshman and sophomore years, the Regimental dance at St. John's High (a military school) was a big event. Diane always went with one of the top officers from the school and took part in the Grand March under arched swords. By the time I got to go to the Regimental I was a senior and it wasn't a big deal, and besides, my date was only a junior and had no status at all. Getting asked to dances at Montgomery Blair High School also had no status, since it was a public high school.

It was the only way we could compete—basketball excepted: with boys and dates and their schools. We could not compete with money, a major sport in society as a whole at mid-century, because we were all so much alike. There were minor differences, but most of us lived in modest houses, our parents drove Fords, Chevys or Plymouths, shopped at the Hecht Company and not at Peck and Peck or Garfinckel's downtown. A few ladies marked as social climbers itched to get out of Silver Spring and move to Chevy Chase or Spring Valley or Georgetown, and a few girls' fathers drove Cadillacs. There were very few girls whose fathers were builders or eye doctors who had money, and they were marked as special people. Even the nuns fawned on them sometimes, speaking of their breeding and refinement. The Status Symbols that were admired were those of the *nouveau riche,* for we were all so far away from the world of real money, of society with a capital S that we were unaware of its conventions and its snobberies. I thought that girls who went to Georgetown Visitation Convent and whose fathers ran plumbing companies were the apex of the social scale.

So our currency was boys. Clare, very early on, developed a fixation on Annapolis, partly because of her father's background and the fact that she had an aunt who was married to an admiral and might be counted on as a source of supply. I developed a subfixation; that is to say I sat entranced, listening to Clare's escapades, being able to provide only a few of my own. Clare's histrionic ability was such that she was able to turn a blind date into a saga that lasted for weeks. Unlike Diane, Clare had to plot and scheme to get to Annapolis. Diane was always getting asked down to June Week or to navy football games.

(Clare and I talked about the good old days in Annapolis recently, and every time she said, "Remember what's-his-name," I would say: "Lee Chastine" or "Bill Simpson." I remember the names of all the midshipmen she ever dated, having listened to every detail of every date for hours on end. We plotted ways to get middies to keep her in mind. She was very big on anonymous letters with supposedly witty sayings. We composed them with great care. "All those hours, all that plotting," she says, "and then Diane would go to Beverly Beach for the afternoon and meet three midshipmen and get asked to June Week and we wouldn't.")

Clare once had a blind date to go to the Army-Navy game in Philadelphia, and got fixed up with a horrible plebe (freshman) who was shorter than she was. The subtle midshipmen had rented a hotel ballroom and had it filled with mattresses so the middies could neck with the girls they brought. Clare refused and the plebe stormed off in disgust, and a pinch-hitter was brought in. His name was Joe Duffy and as Clare described him he was a combination of Tyrone Power, Clark Gable and Alan Ladd. They sat in a hotel room drinking bourbon and necking to a record-player crooning "As Time Goes By" and Clare fell madly in love with him. (She fell madly in love with six other midshipmen that year, as I recall.)

He promised faithfully to write, and he said as he went off to take the train back to Annapolis: "Don't sweat the Tuesday Mail."

Tuesday came. No mail. Wednesday. No mail. Two weeks, three weeks, no mail. Clare started making a novena, going to church every Wednesday evening to get Joe Duffy to write. She suggested that I make a Joe Duffy novena too, and I said that if I made a novena it would damned well be to get *me* asked to Annapolis.

Five months later, her prayers were answered. (Slow service, but there were a lot of novenas that season.)

He asked her down to a dance in Norfolk, where the midshipmen were on summer maneuvers. She had a miserable cold and stuffed herself full of various pills and cold remedies. I inspected her carefully to see if the red eyes and the drippy nose showed improvement. They didn't.

But off she went, with her formal packed for the dance. When she got there, Joe Duffy said that only kids went to dances, so a group of middies rented a cabin on the South River where they could all sit around and drink. Clare was so paralyzed at seeing Joe Duffy again that all she could say the whole evening was "yes" and "no" and she kept blowing her nose the whole time.

He never asked her down again but he did send her an autographed picture of himself. "Dear Clare," it was inscribed, "Here's a picture of me" and it showed him getting his face squashed in during a Navy boxing match. She showed it to me and said, "Isn't he cute?"

And I said it was sort of hard to tell with that other guy's fist in his face.

My first big coup in the Annapolis department was getting an invitation to June Week. It was the result of connections, rather than my girlish charms. (When *I* went to Beverly Beach, all I got was a sunburn.) One of my mother's best friends had a daughter who was engaged to a first-classman (senior) at the Naval Academy and I had just gotten my braces off so she agreed to get me a date with a plebe. Plebes weren't allowed to date until June Week, the close of their first year.

Via my friend, I received a picture of my date, and it was a big boost in status for me. I rushed over to show it to Clare. His name was Bob Schmidt and he came from someplace called Squirrel Hill, Pennsylvania, and he was a handsome, darkish young man who looked very dashing in the picture of him in his uniform.

(I put the picture in my wallet, and I kept it there for

years afterward. I never saw him after June Week, but the snapshot did make a dandy set piece for my picture folder.)

I borrowed a shrimp-colored formal from Clare, who watched approvingly as I put it on, noting that I had a nice neck and shoulders, and now that my braces were off, I could even smile without the gleam of metal. I packed up the dress and got on the bus to Annapolis.

I was to meet Anita Doris, the daughter of my mother's friend, at a "drag house" at the Academy. Since girls were not permitted lodgings on the grounds of the Academy, they had to stay at rooming houses just outside the walls, usually run by spinsters or widows. Girls were not called "dates" at the Academy, they were called "drags."

As soon as I walked into the drag house I knew I was out of my league. The other girls were all older than I, and like Anita Doris, they were engaged to midshipmen, looking ahead to clearly defined lives as navy wives. Many of the girls were from fashionable southern schools like Holton Arms or Mary Washington College and they talked like Scarlett O'Hara. (There is nothing like the absolute mastery of a stiletto wielded by a Southern Belle. A girl was introduced to Diane one day at a dance, and with magnolia and money in her voice she cooed: "Aren't you that *mah vel ous* basketball player from Silver Spring?" This pointed out to all assembled that Diane not only engaged in a sweaty, unfeminine sport, but came from a place where only government clerks lived.)

The girls at the drag house seemed incredibly old and sophisticated. I was a girl, but *they* were Women. There was no scent of insecurity wafting off of them, the sort that I knew floated about Clare and me. They knew where they were going, they wore "miniatures" on their fingers, little diamond-filled replicas of the rings the midshipmen wore, and they had in some mysterious fashion earned the love of these incredibly handsome men I saw walking the cobblestone streets of Annapolis, an old town noted primarily for its proximity to the Naval Academy. I sat very still in the drag house and spoke only when I was spoken to.

The girls at the drag house used a patois that I understood only because I had heard Clare and Diane speak it. A "yearling" was a sophomore, a "tea fight" was a mixer, a "brick" was an ugly girl, so named because a middie who dated one was given a brick by his classmates. I remember that while we were there, Anita Doris opened a package that had been given to her by her fiancé, and took out a pair of navy regulation pajamas that were decorated all over with little pictures and sayings. It was a tradition for a midshipman who was especially fond of a girl to give her emblazoned pajamas. Hers had pictures of gun mounts just at the spot her breasts would be, with the words "revolving turrets" printed over the drawings. The girls laughed over it, and I was awed by the sort of intimacy that it implied. It spoke of a universe of things I understood only in my daydreams about *The Saracen Blade*.

I met Bob Schmidt the night we were to go to a formal dance. He was as handsome as he looked in his picture, and we were introduced and smiled at each other but nothing happened like it did in the movies. He didn't look at me and Know. I didn't look into his eyes and see my future. We shook hands, I think.

We walked to the dance past stately buildings and huge anchors with ivy growing on them, up the steps of Bancroft Hall and into the room where the dance was going to be held. I struggled to think of something to say to Bob Schmidt.

"My father used to be in the Navy," I said.

"Oh, that's interesting," he said. "What year was he?"

"He didn't go to the Academy. He was in the Reserve."

"Oh."

So much for that conversation.

"I'm going to be a journalist," I said.

"That's nice," he said.

"Do you like it here at Annapolis?"

"Yeah. I like it a lot."

So we danced, between the awkward silences, and when the dance was over everybody started to run out of the hall. Literally run. The midshipmen had only forty-five minutes to escort their dates back to the drag houses, cram in what necking they could manage, and be back in their dormitories. I snagged my heel trying to go down a hill and he gallantly picked me up and carried me down, and all I could think was "Hot damn, wait till Clare and Diane hear about this!! Back at the drag house he kissed me, my first real life, honest-to-God-on-the-mouth-kiss, and I was sixteen years old. I tried very hard to be thrilled. It was sort of nice, but not exactly the way Edison Marshall described it, with the tongues of lightening and feeding like a swarthy Arab lost in the desert and all that. Apparently it wasn't for him either. I never heard from him again.

Another time Clare was sort of going with a midshipman named Nick and she got me a date with a middie named Jim and we went out to some tavern to drink (I had ginger ale) and we went back to the drag house and Clare and Nick went to the kitchen to neck while Jim and I made small talk.

"My father was in the Navy."

"Oh, that's interesting. What year?"

"He didn't go to the Academy. He was in the Reserve."

"Oh."

Finally I decided Clare and Nick had been in the kitchen too long. Clare and I had entered into a mutual assistance pact beforehand aimed at the preservation of our respective virginities. Not that either had been seriously threatened, but we knew about Getting Carried Away. It happened in the books and the nuns said it happened, so it had to be true.

I went into the kitchen and found Clare and Nick and a kitchen chair all wrapped up in a tangle. It looked as if she might be Getting Carried Away, so I tapped Nick on the shoulder and I said, "I'm sorry, sir, your three minutes are up!"

Clare and I chortled over that line later on. We thought it witty and sophisticated.

I wonder why they didn't ask us back.

Another time Clare had a date to go up to West Point with Alice's brother Don. He was still carrying a torch for Diane, but Clare and Don were chums, and what the hell, West Point was West Point. She got Don to get me a blind date.

We stayed at the Hotel Thayer on the West Point reservation and the first morning we were there I was awakened by the sound of Clare's voice—in monologue. She had the other occupants of the dorm-style room in a corner, and she was telling them, "You think this place is neat, let me tell you about Annapolis."

Don introduced me to my date, a cadet named Leon who was tall and good-looking in a Tab Hunter sort of way. We shook hands. Nothing happened.

It was a summer weekend, and so we went to a *pee*raid, as I was instructed to call it, to admire the Long Gray Line, and then we went canoeing. I liked canoeing. I grabbed the paddle and started to row-row-row, working up a good sweat. Suddenly I stopped and looked around. All the other girls were languishing in the back of the canoe, letting their cadets row them around. I was sweating and puffing like a galley slave.

I knew I had blown it.

He never asked me back again either.

(I have been back to Annapolis and to West Point in the years since, to West Point to cover a speech by President

Kennedy and to Annapolis just to show visiting friends around, and I always look carefully at the midshipmen. But they are boys! Pimply-faced, peach-fuzz little boys, dressed up in uniforms. They couldn't have been like that then, could they? Those marvelous men, so gorgeous, so old, were they only boys?)

Despite all the talking Clare and I did about Annapolis and West Point, all the plotting and the planning and the retelling and the one-upping, Annapolis and West Point were not places for us. They were male worlds, places invented for men who were to do Important Things, places where women had to stay on the periphery. The focus was always on *them*, not us. A girl's identity sloughed off on the cobbled streets of Annapolis. I was not Caryl Rivers, CYO basketball player, aspiring journalist, Commie-fighter, at June Week. I was Bob Schmidt's drag. Nobody asked me what I was studying or what I thought of the world crisis. Nobody cared. I was expected to talk their language, to admire them in formation, to be towed along in their wake. I remember at one party I went to, the midshipmen started a game in which they would invent letters in navy jargon and everybody would have to guess what they were:

"What's COMPACNAVOP."

"Commander Pacific Naval Operations."

"I got one. What's COMATSUBOP."

"Commander Atlantic Submarine Operations."

And all the girls sat around, bored to death with them and with their silly little game, but nobody had the nerve to say so. It was mid-century, and we were soon to be women, and it was our job to admire.

13 *Aphrodite at Mid-Century*

When I was sixteen years old, on one of those infrequent trips to Annapolis, I went into the Naval Academy bookstore and purchased a calendar date book with a red imitation leather battleship and the words UNITED STATES NAVAL ACADEMY embossed on the cover. I bought it strictly as a status symbol—my social schedule hardly warranted keeping a date book—just as other girls in school sheathed their geometry books in plasticized covers bearing the seal of Georgetown University.

Each page pictured midshipmen doing something nautical, or simply looking splendid in their whites. And to give the whole thing a little tone, each page bore an inscription from Literature. March brought Lord Byron: "Man's love is of his life a thing apart. 'Tis woman's whole existence."

I had never seen the line before, since we never got to Byron in English class. (His morals were lousy.) But I remember the quote very well because as soon as I read it, I had the same sort of reaction that Bobby Seale would have to "Don't those folks have rhythm."

I knew exactly what it was that Byron was saying. I had heard it from a variety of sources, though it was never said with quite the same poetic flourish.

Byron's message, boiled down to the essentials, was this: Men are so fascinating, bold, daring, creative, inventive, stimulating, etc., that women can happily spend their days absorbed in the wonder of it all. Men, on the other hand, have better things to do than sit around thinking about women all the time. Women are dull. (Except in a prone position, and how much time out of a whole life can a man spend doing *that?*)

By the time I had reached adolescence, I was aware that society had carved out a niche for me, now that I was about to become a woman. I was offered one ticket, good for a lifetime, to the bleachers. There, I could cheer for men who did things well. It was assumed that the right order of the universe was for men to do, and women to admire. I realize now that I had been soaking up that message since the old days at the Seco, where the good guy punched the bad guy and the heroine cowered in the corner, and then smiled like a grateful spaniel at the Good Guy (who tipped his hat and got back on his horse. It is no wonder. The horses had a lot more character than the heroines. I remember Trigger and Champion and Silver. I can't remember the names of any of the heroines.)

I had an easy solution to inequitable sex-role divisions back in Seco days. I just changed sex when I played the movie. If anybody objected, I gave him a fat lip, and that was the end of that. The books my grandmother read to me said that little girls were made of sugar and spice and every-thing nice, and I went out and swiped the trash can covers to duel like Paul Henried, and flew the woodpile over Tokyo. I had a tough, sinewy little ego that grew right along with my feet. It was a prickly plant that dug its roots into thin soil and clung like some ratty little desert weed. Its sur-vival, I know now, was my parents' gift to me. They did not stomp on it or weed it up because it was tough and thorny and did not in the least resemble a rose. They wa-tered it and smiled kindly on it, and so I came to the brink of womanhood believing that I was a person who mattered and that my destiny lay more in my brain and my will than my bra size.

The climate at mid-century was decidedly hostile to

prickly ego-cacti grown by little girls. Notions about the
nature of woman hovered over us like an inversion. The air
we breathed was filled with carcinogens more poisonous
to our inner growth than the unfiltered Camel smoke we
inhaled in the bathrooms at school was to our lungs. Society
played on two main themes about how women were constructed.

The first was that women were satellite people; that we
were supposed to shine by reflection, pale silver shadows of
the white heat of the male ego.

The second was that we were infinitely perfectible. It
was a time when everybody was optimistic about the im-
provability of the species. You could Develop Your Personality with Christ or get the hook taken out of your nose
by surgery; and women were more in need of perfecting
than anybody.

The first message spread across an entire page of *Ladies'
Home Journal* in January of 1954. Staring back at me from
the page was the incredible face of Marlene Dietrich, the
square, cruel mouth and the aristocratic, snowy ridge of the
nose. Marlene Dietrich was telling the women of America
"How to Be Lovable."

"Love him, unconditionally and with devotion. You are
a woman and you have a thousand little pockets in your
being where you can tuck away little pains until tomorrow.
A man hasn't got those pockets. His emotional system isn't
as vast a labyrinth as yours. This is not man's personal
achievement. He is made that way. To be completely a
woman you need a master. In him you will find a compass
for life. You need a man to look up to and admire and
respect. If you dethrone him it's no wonder that you are
discontented. Discontented women are not loved for long."

(I read this and it seemed to me that it had a familiar
ring to it. I didn't recognize what it was at the time, but
now I know. It was all those dog books I read—*Lad, a Dog*

and *Lassie Come Home*. They extolled the same virtues:
blind loyalty, doggy devotion, complete selflessness. Marlene Dietrich's lovable woman was a collie!)

And Marlene added, "Like the moon, which gives its light
nursed by the sun, the woman needs the man so she can
shine and glow and make her alive."

Famous women were always saying things like that,
movie stars in particular. They did it in interviews in *Photo-
play* and *Ladies' Home Journal* and *McCall's* and on the
late-night talk shows on television. They came on the
screen, ponderous bosoms heaving, capped teeth gleaming,
purring about shining like moons and wanting masters. And
even *I* could tell they were lying through the caps on their
teeth. They had egos larger than their bra cups. They
basked in the spotlight like fat seals enjoying the Arctic
summer sun. But they believed they had to lie. It was some
kind of absurd party line. They were just simple little girls
who really wanted a neat little cottage and a man to cook
apple pie for, and acting was something they did to while
away the time, like needlepoint.

Famous women weren't the only ones who were telling
me I was a satellite; the Writers were too. Everybody who
wrote a novel at mid-century wanted to be Ernest Heming-
way. I waded through stacks of them, epics of hairy-chested
men and compliant women, those war novels with blood
and gore afield and the shore leaves with horny native girls,
barmaids, prostitutes, titled British ladies, housewives, night
club singers, Red Cross nurses, Italian peasant girls. But
the ladies were only a diversion. It was the hero who kept
center stage.

The hero, typically came from a poor family; he had to
fight in the back alleys or the fields of a rural shantytown,
and he worked his way up the ladder of success, copulating
with a different woman on each rung. Early on, he knocked
up Lula Mae in the shade of a cotton plant, and he left her

because, of course, his manly thirst for adventure and his restless soul weren't about to permit him to sit around changing diapers in a tarpaper shack. He grappled with his night-school teacher, the wife of his first boss, a society matron, and a chanteuse, and he finally found True Love with a young, unspoiled and innocent virgin.

We were all supposed to admire him. Oh, he was no saint, but he had *lived*. This was what a man's life was supposed to be, rolling in the hay and panting after Success. The women all loved him madly and when he left them they were distraught; they moaned and tore their hair, and they never said, "Christ, what a schmuck *he* was!" One presumed they spent the rest of their lives sighing over their lost love or cursing him for wrecking their lives. In scenes where the hero would once again encounter one of his forsaken ladies, they were always saying things like:

"You left me, Edgar, but I didn't forget. I carried your baby and I gave him your name. It was always you, Edgar. I had other men, but it was your face I saw, Edgar. Always You. I knew this town couldn't hold you Edgar. But It was Always You."

OR:

"You bastard, Milton. I hate you. You ruined it for me. I swore I'd get you if it was the last thing I did, Milton. And now I've done it. I've spent my life waiting for revenge, and now I have it. It is I who own the controlling stock in your company. You are bankrupt. You are ruined, like I was! (Suddenly, she begins to sob!) Oh, Milton, Milton, why did it end this way. The things we could have had together! What a fool you were, Milton. If you only knew how I loved you!"

The only function of the women in the novels was to

respond to the hero (i.e. fall in love with him or sleep with him or get pregnant by him). As soon as she got pregnant she got written out, because who wanted a pregnant lady slopping around spoiling a dandy story. If Lula Mae got knocked up, tough luck for Lula Mae, but boys will be boys.

Not once did any of the women in the novels have an independent thought about something that didn't have anything to do with HIM. Not once did they ruminate about the existence of God or the state of the union or the PTA bake sale. Even if they were professionals, HE came before everything. A lady doctor would leave the sponge in the patient's pancreas and dash off to meet HIM for cocktails; a lady lawyer never said, "Not tonight, Milton, I've got to get a guy off on a murder one charge." The Broadway Star never had a matinee when HE suggested the double bed in his apartment.

The women in the novels all seemed afflicted with an incurable case of "The Ripsies." Two seconds after they shook hands with the hero and said hello, they had left a trail of undergarments across the floor of the living room. The sight of the hero's steel blue eyes gave them an ungovernable urge to rip off hats, gloves, skirts, slips, garter belts, bras, and panties, foaming at the mouth all the while:

"She ripped off her bra and freed the incredible lobes of her breasts; they quivered in the breeze from the air conditioner. She moved her hands down to the edge of her beige lace panties. "Take me, Milton," she breathed. "Take me, take me!""

It was all very confusing to me. What was I supposed to be, anyhow. Was I supposed to be an icy vestal virgin, chirping "I am a Child of Mary" when somebody tried to kiss me, gently, on the lips. That seemed very peculiar. On the other hand, nobody I had seen, not even the Annapolis midshipmen in full dress white moved me to any great compulsion to rip off my white cotton 34B. It was very hard to figure out how to be a madonna and a whore at the same time.

Despite the novels and Marlene Dietrich and Lord Byron, I was not convinced that I was a satellite person. But the second message, that was a different story. Perfectibility was hard to resist.

We were all perfectible, of course. Men could get nose jobs as well as women. But there was a difference. The material of which men and women were composed was different. *They* were made of some solid, rocklike substance. It often needed polishing to make it shine, some craggy outer core had to be sanded until it gleamed like a diamond extracted from stone. But its mass held solid.

Women, on the other hand, were creatures whose texture approximated the lump of dough that was the start of my mother's pie crusts. Our material was infinitely malleable. It could be squashed flat or rolled into a ball or squeezed into a trapezoid if one had the time and patience to do it. Since such material could be pummeled and handled and shaped, logically then, it should be. We could be improved —inside and out. Not only could we be perfect, we were morally obliged to take a hand in the perfecting process.

I WAS A HOPELESS FATTY: NOW I'M A MODEL

read the headline in the *Ladies' Home Journal.* I was hooked as soon as I saw it. There was always a copy of the *Ladies' Home Journal* around the house. My grandmother subscribed to it, and since it was large and easy to spot I always grabbed it when I didn't have a book to read. A good place to browse through *LHJ* was on the glider on the porch. I sat and glided, back and forth, smelling the roses in the back yard and absorbing the Gospel of perfectibility streaming from the pages of *Ladies' Home Journal.*

I WAS A HOPELESS FATTY: NOW I'M A MODEL

There she was, in the little black-and-white before picture, all fleshy thighs and stomach bulges in the black bathing suit. Repulsive! Ah, but then, miracle of miracles, there is the same girl, the very same person, in glorious Koda-color, smiling at the camera, swathed in mauve chiffon, bulges gone as magically as if she had been touched by the wand of a fairy godmother and the ugly fat sizzled into nothingness like bacon shriveling in a pan.

She was a *model*. A genuine, honest-to-God model, the next best thing to a movie star. I read it and was inspired. After all, if she could be a model after starting out as a lump of lard, why not me? I didn't even have stomach bulges or baggy thighs. (Although Big Feet were more difficult to get rid of than thigh bags. Amputation of my toes would have taken me down to size nine, but could have hindered my model's walk.)

SHE TURNED HERSELF INTO A BEAUTY

said another headline in *Ladies' Home Journal*. I burrowed into it. It was a "Beauty Biography" by Journal Beauty editor Dawn Norman Crowell.

> Your letter may say (Mrs. Crowell began) "I want so much to have my husband proud of me" or "My children need the security that comes with having a nice-looking mother." Beauty is not merely a personal gratification, great though that may be. It can also be a source of joy to others. Many of us have handicaps to overcome and are stirred to admiration and action by stories of women, who, against even greater odds, have taken practical steps to make their beauty dreams come true. The following is such a story:
> "Dear Miss Crowell (the letter began):
> "Recently someone described my daughter, Delores, as being slim and attractive, and the words filled my heart with unspeakable joy."

The saga of Delores was unveiled before me. It was gripping, inspiring. What obstacles Delores overcame to Turn Herself into a Beauty! During her teens, she was, her mother says, "a hopeless fatty." And not only that, a ruptured disk in her back required nine operations to cure a limp. *And* she had a serious case of acne. *And* a fall from a horse caused a nose deformity that had to be cured by surgery. But she did it, she turned herself into a beauty. There was the undisputable evidence: Delores in Kodacolor after a nose job and dermatology, with a nose as fine as Deborah Kerr's, skin as smooth as new-ironed sheets. I looked at her and felt guilt pangs. I *had* to turn myself into a beauty.

I had plenty of advice. They were all there to help me: *Ladies' Home Journal* and *Glamour* and *Charm* and *Seventeen* and *McCall's* and *Mademoiselle*. I tried to keep up with it all.

"Do you have gritty elbows?" *Glamour* asked. (I looked. Oh God, yes, I had gritty elbows. They looked like cobblestone streets that hadn't been washed in years.) Use a pumice stone each night to keep them smooth.

"Do you have ugly feet?" (I looked at them. Blaugh. Ugly feet. Not even a mother could love such feet.) Use skin oil daily and keep your toes well groomed and polished.

"Do you want shining Hair?" (YES YES YES!) Brush at least one hundred strokes a night.

"Are your eyes small and beady?" Beauty Advisor asked. (I peered in the mirror. Definitely small and beady. Like a myopic snake.) Apply three shades of eye shadow: Blue Coral, Misty Ash and Tahiti Green, white near the corner of the eye, liner three quarters of the way under the eye and use waterproof Roman Brown mascara.

"Is your skin caressable?" (I slid an index finger down my arm. It did not feel remotely like velvet. Uncaressable.) Bathe in Sardo Oil.

Does your hair need sheen? (It needs something) Try Moon Glow Rinse. Are your knees bumpy? Teeth white? Hips big? Calves curvy? Do you have dandruff? Bad breath? Body odor? Psoriasis? Split ends?

I read, sitting there on the glider, and I believed. I was perfectible. After all, had I not seen perfection emerge like a statue by Praxiteles out of human clay in *Glamour* Make-overs and *Ladies' Home Journal* Beauty Biographies? It could be done!

So I pumiced and I brushed and I sprayed and I bleached and I rinsed and I polished and I trimmed and I squirted and I slathered and I rubbed. And I discovered a terrifying fact. If I did all the things all the magazines told me to do I would spend my entire life in the bathroom. I would be a shining, perfect creature, but the only people who would ever see me—briefly—were members of my family and the occasional guests who came in to the john to answer nature's call.

My mother could write to Dawn Norman Crowell:

"Somebody recently described my daughter as slim and attractive, and it filled my heart with unspeakable joy. That person was the plumber who had come to put a new clamp in the back of the toilet, and he saw her just after she had gargled with Listerine and was about to start her hour of Yoga exercises to get rid of blackheads through inner peace. If you would like to photograph her for Beauty Biography she will be out of the bathroom for twelve minutes on the evening of July 17 while her plum passion nail polish dries under her GE Home Beauty salon nail dryer."

Not only did we have to keep the basic machine in shape —hair shiny, armpits shaved, elbows smooth, feet caress-able—we also had to manage everything that went on top of it. As *LHJ* and *Glamour* and *Charm* and the others told us, Dressing Right was half of being a beauty. The models in the magazines were sent to guide us. There they were, gliding down a city street like classy limousines, white teeth bared to the wind, not a curl out of joint, gloves the exact shade of persimmon as the high-heeled pumps, no run-down heels, no mustard stains, no crooked stocking seams.

The serene smile of perfection glided across faces done as expertly as a Picasso blue period painting.

And for our edification, the magazines also showed us the opposite virtue: imperfection. *Glamour* had a section it called "Fashion Don'ts" in the back of the magazine. They sent their photographers out to stalk imperfection, and they found it, snapped it and printed it for us to see. The girls whose pictures were used had little black squares over their faces, like the newsmagazines sometimes used in stories about prison inmates, mental patients, prostitutes, or other social outcasts. The little black squares may have obscured their faces, but their sins were bared for all the world to see: ill-fitting slacks on a rump that was definitely not model size; pleats perching on wide hips; a slip hanging, a stocking running, fat knees in short shorts, a dressy coat with slacks, earrings with sneakers.

I wanted, of course, to be one of the creatures in the front of the magazine, the ones with good bones and no hips who got photographed in color. I saw myself, walking down a city street one day and a photographer would jump out in front of me and *snap!* I would be on the cover of *Glamour*. And all my classmates in the convent school and the boy at the CSMC convention who looked like Carleton Carpenter and the midshipman who never wrote would eat their hearts out.

But in my heart of hearts I knew that I was not destined to make the color pictures in *Glamour*. Like some character from Kafka, I was destined at birth for the little black and white pictures in the back of the book. If a roving photographer ever did snap me, I would wind up with a little black square across my face. I never could quite get it all together. If my shoes were polished, my slip hung; if my hair curled, my shoes were crappy; when I put on make-up I never got it even, so I looked as though I had some horrible mottled skin disease; and when I used medicated

233

make-up to keep my skin from breaking out, it dried up and cracked so that it resembled the floor of Death Valley. What was Fashion on other people made me look like I was going out for Halloween. Even when I bought something as simple as a polo coat to go off to college, something went wrong. How I could screw up something so simple as buying a polo coat still mystifies me, but the one I got was too big and it looked like I had wrestled it off a cossack on the Eastern Front.

But I tried. I tried because I knew it was important to be beautiful, or at least to get as near to that condition as time, money and the largesse of nature permitted. The magazines wanted us to be beautiful. Men wanted us to be beautiful. Beauty equaled success. Did anybody ever get crowned Queen of the Prom for a generous soul? Did anyone ever get a Hollywood contract for compassion? Did Dawn Norman Crowell ever write "She Turned Herself into a Nice Person"? Did songwriters ever compose lyrics that went:

> The most intelligent girl in the world
> Isn't Garbo, Isn't Grable
> But she's able
> To outline the Atoms for Peace plan, compute the square root of 4742, recite *Evangeline* and discuss the implications of the Treaty of Versailles.

Ladies' Home Journal took a poll of happily married men and eligible bachelors for an article called "How Lovable Are You?" *LHJ* asked the men what they found lovable or not lovable in women. The answers:

> The more feminine the better. I don't mean a girl has to be a helpless bundle of curls and frills. But there is something mighty appealing about a girl who softens her appear-

ance with a pretty color, or a ribbon for her hair, or a flower to keep her suit from looking too businesslike.

* * *

Freshness in appearance is loveliness itself. Hair that shines, clothes that are band-box trim are pretty pluses for any girl. Some girls underestimate the value of these things. They go around with soiled gloves, hanging slips, run down shoes. It's an "I don't care" look that prompts a man to feel exactly that way about her.

* * *

You think men never notice little things. I met a girl at a party and thought she was a knockout. I invited her to join me for a cup of coffee afterwards. I was appalled to see her hands. The skin was rough and the nails ragged. Why would a girl stop her grooming at the wrists?

* * *

I like a girl who is romantic about how she dresses. Maybe because I'm in love with one who has the fetching habit of carrying little perfumed chiffon scarves in pretty colors to go with what she's wearing. And when she wafts the chiffon into the air it looks pretty and I'm intrigued.

* * *

A man wants to help and protect a girl. To carry her packages, open the door and see that she's comfortable in her chair. But there are women who are so anxious to prove they can take care of themselves that they insist, "Oh no, let me do it!" They make men feel totally unnecessary. Their effort not to seem imposing boomerangs by making them seem overly competent.

There was TRUTH, plain and simple. Nobody gave a damn if we were kind; better to wave little chiffon scarves into the air. Courage was unnecessary; what we needed were clothes that were band-box trim. If we could talk brilliantly of Kant and Joyce, but our grooming stopped at the wrists, HE would turn away in disgust. And God help us if we appeared competent.

We were being programed, by the *Ladies' Home Journal* and Dawn Norman Crowell and *Glamour* Makeovers and Fashion Don'ts and *Charm* and *McCall's* and all the others, to be phonies. Our main purpose in life was Catching a Man, and the process seemed to resemble building a better mousetrap. Honest human relations had nothing to do with the whole mechanistic process. Honesty was anathema to success. For if HE knew—before we caught him—that our eyes were too small or our hips too big or that we screeched when we got mad or turned stubborn when crossed, HE would not fall into our trap. Better to cover up with wide skirts and mascara, and contort ourselves like unbaked pretzels into any shape that might seem efficacious in entrapping him. *Ladies' Home Journal* advised "How to Catch a Valentine," outlining strategy for different types of males:

PLAYBOY: It hasn't occurred to him that life doesn't naturally begin at midnight. *Strategy:* Get twelve hours' sleep the night before. Wear durable dancing slippers.

SOLID CITIZEN: He smokes a pipe and wears his frat or lodge pin out in plain sight. *Strategy:* Bring out the family album. Have dog-eared copies of civic league pamphlets inconspicuously conspicuous.

SPORT: He doesn't own a dinner jacket and he feels stifled unless he's out of doors. *Strategy:* Give yourself a sporting chance, but when he wins, don't be upset. He won't be.

BUDDING GENIUS: He's writing the Great American Novel. *Strategy:* Show him how fast you can type.

And for all types of males, *LHJ* advised, one line of dialogue was indispensable: "You're wonderful!"

I sat there on the glider, reading all this, the novels and the magazines, and the more I read, the more the suspicion began to dawn on me that I was being propelled into a game I had no chance of winning. Everybody was telling me what I ought to be, and everybody was very certain, but the upshot of it all was a mass of contradictions. I was supposed to have all the surface perfection that artifice could produce, and if I didn't, I would be called slovenly, unattractive, uncaring. And at the same time, women were condemned for being vain, artificial, overconcerned with appearance. If I opened my own door, I was overly competent, and men didn't like that. If I was ambitious and too aggressive, men wouldn't like that. But if I sat back and let men open the doors and do all the work I would be called lazy and greedy, pushing my husband (when I got one) into a heart attack working too hard to buy things for me. But if I went out to work so that he wouldn't have a heart attack trying to meet the mortgage, I would be turning my children into juvenile delinquents. I was being urged to stay home, to pour all my energies into molding the children I would have; but then Philip Wylie came along and attacked Momism, and said American mothers were castrating their children by being too possessive. I was told I shouldn't be too brainy, because men didn't like smart women; but then I was told that men got bored with women because all they talked about was housework and babies. And if a woman stopped being dull and got passionately involved with something besides home and family she was blamed for being selfish and for tearing down her husband's ego by "dethroning" him. There just wasn't any way at all a woman could win.

The world of the *Ladies' Home Journal* blithely ignored the contradictions. In its world, a woman could win, a big, fat glittering prize wrapped in pink paper with cherubs on it. LOVE AND MARRIAGE, read the label.

Love, in the land of *LHJ*, could cure everything from obesity ("A reader writes, 'I reduced on Love'") to general sluggishness. ("Doctors tell us that love heightens the metabolism and quickens all the body's vital processes.")

In "Love Can Make You Beautiful," Dawn Norman Crowell told me how it worked for Queen Elizabeth:

"These before-and-after-Philip pictures show how love and conscious effort can work beauty miracles. The radiance of her smile is from the heart, but a reducing diet combined with more tasteful attention to clothes, hairdo and makeup has transformed a plain princess into England's beauty queen."

And love, Mrs. Crowell continued, was "just around the corner for the girl who confidently expects it and who radiates belief in herself. This girl dresses appealingly at all times, wanting to be deliciously ready for the magic and unpredictable moment when HE sees her across a crowded room."

And what if she keeps dressing right and radiating confidence and going to crowded rooms, and nothing happens? It is her fault, that's what. A woman who was not lovable with all the help she was getting had only herself to blame. But she was not alone. Who would come riding to the rescue like the masked rider of the plains with his faithful Indian companion?

Psychology, that's who.

Armed with an invincible belief in the perfectibility of women, psychology stepped in to play Pygmalion to a collective Galatea: The women of America.

And the *Ladies' Home Journal* brought its message. It told me "How to Be Marriageable":

> The natural wish of the average young woman to marry, to have a home, to bear and rear her own children is sometimes thwarted: by circumstance, by unfavorable personality traits formed in childhood, by half-conscious fears and resistances. Yet many of these young women would make good wives and fine mothers. It is to the advantage of society as well as themselves that they conquer these barriers

in order to be fully happy and to make their maximum contribution to society. This problem is being realistically and honestly faced by the Marriage Readiness course conducted by the American Institute of Family Relations. The successful results are here reported for the first time.

The philosophy of the American Institute for Family Relations came pretty clear right off: Single women, look into your souls! Face up! Brace up! The fault, Dear Brutus, lies not in our stars, but in ourselves. Or, in the words of Paul Popenoe, director of the institute:

> Unmarried women all share in not realizing that they have traits which are unlovable, or in having failed to acquire traits that are lovable. It takes most unmarrieds about a year to face up to this fact, and to be able to bring themselves to the point where they will work at achieving lovability.

I was still under twenty, and I was safe. Nobody could call me a spinster yet. But was I lovable? I thought so, and so did my mother. But we could be wrong. I heard the message, loud and clear: Spinsters of America (even potential spinsters) begin now to blast away at all those unlovable traits: Be merciless with that stubborn streak, or the barbed wit, or the drive, or the arrogance, or the bluntness, all those peculiar traits that make you different from the cheerleaders with the curly hair who all get asked to get married. Listen to Marcia Carter (A pseudonym, but a real Case History):

> I squeezed the orange juice, popped hot toast onto two plates, splashed scalding coffee into the cups and called through the hall door: "Eggs will be done in thirty seconds, dear!" A few minutes later we said morning grace and I was

eating breakfast across from the man I love most in this world.

It still seems incredible to me—that I have so much. I still catch myself sitting cross-legged on the couch, naively surveying our domain with abandoned delight. Everything just as I had hoped for: blue and yellow provincial print on the wing-back lounge, braided oval rug on the floor, maple rocker and cobblers' bench, bookcases loaded with our favorites, a golden splash of sunshine coming through the curtains. Four years ago I had tried to quell what seemed to be the hopeless desire for these very experiences of happiness. I asked myself, if I am not going to live them, why do they keep torturing me?

So Marcia Carter took action. She went to the Institute of Family Relations to learn how to be lovable. She rooted in her family tree to find out if unlovableness might be a bad gene ("On the surface everything for an early happy marriage seemed to be in my favor. There were no bad examples around me. My parents and my brothers were happily married") and she also took a battery of personality tests to see how she rated on such traits as Nervous; Aggressive; Submissive; Cordial; Hard-boiled; Sympathetic; Quiet. And she dutifully went to work on the rough edges; a little too shy, a little too proud; a little too demanding, not really a "fun" person. She worked very hard, and finally her file was closed up and stuck away forever in a file marked "Success." Marcia Carter, twenty-nine, spinster, became Marcia Carter, married lady.

I wonder whatever became of "Marcia Carter." Does she ever sit on the blue and yellow print of the wing-back lounge, looking at the braided rug, saying: "Is this all there is?" Or is she lying on a bed someplace in a motel in Reno, her ring finger newly naked and bewilderment on her face?

"Marcia Carter" in the *Ladies' Home Journal* seemed not a mature person, but a child delighted at the gift of a pretty package. Her description of her new life is a page from a child's coloring book; everything is colored in; the print on the lounge, the maple rocker and the cobbler's bench, the sheer curtains. Everything is filled in—except HIM. He remains a white, uncolored section of the page, something a child missed in her haste.

Marriage, as the magazines presented it to me, was not simply a relationship with another person. It was a condition. Being Married. How to Be Marriageable. It was a little flower garden to which the man was the door. Once inside, the lady of the house selected the blooms and planted and tended and took charge of the children and kept HIM from straying by wafting a pretty chiffon scarf in the air or bathing in Sardo. If only I had a dollar for every article I read on "How to Keep Your Husband." But the rationale for keeping him was not for any admirable personal qualities he might have, but because he was indispensable to the condition. He paid the bills and fixed the screens when they got holes in them and took the lady out to dinner. One had to keep him because there were other women on the prowl who might find him useful for establishing *themselves* in "The Condition."

Under the gossamer clouds of romance in the ladies' magazines, under the emphasis on how important men were to women in articles written by ladies with three names, there was an undertone of contempt, veiled though it might be. Men, it seemed, were logical, builders and creators, aggressive and self-reliant, but they were also rather stupid. They were so easily manipulated. If you could catch a Valentine just by typing his novel or knitting his sweater and breathing "You're wonderful!" how bright could the Valentine be?

Women were supposed to manipulate men, the message came. And men, peculiarly enough, were supposed to like it. Eligible bachelors told *Ladies' Home Journal* they like to

241

be flattered and wheedled. But did they not know that lurking behind the dewy lashes and the waving chiffon was the scent not of Chanel, but of contempt. People who manipulate others must believe they are superior. The little groups of women who have knotted together today to do battle with women's lib, with absurd names like "Men Our Masters" and "The Pussycats" are scared silly of being equal. They like being superior. They figure they've got a good thing going. Equality is tough, and honest, and hard; it takes giving as well as taking. And like the ideal woman of mid-century, these women have discovered Power through Weakness. They can get a lot by giving something as trivial as a whispered "You're wonderful" and a skin daily dipped in Sardo.

Women, the *Ladies' Home Journal* told me, needed to be helped not only in achieving The Condition, but in maintaining it. If the ladies with three names opted for subtle manipulation, the psychologists took another tack entirely. Obsessed as they were with molding us, they set out to produce little replicas of the ideal woman; every home should have one. It was a lucrative era for psychologists. The *Ladies' Home Journal* had Clifford R. Adams, Ph.D., and the other magazines had their Dr. Cronehardt and Dr. Greenglove and Dr. Willmark and Dr. Blatbark, all men, all spooning out exactly the same sort of crap to the budding females of the fifties. There was no way we could escape it; Dr. Adams was relentless; month after month he urged us to examine and re-examine our faults, with the intensity of a Trappist nun hunting down her sins. "The fault, Dear Brutus, lies not in our Stars, but in our selves."

Is wifey bored and restless? A sign, said Dr. Adams of emotional immaturity. His solutions:

"Fulfill duties to husband, home and marriage above all other. Discontinue activities that interfere. Marriage is a career in itself. A job does not relieve a wife of household responsibilities.

"Cultivate household skills. Efficiency will relieve tedium.

"Plan your social life to include activities adapted to your husband's tastes as well as your own. Excursions off the beaten path may be hazardous.

"If you are restless despite the security your husband provides you, the standards he respects and the love he bears you, you may be bored with yourself. But a man like this will do his best to help and encourage you. With him beside you, you may still grow up to be a happy wife."

Does wifey nag? Self-help is the answer:

"One of the most common grievances discussed by husbands who write in to us is their wives' habit of scolding. Naggers take the joy out of marriage."

Married ladies, be alert. Dr. Adams suggests: "Try being your own tape recorder for a day or two. Listen to yourself as you talk to your husband and children. You may be surprised by the tone of your voice, the impatience of your words—the number of orders that you give."

Is wifey irritable? Dr. Adams has a little quiz:

1. Are you grouchy early in the morning?
2. Do you lose your temper easily?
3. Are you somewhat on the impatient side?

(The grilling goes on for 14 questions, and wifey totals up her score. If she has a score of 10 or more "You may be too irritable to make or hold friends. Try to be less temperamental and more tolerant.")

Is hubby a malicious tease, always making little stinging remarks to wife and kiddies? The problem: wifey doesn't build his ego enough. Dr. Adams has a quiz: Do You Build His Confidence?

Do you:

1. Cheerfully adjust your wants to his earnings?
2. Suggest he isn't the man he was?

3. Find much to praise, little to criticize?
4. Urge him to be like somebody else?
5. Kiss him because you want to?
6. Point out his luck in marrying you?
7. Always have time to talk to him?

And so on. If wifey doesn't score high enough on building his ego, she is advised to "find ways to show your appreciation and affection. Both his personal happiness and his business progress are at stake."

Is hubby chubby? That's wifey's fault too.

"The average wife would deny indignantly that she neglects her husband's health. She probably doesn't when he is actually sick. But it is equally important to see that he follows a wholesome routine when he is well."

Wifey must watch his weight; if he puts it on she must revise menus, supervise his diet, provide time for rest ("Some husbands are chronically tired because their wives schedule too many activities for weekends"), encourage him to relax.

"Try to understand, appreciate and lighten his burdens. Under the terrific strain of financial responsibilities, many endure a greater strain than wives know. Relieve his money worries as much as you can by thrift, good management and by moderation in your requirements."

Now and then I see a note in the Letters column from a woman who asks plaintively why Dr. Adams never says anything about what men ought to do to Make Marriage Work. Why does he never suggest that *he* encourage *her* to relax, or try to understand the strain *she* is under or try to build *her* ego. But Dr. Adams never does. Men are not so malleable.

(If I were granted the powers of Jehovah, I would wait, salivating, for Dr. Adams and Dr. Cronehardt and Dr. Greenglove and Dr. Willmark and Dr. Blatbark to come tripping up to the throne. I would pronounce sentence. I would turn them all into women and I would send them back to 1954 and give them teasing, overweight, grouchy, inconsiderate husbands with egos in need of fortification. They would have to build those egos for Eternity. And I would remind them of Sister Angela's definition of eternity: If a swallow flew by a mountain and brushed it with his beak once in every million years, the time it took the swallow to wear away the mountain would only be an instant in eternity.)

After all the helpful hints, the self-improvement regimen and the lectures, Dr. Adams unveils what should be the result of all his labors: The Perfect Wife:

(FANFARE)

SHE IS ADAPTABLE: The happy wife adjusts her mood to her husband's. (She feels like talking, he is uncommunicative.) She conceals her disappointments. (He is too tired for the movie she'd looked forward to, so she puts the big chair by the fire even though it spoils the effect she'd planned for the room.) Adaptability means more than weakly giving in. Rather it means the ability to understand his needs, to see his point of view, and to identify with him so fully that his wishes are usually hers.

SHE IS RESPONSIBLE: No one will see if she sweeps dust under rugs or hides overdue bills. But it is not personal fastidiousness or fear of detection alone that restrains the responsible wife from such behavior. She performs her tasks faithfully and admits shortcomings honestly because she accepts her obligation to run the house, as she expects her husband to earn a living. The woman who wants a dependable husband proves to him that she is trustworthy.

SHE KEEPS UP WITH HER HUSBAND: Her husband's promotions and salary increases bring her new responsibilities and opportunities as well. By improving her household methods she does a better job and still has time for outside activities.

She tries new recipes, rearranges her furniture and invites new friends to dinner, follows sports and tries her luck at a new game. Her development is measured not by a pay check but by her husband's growing admiration, appreciation and love.

And there she is, folks, Aphrodite at Mid-Century: Adaptable as Play Doh, possessed of no ego at all, fetching and carrying for hubby with her hair freshly done and the beef bourgouignon simmering on the range, a pal who likes hockey, football, lacrosse, craps (you name it) because HE does, who never nags, who keeps hubby thin, puts the big chair by the fire for him and slinks about in a black negligee if HE is in the mood. And she always, *always* spends an hour a day cross-examining herself to make sure she is Making Marriage Work.

She makes me want to throw up.

14 *Gaudeamus Igitur*

One afternoon during my senior year at the convent school, I walked into Sister Superior's office. I handed her four college application forms that I had filled out. I had arranged them strategically, and I watched her face as she looked at them.

She frowned at the University of Maryland. She frowned at Cornell. She frowned at Swarthmore. Finally, she came to the last one, and she smiled. It said Trinity College, Washington, D.C.

Trinity is a small women's college tucked into several acres of greenery in a section of Washington that is so jam-packed with seminaries it is called "Little Rome."

Trinity had a high academic standing, a reputation as a school for Catholic girls of the upper middle class, and it was close enough for me to commute. (The University of Maryland was even closer, but I had a neat, rational list of reasons why I didn't want to go to Maryland. The campus was too big, there was too much emphasis on football, etc. The real reason was snobbery, though I wouldn't have admitted it at the time. It was not my immortal soul I was worried about, nor even the nurture of my mind. A classy women's college offered much more in the way of status than a state university.)

Trinity offered me a scholarship, and off I went to the campus in the autumn of 1955. I discovered to my surprise that I had moved up several rungs in Catholicism as well as in society. The old, familiar cast of characters vanished; I had thought them universal. Maria Goretti and Our Lady of Fatima and Marylike Dresses and the Marriage Act were no longer. It was like moving from vaudeville to Grand Opera. The old standbys were O.K. for the hoi polloi but the carriage trade liked its refinements. Religion was now St. Thomas Aquinas and metaphysics and theology.

I adjusted to the new style as quickly as I adapted to the little snobberies of an upper-middle-class girl's school. I retired Maria Goretti about the same time I packed away my angora sweaters, though I regretted the loss of the latter much more. The sweaters were fuzzy and soft and comfortable, with the feel of sweet little rabbits, but I wore an angora sweater to Trinity one day, and though nobody said anything, I could feel the sidewise glances. I never wore one again.

At Trinity, certain assumptions were made about our moral character. It was assumed that after twelve years of Catholic education, capped by a decision to attend a Catholic college, we did not need the sight of a Madonna or a haloed saint every 2.5 feet to guard us from the ravages of atheism, nor the steady smell of brimstone to protect us from the sweaty hands of young men in the clutches of satanic lust. (By now, we were too stuck-up and too smart to Do It without a six-hundred-dollar diamond on third-finger-left-hand.)

And so the hardy and vigorous peasant brand of religion of the convent school was transmuted, at Trinity, into a classroom exercise as disinterested as a mathematical theorem. Theology was at the opposite pole from Our Lady of Fatima and Moral Guidance. Those things had been twined into the fabric of our adolescent lives, and that they were of little help in our attempts to come to grips with reality was hardly due to their distance from us. But the antiseptic scent of the cloister drifted about theology. It seemed to consist of monks wrestling with syllogisms, the content of which we were expected to memorize. We were taught theology by a Dominican priest with eyes as cold as the weathered stones of the main building and the air of a man tossing pearls before swine. He did not expect to be challenged on any of the points he laid so neatly before us. When one girl had the temerity to question him sharply, he brushed her off with the same annoyance he might have shown a fly who alighted on his shoulder. When she persisted, his annoyance flared into anger. The rest of us—in the true intellectual spirit—just wished she would shut up so we could go on taking notes. We were on to the College Game. If you took copious notes, and regurgitated back what the lecturers had said on your exam paper, you would probably be O.K.

The channels between theology and the bustling twentieth-century world outside our doors were not explored. What did theology have to do with Joseph McCarthy or nuclear weapons or Brown versus the Board of education? The connections were there, of course, but they were never made. I memorized the notes I took in theology and forgot them two days after the exam. I was not motivated to retain them, though I gobbled up what I was learning in ancient history because it seemed so real, so full of humanity and passion.

Aside from theology, the course of study at Trinity was in the classic liberal-arts tradition. In retrospect, I would have to say that the education offered to Trinity students was quite good, particularly in the era where the quarterback and the baton twirler were the national symbols of college U.S.A. It was limited; our courses were predicated on the universally accepted assumption that the civilization of Western Europe was the only one that mattered, and our green and gray-stone world stood aloof from the events of the day. But I remember that I felt in my first year at Trinity that a window had suddenly swung open on the

world for me. After the convent school, with its pious homilies, its rote learning and acceptance of authority, Trinity
seemed like Harvard, Cambridge, and Oxford all rolled
into one.

The nuns at Trinity took some getting used to. At the
convent school I had slipped into the habit of being very
tolerant of the nuns. My classmates and I had accepted
the fact that the nuns were holy and sheltered women and
if they said things that didn't sound very bright it wasn't
their fault. When a nun at Trinity began to expound on the
intricacies of the Gross National Product, I went into culture shock. I kept waiting for her to say that recessions
were caused by the Holy Ghost.

I came to understand that the nuns at Trinity were for
the most part more inquisitive, more open, less encrusted
with Catholic middle-class morality than the students. For
many of the girls, Trinity was just the frosting on a cake
already baked and starting to dry. It was a place where a
top layer of education was supposed to settle on the psyches
of dentists' daughters who were out to marry Georgetown
boys.

A magazine writer, Jane O'Reilly, did a profile on Trinity
for *Mademoiselle* shortly after I graduated, and she observed that all the girls seemed to have been stamped out
by the same cookie-cutter. It was an apt observation.

I remember that when we arrived as freshmen, we were
a motley assemblage, reflecting the disparate high school
chic of Chicago and Boston and Miami and St. Paul. It took
only one week, and we all looked alike. I wore woolen knee
socks despite the fact that they brought out red scaly rashes
all over my calves. I gave away my triple-roll bobby socks.
I bought a little circle pin and shetland sweaters and I
lusted after a genuine scarab bracelet. They cost forty dollars, so my wrist stayed bare. Forty-dollar bracelets were
out of my league.

Nobody *very* rich went to Trinity, though I remember hearing girls talking about their debutante parties. It seemed romantic and marvelous and I wished I could be a debutante too. I once spoke rather wistfully of it to my father. He was then a member of the Parole Board in Washington, and he said that he could arrange a bang-up debut in the rec room at Lorton prison, with the biggest stag line in town.

So much for that fantasy.

Nobody *very* poor went to Trinity either. As a dayhop and a scholarship student, I qualified for the poor side of Trinity's economic scale. We all dressed alike, we talked alike, and I guess we thought alike. We were suffocatingly the same.

The rough edges of a world different from ours, which so many people lived in, rarely impinged on our lives. We were in a city that was turning into the power center of the planet, and we might as well have been in Dubuque. We did go to concerts and art galleries, but we were oblivious of the workings of the vast machine called the federal government that cast its shadow almost to the gates of Trinity. Outside the stone walls, the drama of a white, southern city turning black was being played out and we took scant notice. We saw only that it was not safe to walk alone to the Hot Shoppe six blocks away. A few Trinity students spent a few hours a week teaching catechism at settlement houses run by various Catholic charities. There is a picture in one of my yearbooks of Fifteen Lady Bountifuls from Trinity, each one wearing a polo coat and a long woolen striped scarf, standing in a semicircle in front of a settlement house. Squatting on the ground in front of them is a gaggle of black children in tacky clothes, grinning.

It is enough to choke even Uncle Tom.

It was not only the past and present of Trinity girls that seemed predictable, but the future as well. I see it now flipping through the alumnae journal where all the entries seem to blend into one. The kids (four-six-eight) are in school, Joe or Dick or Frank is moving up in the firm, and the family went to Puerto Rico last winter. The alumna notes that she is teaching catechism and working for the sodality or Girl Scouts.

Which is not to knock kids (I have two who are charming when they are not being impossible) or Girl Scouts or Puerto Rico. But how is it that so many lives fit a single pattern? So few Trinity alumnae seem to be moving beyond the safe borders of home and parish. So few seem to be stretching to find the limits of their capacities. So few Trinity women seem to be taking any chances.

Perhaps it is because Trinity didn't really prepare us for taking chances. It was a cocoon—an enlightened one, true, but a cocoon nonetheless. Trinity was supposed to produce Good Catholic Women, and the Good Catholic Woman wasn't a prick like the Good Catholic Girl, she wasn't very interesting, either. She was accomplished and charming and educated and polite and she didn't raise her voice and her hem was straight and nobody but a Grand Dragon of the KKK could have objected to her.

It has always been interesting to me that the late Joseph P. Kennedy sent his daughters to Catholic schools but his sons to Harvard; because it was what the men did that mattered. Good Catholic women might teach catechism at settlement houses, but you wouldn't find them organizing rent strikes. They might work for a candidate, but they wouldn't run for office. They might write poetry, but not politics. They were always Helpful, and Polite.

Perhaps it is not fair to expect too much of the Catholic woman college graduate. She was trained to be a charming senator's wife, not a senator, or a lawyer's wife, or a PTA executive or a Girl Scout leader. Does the cookie change its shape after it comes out of the cookie cutter?

I was not really aware of all these things when I was at Trinity. I knew that the hard lump of ambition inside me would chafe until I exercised it in action; but I felt no guilt pangs about the fact that I, the budding journalist, rarely picked up a newspaper except to scan the headlines. I was woefully ignorant of the issues of the day. No one really expected me to know, or care. I directed my energies toward study and toward acclimating myself to the new society I had entered.

My friends in the convent school had scattered in various directions. Sally had gone off to a small Catholic college in Maryland where she would cultivate an already pronounced talent for drinking beer. Clare was at Maryland, acting in campus theatricals and vowing to become editor of the campus paper, *The Diamondback*. Alice and Diane went off to Notre Dame College in Baltimore. (Diane, after graduating from college, fulfilled all our fantasies of baseball players and midshipmen by marrying the captain of the navy baseball team.)

I was making new friends at college: Margie, who was tall and dark-haired, the only girl in a family of five children from a small town in upstate New York. She was just recovering from a seizure of piety in which she had thought she wanted to be a nun. Mary, tall and willowy, had red hair, played guard on her high school basketball team and wanted to be a doctor. Jean, from a small town in New Jersey, had long legs and dimples and the habit of falling in love with about the same frequency as Clare. We formed the nucleus of a clique that spent the next four years doing almost everything together.

In my sophomore year at Trinity, I became a sophisticate. I suspect that I also became impossible.

I turned my nose up at the Hecht Company. Trinity girls did not shop at the Hecht Company. They shopped at Julius Garfinckel's. In Garfinckel's the elevator girls wore white gloves and the salesladies acted like the Duchess of Windsor. The first time I went in I had the urge to genuflect. Garfinckel's inspired reverence. I bought a Pringle cashmere on sale and I knew I had finally outgrown the convent school. I wouldn't touch Orlon with a ten-foot pole.

I cut my hair very short and bleached it very blond, which meant that my mother had to spend every Thursday night swabbing "Turn Blonde" on the roots. I discovered drinking.

I had been scared to death of drinking in high school. I was convinced that more than three sips of beer would lead to Getting Carried Away, or more likely, making a fool of myself. But in my sophomore year at Trinity I signed up for a ski weekend in the Poconos sponsored by Trinity and several other colleges. I departed with visions of handsome young men in ski parkas and romantic evenings by a roaring fire. But the lodge was jam-packed with other college girls with the same visions. The girls from Trinity spent the evenings drinking in our rooms. When we played Buzz I gulped down bourbon when I lost. Then I gulped down bourbon when I didn't lose. I was the life of the party; gay, boisterous, and soused.

Then I threw up.

It set the pattern for my life as a drinker. I inevitably got by turns merry, dizzy, and sick as a dog. I finished off most weekend evenings in somebody's bathroom, throwing up. I remember one night I had a date with a sophomore at Georgetown who had a car. After a party, he drove to a woodsy spot and parked. I started to feel squeamish.

He moved closer.

All I could think about was my stomach.

He blew in my ear.

"'Scuse me!" I said, and leaned out the window.

He kissed my ear passionately as I threw up out the window. It wasn't exactly the way Alan Ladd and Ava Gardner used to do it.

Now that I was moving deeper into nubile young womanhood, I began to realize that I must contend with more serious assaults on my Temple of the Holy Spirit than heretofore. Not that Trinity was a hotbed of passion. The school's nickname among young men on the spoor of compliant female flesh was "The Cherry Orchard." It was not the sort of image that attracted the Lothario.

The rules were also discouraging. Boarders had to be on the grounds by 7 o'clock on week nights, and midnight on Saturdays. As a dayhop I had considerably more freedom, but I didn't need a curfew to keep me a card-carrying member of the Cherry Orchard. I had my reasons.

One. I didn't want to get pregnant. No Way. I knew perfectly well that the outcome of all that stuff I read about roaring loins and heaving bosoms would be, for me, with my luck, just one unaesthetic fact: a pile of dirty diapers.

Two. The double standard. When a boy did it, it was Scoring. When a girl did it, it was Putting Out. The imagery was straight from the athletic field and the rites of war. *We* were the fortress, *they* were the attackers. *They* were the fullbacks, *we* were the goal line. When a Georgetown sophomore came in from a date, his roommate said, "What did ya get?" as though he was talking about a pound of hamburger. I figured I was sirloin, not hamburger.

Going All the Way was perilous, bad for the reputation and probably sinful. Necking was another story. Everybody necked. It was considered quite respectable. Necking—in Trinity parlance anyhow—generally meant activities above the neck or on the outside of one's clothing. The rules of necking might permit a fleeting touch of bosom, an awkward pat of buttock or thigh, but usually things stayed buttoned and zipped.

The contest was to see if we could stay zipped or if he could entice us into something more daring. A number of different strategies were employed:

The Animal Attack: This strategy required the young man to grab you and begin to kiss and hold you like a linebacker in the hopes that you would be overpowered. Grunts and panting usually accompanied the animal attack, as if he were transported by passion beyond the sound of your entreaties to cease and desist.

I was not fond of the animal attack. It had no class, except when Marlon Brando did it, but I never went out with Marlon. Since I was five-eight and had a passable left jab, I was not overpowered.

The Weak Point Theory: Legend had it that there were clever Byzantine and irresistible tricks that would reduce even the most frigid female to a helpless pool of passion. Blowing in the ear was one. Caressing the back side of the knee with a fingertip was another, and then there was the gallic classic, the tonsil-swab.

Blowing in the ear made me throw up. The knee-back caress tickled, and as for the tonsil kiss, while he dreamed of unbridled sensuality, I thought about mononucleosis.

The Logical Approach: This gambit had as its aim to talk you into a prone position by sheer force of argument.

"What if you died tomorrow?" The Georgetown sophomore would say. "You would die Never Knowing."

I would state that I had no intention of departing this vale of tears in the morning.

He would fortify his generous offer to initiate me into the ultimate experience with a line from Omar: "'The moving finger writes, and having writ moves on . . .'"

I too knew Omar.

"'Nor all your piety nor wit shall lure it back to cancel half a line, Nor all your tears wash out a word of it,'" I recited. "So get your hand off my zipper."

I have an ambivalent attitude toward every girl's dream of falling in love, which everybody around me seemed to be doing with alacrity. I wanted just as desperately as they to hear the violins, to sigh the gentle sighs of True Love. But at the same time I sensed in the music and the sighs a tender cage, made of a misty mesh as strong as any wire. My bright dreams of what I might be and do were merely little green shoots, and they could be cut down so easily. I wanted to soar, to test my wings. Only when I had flown on my own could I stand on the ground and be content. I dreamed of the faceless man who would love me forever and yearned for him as much as any girl. And yet at times in my dreams he turned into giant scissors to clip my wings; castration in reverse. It was always said that men "lost their freedom" when they married, but I saw the women hanging out the wash and dragging crying children along the aisles of the supermarket and I wondered whose freedom it was that *really* ended. I saw the seniors at Trinity extending their delicate, sparkling third fingers, talking of June weddings and jobs as secretaries while *he* went to med school. Their futures seemed so safe, so empty of challenge, firmly clipped to the trajectory of a man's arc through the world.

So I dreamed, but fearfully. If only Mr. Right would just hold off for a while. But what if he never came at all? What if nobody wanted me?

At least I no longer had to spend my weekends at the Silver. There were plenty of young men to go around, and now Georgetown, not Annapolis, was Valhalla. Catholic University, down the street from Trinity was not in the same class as Georgetown. C.U. boys were Catholic all right, but they didn't drive MG's like the Georgetown boys. Even the most forlorn of them shared in the *élan* of a rich man's school. My first date with a Georgetown boy had been when I was a senior in high school. It was a blind date, and I looked forward to it with breathless expectation. He turned out to be a football player with a body that was square and muscular and a mind to match. I guess he thought himself a man's man, because if he said anything at all, he leaned past me to joke with one of his male friends. We went to a dance at the convent school, and in the middle of the traditional last dance to "Goodnight Sweetheart" he stopped dancing and began to howl like a wolf. I was mortified. He just stood and howled and I turned lavender and wanted to die on the spot.

Margie's brother, who went to Georgetown Law School, was regarded by us as a potential gold mine. But he still looked at his younger sister as if she had pigtails and scrapes on her knees. We worked on him. He held out through freshman year, but buckled when we were sophisticated sophomores. Five of his friends were renting a house in nearby Virginia, and the house was usually filled with an ever-changing mélange of government girls out to marry law students and law students out to make G-girls.

We drank scotch and water and looked down our noses at the G-girls (we *knew* Georgetown men weren't going to marry *them*) and sang risqué songs. Nobody minded if a couple left the door ajar while they were making out or if somebody else collapsed in a stupor on the stairs. I thought the whole thing was marvelous. This was how *adults* lived. I felt more sophisticated than ever, old and worldly. I can see it in retrospect for what it was for the G-girls and the older "students," several of whom were pushing thirty-five: an endless, boring, aimless activity, repeated each weekend for lack of anything better to do.

I went out with a series of different boys, many of whose names and faces I cannot recall. One was Kim Novak's cousin and another was the son of a congressman and another came from a poor neighborhood in Newark and another was a good dancer from Villanova. I am sure I was as forgettable to them as they were to me. I told them I was going to be a journalist. After all, I had even had a few things published. I had written school sports for a Washington paper, and I had worked one summer as a copy girl in the

Washington office of the New York *Daily News*. I got to go to the White House and the Hill and the Supreme Court. True, it was only to pick up the press releases, but I thought I was—in the parlance of the times—Hot Shit.

Still, no one except my trusty parents seemed to take me seriously. The boys I went out with were polite about it, but clearly they regarded it as the sort of thing a girl did, playing around while she waited to get married.

I tried my hand at politics in 1958, which means I helped plan a student party to swell the campaign chest of Adlai E. Stevenson. I was motivated, alas, by the fact that the chairman of the committee was a very handsome law student who had a sister at Trinity. The party was a great success and the Georgetown boy asked me to give my phone number to his sister.

I approached her in the hall, trying to appear nonchalant.

"Oh, Ellie, your brother asked me—uh—well he may have to call me—about the campaign, you know. He can reach me at this number."

Stevenson lost, and the Georgetown boy never called. I gave up politics.

I joined the International Relations Club because it sounded like something a journalist ought to know about. I was picked as a member of a student panel to interview Israeli Ambassador Abba Eban on a TV show, but when I first heard his name I thought it was Ali Baba I was supposed to interview. I figured he was the President of Egypt or something.

I also attended the National Convention of International Relations Clubs at a Washington hotel. But while it was International Relations that we were supposed to be discussing, it was interpersonal relations that consumed most of our time and energy.

The rooms occupied by the out-of-town students became the social center for the convention, and very quickly the pecking order was established. I met a very nice, homely, lanky boy from Philadelphia who was a wonderful dancer. We had a marvelous time dancing between the twin beds in his room and I promised to go out with him after the late meeting for Chinese food.

In the meantime, I had attracted the attentions of a very good-looking and self-assured boy from Villanova, who was clearly one of the "wheels" at the convention. He asked me to come to his room for a drink. I told the tall, homely young man I had a terrible headache. I went with the boy from Villanova, and later, while we were necking, there was a knock on the door. I opened the door, my hair tousled and my Cherries in the Snow lipstick smeared across my face. The homely young man stared at me. It seems *he* was the roommate of the Villanova boy. I will never forget the way he looked at me, like a dog I had just kicked. He walked away and I went back to the room, knowing I was a Traitor to My Class. It wasn't with the beautiful self-assured people that I belonged; the lanky, homely, rejected young man was my kind of people. I knew how he felt. The handsome young man I couldn't fathom. Even when he was kissing me he was thinking about *him.* (I am never completely comfortable around winners. Maybe it was too much exposure to the Washington Senators or having big feet. I think maybe I picked journalism because it is a job for Outsiders.)

Since the hour was getting late, I told the boy from Villanova that I had to drive home. (I had my mother's car.)

He insisted on going with me, which I thought was very gallant. He drove, and when he pulled up in front of my house he put on the emergency brake and unzipped his fly.

"What are you doing?" I asked nervously, though it was perfectly obvious what he was doing.

He slid off his pants.

"*What are you doing?*" My voice croaked like a frog's.

His hands went to the top of his jockey shorts. And this was a Good Catholic Boy!

I leapt out of the car, horrified. My God, he was going to take It out, right there in my mother's car, in front of my house!

"Put your pants back on!" I hissed through the window.

"Why?"

"*Why!* That's a dumb question! You just can't take your pants off in front of my house."

He sat and considered whether he could or he couldn't. He had his shorts in his hand and his you-know-what stuck up through the spokes of the steering wheel. I stared at it, fascinated.

"Will you get back in the car?"

"Not if you don't put your pants on."

"I don't want to!"

I left him sitting in the car. The next morning he was gone. I hope he put his pants on before he caught the bus.

I knew, by this time, something of the preliminaries that were supposed to precede the Real Thing, but the Real Thing itself remained a mystery, in the province of imagination and war novels. Knowledge was generally accepted to be the dividing line between girlhood and womanhood. I remember one afternoon Clare picked me up in her car and we drove out to Bethesda Naval Hospital. She was engaged to a law student at Maryland, and it was the week before her wedding. We were on our way to pick up a carton of condoms that she could get free because of her father's status as an ex-navy officer. We felt terribly daring and grown up. How sophisticated! A whole carton of them!

The night before the wedding the ushers went out to get drunk with the groom, and the bridesmaids went out to get drunk with the bride. The husband of one of the bridesmaids came to pick us all up at the end of the evening. He dropped his wife off, then went to take Clare and me home.

He walked Clare to the door and I could see that something was happening. Then he came back to the car to drive me home.

In the meantime, Clare called my mother. I was in mortal peril. The married man had accosted her at her very door step. It had probably been a woozy peck on the cheek, since none of us were feeling any pain, but in Clare's retelling it sounded like he had attempted rapine on the welcome mat.

He pulled his car up in front of my house. In a glow of alcohol, he felt like talking. In a glow of alcohol, I felt like listening. Five minutes passed. My parents started to peer out the window.

Ten minutes. My father leaned out the front door.

Fifteen minutes. They started to flick the front porch light off and on.

I entered the house, unsteady but enraged.

"*How dare you!*" I thundered. "All these years and you don't trust me, your own daughter! I am an *adult*. I am no longer a child! I will not be treated as a child!"

My father observed that perhaps I had had a bit too much to drink.

I drew myself up to my full height, indignant. It was a calumny, a libel.

"I have most certainly *not* had too much to drink," I said haughtily.

I turned to march, with dignity and indignation, to my bedroom. I missed the hall door. *Smack!* I crashed right into the refrigerator.

The next week, Clare and her new husband came back from their honeymoon in Ocean City. They walked up to my front door, hand-in-hand. I looked at her closely. She *knew!* I don't know what I expected to see that was different about her. Maybe something like a birthmark that you got when you *knew*. There was a chasm between us now. She was a woman, and I was still a girl.

Margie and I, both girls, tried to make up in insouciance what we lacked in knowledge. We sang racy songs like "Roll Me Over in the Clover" and we drank like fish and told raunchy jokes. We both signed up for a student trip to Europe in the summer of 1958. At long last, I would visit the foreign lands I dreamed of! Romance and adventure surely would await me.

On a hot June day we boarded the S.S. *Zuiderkruis*, an old liberty ship sold to the Holland-American line. It plowed along at the blinding speed of eight knots, and three days out we ran into a hurricane. Margie and I shared a bunk-bed cabin with six girls from Mary Baldwin College in Virginia. The ship pitched and tossed, and we struggled to stay in our bunks while one of the Mary Baldwin girls chanted, rythmically: "We are all gonna' Diaaaah! We are all Gonna Diaaaaaaahhhh!"

Still, the Heinekins beer only cost fifteen cents and the social life was lively. Formal manners were observed. That meant you met someone and you shook hands and *then* you started necking. At night the lifeboats on deck were filled with grappling couples. You could hardly move without stepping on them.

One night I was with a Yale basketball player and Margie was with an NYU senior and we polished off a bottle of blackberry brandy her father had given her for medicinal purposes.

(Margie's father had been leery of sending his daughter wandering in the wilds of Europe. He ran a general store and he had rummaged around in the merchandise and come up with a money belt, circa 1920. He had instructed Margie to wear it under her clothing at all times. But the day before we were scheduled to leave the clasp broke as she walked across Forty-second Street and a Greyhound bus ran over her traveler's checks.)

The use to which we put the blackberry brandy was not at all what Margie's father had in mind. There is nothing worse than a blackberry-brandy drunk. I threw up and felt better. But Margie fell into a zombielike trance. Her eyes did not blink and she did not respond when I called her name. I marched her into the shower, turned on the cold water and pushed her in. For a few seconds there was silence. Then I heard a terrible scream. I knew she was alive.

Margie, with my encouragement decided to become a "modern woman" on the trip to Europe. She threw out all her big boxes of Kotex and bought little boxes of Tampax. On the first day she got her period, I came into the john to offer my advice.

From inside the stall came muttered incantations.

"Oh shit! Damn! Damn! Shit!"

"What's the matter?"

"It won't go in!"

"Of course it will!"

Silence.

"No, it won't."

"It has to."

Silence.

"It just won't." (A tinge of panic in her voice.)

"Well, shove."

"I am shoving, dammit!"

"Well, shove *harder!*"

"Oh shit!"

Margie never did make it as a Modern Woman that trip. We bounced around in a touring bus, in search of European men. We found them. I was sunbathing on the beach at Rimini and when I opened my eyes I saw another pair of eyes, big brown ones, peering back into mine. The eyes were set in a handsome face that was attached to a magnificent body belonging to a tall Italian man named Lucho.

"Bella," said Lucho.

"Bella yourself."

Margie got one called Luigi. They didn't speak any English except "Hi, American girl," and we could only say "Arrivederci, Roma."

We had a grand time, but stayed zipped, much to the chagrin of Lucho and Luigi. So much time and heroic effort had gone into defending our virginity we were not about to abandon it on foreign soil, to somebody who couldn't say anything about it except "Hi, American girl."

Margie and I were both taken to a movie one night by our Italian student guide. It was a vintage Paul Henried pirate movie, with dubbed Italian, so Margie and I couldn't understand a word. As I sat watching Paul Henried dueling with Basil Rathbone, and trying to read their lips, I felt somebody's tongue in my ear. Then it went away. Then it came back again. Our Italian guide was switching off between the two of us.

The Seco was never quite like that!

Back at our hotel, a party was in progress. I was tired out from the day's events, so I got into bed and turned out the light. All the rooms were connected by a balcony, and the party started to spread out. A shadow climbed in my window. It was one of the girls on the trip. Another shape. A blond boy named Jim, who was also on our bus.

The girl went out the window. So did Jim. A minute later she came in again, without her blouse. Jim came after her, minus his pants. They kept climbing in and out of the window, shedding an item of clothing each time, like a Marx Brothers routine. They tried to get in bed with me, and muttered "spoilsport" when I demurred.

For Jim, the entire trip was just a prelude to Sweden, anyhow. He was planning to leave the tour at the end of the summer and strike out for the land of liberated women. He kept complaining that American girls were too dull, French girls too uppity, Italian girls too virtuous, Swiss girls too cool. He talked of Sweden in front of the Pietà and in Notre Dame cathedral, and in the castles in Heidelberg and picking edelweiss on the Alps. "Just wait till I get to Sweden!" he would sigh, and a faraway look would creep into his baby blue eyes.

We found out later that he came back from Sweden with gonorrhea. It was a fringe benefit not mentioned in the National Student Association tour booklet. (Margie and I chortled maliciously when we heard about it. Virginity, it seemed, offered certain health benefits.)

In Paris, Margie had a date with an Algerian folk singer who spoke only French and I had a date with a young man named Pierre who claimed to be half Danish and half Jewish and came from Tahiti. He suggested that I go with him to the Riviera for a week of bliss, but I declined. I didn't want to miss the Houses of Parliament, next stop on the tour. Unbridled bliss lost out to Big Ben. What the hell, I figured, I could always get bliss in the back seat of a Plymouth in Silver Spring; but the Hecht Company didn't have Big Ben.

We went to a left-bank bistro where there was a single bathroom shared by men and women. Margie and I, with our American hygienic habits, were horrified. But the call of nature is not to be denied, so off we trudged to the john. There were no locks on the doors so I went into one of the little wooden stalls, making Margie promise to defend the door at the risk of life and limb.

While she stood, braced faithfully against the door, a young American came up to her and said, "Hey, are you American?"

She nodded, not quite sure of formal etiquette in the particular situation.

"Maybe you can help me. I've got this homo who's been

following me and I can't convince him I'm not queer." He pointed to another young man standing in the corner of the john.

"But what can I do?" Margie asked.

"This!" the young man said, and he grabbed her in a passionate embrace. The door rattled.

I grabbed my pocketbook and held it across my privates. "What's going on out there!" I shrieked.

At that moment, Margie's date walked in, took one look, and started yelling at her in rapid-fire French. But since our entire French 101 class consisted of memorizing a book by Antoine de St. Exupéry, all she could think of to say in French was: "I have always loved the desert."

It did not seem quite appropriate.

We took home with us from the continent a cache of stories to tell the next year over bridge hands in the smoker at Trinity, and a number of European affectations, such as eating with the fork in the left hand. I had blown all the money I earned from summer jobs on the trip, so the summer after graduation I had to hustle out to look for a job. I had plans for graduate school already made, but I did not confide them to potential employers. I got a job as assistant to the personnel manager at the Sheraton Park Hotel in Washington, a position that consisted mainly of hiring "warewashers," the hotel's euphemism for dishwashers. The warewashers were usually black men who could get no other work and signed up for a few days to wash the hotel's china. They were silent, sullen men, ill at ease in the air-conditioned office where I showed them how to fill out the required tax forms. I was absurdly polite with them, as polite as I would have been with visitors from Mars who had little green antennae sprouting from their ears. I had no understanding of what they wanted, of what sort of things their dreams were made of, but I could see the chasm that yawned between myself and them. Tomorrow, for me, offered hope, excitement, the scent of incredible possibilities. For them it offered only the humid basement of a hotel, scrubbing the lipstick from whiskey-sour glasses used by white people. It did not seem fair that life should deal such unequal hands.

The social life at the hotel that summer was gay and lively, though at times I felt an undercurrent of desperation that was never present at the college parties I had attended. These people, some of them at least, were playing for keeps. Their futures hung in the air along with the stale cigarette smoke at the parties. The staff was a clique with international touches: Pierre, the assistant chef, was French; Rudy, from food and beverage control, was German; Court, from public relations was southern gentry; and Curt, the son of one of the executives, was a blond All-American boy. The girls were secretaries, young women in their twenties. There were lots of parties where people necked indiscriminately in corners, but the hotel parties lacked the rather touching innocence of the college parties where exactly the same thing happened. In those parties, it was an exercise among equals, and nothing hung in the balance. But at the hotel parties I watched the married executives fondling the pretty girls and I was revolted. I thought them old men, though they were perhaps pushing forty-five, but they had paunches from rich food and lack of exercise. The secretaries were my age, their perceptions must have been the same as mine; I saw in the corners a mutual exploitation that offended my tender conscience.

I developed a mad crush on Curt, who was the assistant director of food and beverage control. But in the course of the summer he threw me over for a pretty secretary named Nancy who had been photographed by the Washington *Post* for its Beauty Behind the Desk photo feature. (Later, I heard, she dumped him to marry one of the executives, who divorced his wife and gave Nancy a white Cadillac as a wedding present.)

At one of the last parties I went to that summer, Curt left my side during a game of Buzz in which we were supposed to name all the Sheraton Hotels in existence, and he was discovered later in the kitchen necking with Nancy. I took a cab home at 2 A.M., and I remember that the cabbie had the radio on, and Debbie Reynolds was singing the season's big hit, "Tammy."

Debbie crooned about love, and I sat in the back seat of the cab and dried silent, copious tears. I tried to believe myself a tragic heroine who had been disappointed in love, but there was luxury in the tears and I enjoyed them thoroughly. I already had in my possession my acceptance to the Columbia University School of Journalism, and even as I cried over Curt, I knew damn well that I, who dreamed of Glory, was not about to settle for a man whose horizons were the carpeted lobbies of the Sheraton Hotels.

15 *Childhood's End*

The gigantic torso of the George Washington Bridge crouched directly ahead in the center of the highway, a behemoth about to swallow our family car in its navel. My father was driving, my mother was sitting beside him, and I was sitting in the back seat. As we slid smoothly into the metal entrails of the bridge, I felt a shiver of excitement. There was portent in this crossing; the George Washington Bridge was a birth canal to a new life. When we reached the other side of the Hudson River, my life as an adult would have begun.

I peered through the mists drifting up the Hudson to try to get a glimpse of the Manhattan towers; everything was suffused with the rose-gold glow of my imminent rebirth. Manhattan, off somewhere in the mist, seemed to me to be an enchanted place, as full of secrets as the heart of a flower, that would unfold to me in the fullness of time. The brick and glass apartment houses on the Jersey shore, ordinary places where insurance salesmen and bank tellers lived, seemed to me flushed with all the mystery of the curving arches of the Alhambra.

For this was it; the break, the flight from the nest. I had been away before, traveled to Europe, worked in Washington, gotten drunk on planter's punch, weathered the back-seat wars. I felt myself much experienced. But I had not really left home to cope with the world on its own terms. Now I was leaving my own little snug haven, Silver Spring, Maryland, for the fastness of New York City; not the New

York of the Polo Grounds and Grant's Tomb that Diane and I had visited on our eighth-grade graduation trip. The New York I expected to cherish was the one I had seen so many times through the broad white window of the screen of the Silver. In New York, people sipped champagne in penthouses and wore Dior dresses popping in and out of big yellow taxis, and when they spoke they said clever things to each other. They never said, "Hi, what did you major in?" or "Blatz? Are you any relation to Miriam Blatz, from Shaker Heights? She was in my class." Or "Wanna go to the movies?" Just being in New York would transform me, I was certain. If I bumped into a handsome, debonair young man in the shadow of a skyscraper, I would have on the tip of my tongue a bright remark—something spirited, a little bit wise-ass, graceful—the way Katharine Hepburn would do it. And the young man would look at me and say something equally witty, but in his eyes the light of true love would shine forth. That was how things happened in New York.

The first glimpse of my room in the dorm at Columbia took some of the luster off my fantasy. In the picture in the catalogue the rooms had looked graceful and airy. But the picture had been taken shortly after D-Day. The cracking paint on the walls was institutional pea green and a slouching armoire masqueraded as a closet and the floors were brown linoleum. But I cheered up when I looked out the window. From my bed, I could actually see Broadway; though by the time it got this far uptown, Broadway wasn't much.

I kissed my parents good-by, and then Margie arrived, and we started to settle in. She was taking studies toward a master's degree in Middle Eastern studies at Columbia. The first thing we did after unpacking our bags and getting something to eat was hop on the subway and head for Times Square. The sun set while we were in the IRT and we emerged into a glare of neon. I clutched my pocketbook, sensing the unseen presence of a legion of pickpockets nearby. We looked about us and blinked, and moved closer together, we two sophisticated Trinity women who liked to drop such phrases as "When I was in Firenze last year"— and we gawked like the two greenest schoolgirls from Kansas.

I did get to meet some of the famous and rich people that year in New York, but it did not turn out as I expected. I remember that one day when I was out on assignment at journalism school I tracked down Charles van Doren, who was then in seclusion after the discovery that his performance on "the $64,000 Question" program had been a charade; he had known the answers all along. The press was on his spoor, and on a tip from a fellow student I found him on the first floor of a house in a nondescript neighborhood of the city. But when I found him, I didn't know what to ask. He had the face of a hunted animal, I thought, one who knew the game was up and shivered by a hedge someplace awaiting the inevitable. I asked him a few questions softly. I felt derelict in my duty, because I knew I was supposed to be tough, to bore in with questions. His hangdog look made me feel like an intruder in some private country of pain. I was glad to hurry out of that house.

I went to the April in Paris Ball, where café society was supposed to gather, and I saw Elizabeth Taylor, wrapped in silver sequins and the glare of flashbulbs. I was amazed that she was so small. I had been so used to her in Cinemascope, where the entire entourage at her table would have fit in one bra cup.

I watched a fat, aging lady in a beaded dress interviewing Mrs. Tina Onassis with a tape recorder. Mrs. Onassis was a stunning redhead surrounded by a coterie of young men who hopped about to get her a drink or a cigarette. I listened to the things she was saying into the tape recorder. They were so banal, so ordinary. When she laughed, it was an affected little trill, the exact replica of the one that belonged to a lady from the sodality who was a climber and who wanted to move from Silver Spring to Chevy Chase.

One time I sneaked through the kitchen of a New York hotel to get right next to the room where Carmine DeSapio, the head of Tammany Hall and Senator John F. Kennedy, a strong contender for the Democratic nomination, were having a much publicized meeting. DeSapio and Kennedy were alone in the room, sitting at a table talking intently. Visions of instant fame danced in my head.

JOURNALISM STUDENT SCOOPS NEW YORK PRESS said the headlines in my mind. I cupped my ear and leaned against the door jamb. All I could hear was the clattering of cups in the kitchen. So much for my scoop.

The people I remember most vividly from that year in New York were not the ones in the headlines; not the people in Dior suits popping out of yellow taxis as in the movies. They do not, after all, make movies about sixty-five-year-old Armenian ladies who make paintings with the lint from vacuum-cleaner bags, even if that lady has a zest for life that would make Rosalind Russell seem like Minnie Mouse. There are no headlines about a black city rat inspector who carried on his private and unrelenting war in the anonymity of the back alleys; MGM never featured a Puerto Rican woman ex-junkie who struggled to transfuse her own inner drive into the trackmarked veins of other addicts on an express trip to the morgue.

And I remember a certain section of the anatomy of Mr. Jacobzeiner.

One of my first assignments in a documentary film class was to make a film about health hazards in the city. Poison was decided on as one of the hazards of living in Gotham, so our inept little band of film makers arranged to interview the head of the Poison Control Center.

The first time we interviewed him our cameraman forgot to take the lens cap off the camera.

The second time we dropped a light bank on the floor of his office and there was broken glass all over the place.

The third time everything seemed to be fine. Back at school, we sat in the screening room to see the fruits of our labor. The sound was perfect. The light was just right. The picture was clear as a bell. Mr. Jacobzeiner spoke with great clarity. There was only one problem.

All we had on film was his mouth. His mouth, cavernous, opened and closed. His tonsils jiggled. His jaw went up and down. It was the funniest film I have ever seen. We all collapsed on the floor hysterical. Jacobzeiner's jaw went on, undaunted.

We didn't have the nerve to ask him to do it again.

Another health hazard we trained our cameras on for our film was rats; and it was in the fetid alleys, amidst the trash piles and the patter of infested little feet, that True Love blossomed.

It was not exactly the way MGM used to do it. I couldn't picture Kathryn Grayson warbling "My Romance" while trying to get a light reading on a sprinting rat.

My Romance was tall, slim, handsome—and Jewish.

He was the director of the rat section of the film. We first held hands looking at film closeups of three-inch roaches and foot-long rats. We rendezvoused on street corners carrying shovels and light meters. I thought him terribly exotic after the Irish Catholic boys from Georgetown bent on upward mobility and a barbecue grill in a backyard in Chevy Chase. He wanted to cover revolutions in Latin America and had even been in a gang fight once.

I knew he was my type when I invited him to a reception for some Spanish dignitary given by the New York Newspaper Women's Club, which had given me my scholarship. He wore white athletic socks with his suit and we spent the evening standing in a spot near a fake Corinthian column where we could get the waiter with the hors d'oeuvres tray coming *and* going.

He took me on a tour of the Lower East Side and I munched potato knishes, mesmerized. Our dates were places like night court, meetings of the Dominican Revolutionary underground (his thesis) or Narcotics Anonymous (mine).

He was living in a grimy basement apartment on the Upper West Side. One night we were necking on the studio couch. (He lost the toss, so his roommate got the bed.) I made a decision. I was twenty-one years old. It was time to become a woman. The ingredients were there. The spirit and the flesh were willing.

He hurried out to the drugstore. In the interim, I sat on the studio couch feeling the same sort of excited expectation I used to feel when they played the national anthem before the ball game.

When he came back, nature took its course. It was as though tongues of lightning, shot from opposite horizons, collided in the sky. I fed, as a wanderer in a wasteland. I drank as a swarthy Arab lost in the desert sands. I felt his lips opening under mine like the petals of some great flower, exotic and sweet. Then the flames suddenly, reaching, searching, clinging, until all the drums in my veins rolled in one gigantic thunder.

I felt a stabbing pain.

In my right buttock.

He had neglected to tell me that the reason he got the studio couch when he lost the toss was that it had a two-inch nail sticking out of the frame on one side.

Our trysts were never quite as idyllic as Alan Ladd and Rhonda Fleming's. Once we planned a romantic weekend alone. I had moved into an apartment, and my roommates were away for the weekend. There would be soft lights, candlelight, and solitude.

He got the flu. He bought a bottle of Old Mr. Boston bourbon as a medicinal remedy. He gulped Bufferin and Old Mr. Boston in hopes of a miracle cure. He was reduced to babbling incoherence in the space of an hour.

I tucked him in my roommate's bed, with a sigh, and went off to sleep in my room. The next day the flu was gone, probably stunned to death by Old Mr. Boston. But he was covered with funny red spots. He went to a doctor.

The doctor said measles. The red spots didn't go away. A friend took one look and said The Clap.

He went to another doctor. The doctor laughed and said, "Bed bugs."

We had by that time discovered the invasion; it had come from the apartment above where a man shared an apartment with a Great Dane and three years' worth of undiscarded dog bones.

After graduation, when we both got jobs on a small but excellent paper in New York State, our relationship did not abate. He likes to say now that we were in the vanguard of the sexual revolution. After all, we lived together before it was the chic thing to do. I suppose that is true—if you don't worry about the fine points.

The town he covered was thirty miles away from the town I covered. He took a room in a house belonging to a nice Jewish family, where the beds squeaked. So living together meant my apartment—when he could get there after covering night meetings where village boards were locked in epic struggles over sewer pipes. My apartment had a single bed under a huge grease spot on the wall, the exact contours of which are still imprinted on my brain. It was the first thing I saw when I opened my eyes each morning.

If we started out romantically twined in the single bed, I

would always wake up suddenly when I fell out of bed. I would then swear and drag the blankets off to the couch in the living room. Neither the crash of my body on the floor nor the loss of blanket would even make him turn a hair off there in dreamland. It was always *me* who fell out of bed, and besides, he wouldn't fit on the couch. I fit, but only with my neck on the armrest. It was a good thing that we finally got married and moved to the apartment downstairs, which had a double bed, or my neck would have congealed permanently at right angles to my body.

Our parents were apprehensive. His parents worried that if we had an argument I would call him a Dirty Jew. (A Good Catholic woman would never do anything so impolite. I would sooner have spit in the subway.)

My parents worried because I would be an outsider to his Jewish family and friends. (When his mother wants him to do something she calls me and says, "Can't you make him get those awful sideburns cut?")

The mechanics of getting married were something of a problem.

I knew he was not going to come rushing in one morning while I was burning the scrambled eggs and announce, "I want to become a Catholic!" like all those husbands of the nuns' fables. He was proud of being a Jew. His heritage was an inextricable part of him. It was not so much a matter of ritual, but a sense of being a part of a culture, the use of an inflexion in the voice, a way of looking at the world.

(Once he had gone to Mass with me, and the priest who gave the sermon had just come back from Latin America. The priest told the story of a group of Protestant evangelists who were preaching from a sound truck when a procession devoted to Our Lady passed by. The Catholics turned over the sound truck and beat up the Protestants. And the priest gave the *Protestants* hell for trying to spread Error in a Catholic country. And one time, when I was in college,

Margie and I were accompanied by a couple of non-Catholic boys to Mass, and the priest gave a sermon about Saint Somebody-or-other and his hair shirt with the maggots in it and we could see our dates looking at each other edgily. Why was it, that whenever you wanted to impress a visitor with the dignity and solemnity of your chosen religion, *that* was the time you always got the nutty priests with the hair-shirt sermons?)

I had by this time moved beyond the narrow borders of the world of the convent school to a philosophy that would now be called ecumenical. By the time I graduated from Trinity, I had come to a selective acceptance of the things that I had been told all came lumped under the heading Catholic. This was true, also, I think, of my closest friends at college. We retained the things that seemed important to us and had begun to slough off the rest. I could no longer fathom a God who sat like a giant Buddha staring at the giant superhighway of Catholic dogma that ran smack into his navel, and did not even glance at all the other roads traveled by all his other creatures who ended up lost somewhere in the mist. My theology, while it was not defined in any academic sense, had veered from the Baltimore catechism toward more of the cosmic optimism of a Teilhard de Chardin; an idea that man had a rendezvous with God someplace in the future, and the human drama is all a part of this journey. Where it will end is beyond my range of vision, but my Catholic education left me with enough of a residue of mysticism to find the idea of a blind, accidental universe both unaesthetic and terribly, terribly dull.

I did not want to sign a paper promising the future of my children to the Catholic Church. I did not believe that was a decision I should make for them. I did not want to convert to Judaism, as the rabbis required. Organized religion stood in the path of True Love like Oilcan Harry in the old silent flicks. I know of many young men and women in our position who simply said "A plague on both your houses" and never darkened the door of a church or synagogue again. But since we both did want a religious ceremony, we hunted around until we found a reform rabbi who would marry us. He said he could fit us in one Sunday between a TV panel show and a groundbreaking.

Since our families were in other cities, we had to do all the arranging ourselves. Eisenhower had an easier time with the D-Day invasion. The call to Schrafft's to order a wedding cake was right out of Kafka.

"Hello, I'd like to order a wedding cake, please."

"Just a minute, please. Click. Hello."

"I'd like to order a wedding cake."

"What kind?"

"Just a plain ordinary one with white frosting."

"We have jelly roll, mocha, peach, strawberry, Fig Newton, sponge, marble, cherry—"

"Just a plain white one, please."

"We have jelly roll, mocha, peach, strawberry, Fig Newton, sponge, marble, cherry—"

"Just vanilla. Do you have vanilla?"

"We have jelly roll, mocha, peach, strawberry, Fig Newton, sponge, marble, cherry—"

"Lady, lady, please stop that! Vanilla, I want vanilla!"

"We do not have vanilla. We have jelly roll, mocha, strawberry, Fig Newton, sponge, marble, cherry—"

We ordered flowers from the first place we came to on a New York street. It didn't seem to be the right kind of place. I was convinced the flowered canopy would spell out WE'LL MISS YOU, BUGSY, in lilacs. All the invited guests came, except one girl whose mother called and politely declined, saying "We're not coming because Caryl is going to go to hell."

We lavished most of our attention on the food. We ordered stuffed cabbage and knishes and chicken wings and egg rolls and hot pastrami. A photograph of our reception shows all the guests standing up, cocktails in hand, chatting. The bride and groom are alone at the table, stuffing themselves. I was pleased to have established relations with a culture that had produced both the ten commandments and the meat knish, and had commandeered the egg roll, to boot.

There was an emotional wrench at coming out from the sheltering roof of Catholicism that I had known for so much of my life. At times I would be seized by atavistic guilt from third-grade catechism; there we would be, frying away, Hitler, Mussolini, Jack the Ripper, Attila the Hun, and me. It did not last longer than an instant. I no longer believed in the medieval terror of demons and brimstone, and I have a temperament that is not congenial to guilt. But in those brief instances I could get some idea of its power.

I could distinguish, now, between the religion and the Church, the institution. There was a curious dichotomy between the joyous mingling of God's love and man's love that infused much of the early Catholicism that I knew, and the rigid, humorless, monolithic bureaucracy of the Church. It wasn't that the Church didn't really have all the answers—it wasn't even asking the right questions. It still seemed wrapped in a sac that was a peculiar mix of myopia, arrogance, and terror of the rest of the world. It seemed bent on frittering away its immense power for moral good on such trifles as celluloid cleavage and the domestic agents provocateurs of Karl Marx. Christ, the befriender of whores and thieves and fishermen, would have felt more at home at a meeting of a Rotary Club than in most Catholic churches, so enmeshed were they in middle-class self-satisfaction.

We were often told in catechism class that God gives a special protection to the Catholic Church. Perhaps He does. Perhaps there is a limit to His tolerance for bureaucrats and fools. For the spirit of renewal that now sends its wind through the Church has shaken the stolid, stagnant institution I knew to its very foundations. If you had told me—or any of my classmates at the convent school—that the future held Vatican II or any of the things that followed, we simply would not have believed it. We thought the Church as we knew it would endure, like the relic of a saint preserved under glass—unchanged until the end of time.

It still amazes me that so much has changed so fast. There is much in the contemporary Church that seems light-years away from the Church of mid-century, the ally of Dulles, the censor of necklines and navels, the guardian of suburban real estate and overlord of Bingo. There are some who lament the changes in the Church, but I see them only as revival, renewal, a move toward a more compassionate, more human view of reality, and it is to that movement that I feel drawn. When I write down "Catholic" on any form that asks my religion, I do not mean that I obey a set of ritualized rules. I do not. I speak of an understanding that transcends the details of ritual and even dogma; an awareness of a relationship between Man and God, a universe with order, and a requirement of decent relations with one's fellow creatures, all tied up for me by the scent of incense and the sound of bells.

I have heard serious predictions—by theologians, no less —that the Church as an institution will not survive the year 2000 in its present form. But it is the *idea* of God and Man, not the form that really matters. The Church is no longer the prisoner of the status quo, discomfiting as that may be to some. The Berrigan brothers afflict the nation's conscience, and one may agree with them or not, but they are gadflies to the established order, as Christ was. The new theologians are pushing back the old, narrow walls of the Church, demanding a more human look at sexuality and marriage, realities that are at the core of life and cannot be dealt with simply by Thou Shalt Not. They are retooling the Catholic version of the Chosen People to include all men and women who seek God or Good in a world filled with machines and loneliness. The future does not belong to the Old Men of the Vatican, except to those who are wise enough to see that change is in the natural order of things.

And yet, I think I understand why change is so unsettling to so many Catholics. In a world that seems to be hurtling like a diesel train into an unknown future, the old things are something to grab onto. I remember Growing Up Catholic with affection, even in the days of the old pre-Vatican II insulated and insular Church. There are Gothic strands of love and ignorance, of faith and superstition woven into my past, and I remember: the sudden hush and three clear bells when the priest held the host aloft and it seemed sacrilege even to breathe; the hypnotic drone of the rosary; the Latin words in the Mass for the Dead clanging with the mystery of a world on the bright side of the dark, and the breezy oompa-oompa of "Mother Dear, Oh Pray for Me, Whilst Far from Heaven and Thee" which I discover myself singing yet on days when the sun is out and the air is full of spring and all is well with the world.

27